Teaching *with* RESPECT

Inclusive Pedagogy for Choral Directors

ISBN 978-1-70517-298-8

Visit Hal Leonard Online at
www.halleonard.com

World headquarters, contact:
Hal Leonard
7777 West Bluemound Road
Milwaukee, WI 53213
Email: info@halleonard.com

In Europe, contact:
Hal Leonard Europe Limited
42 Wigmore Street
Marylebone, London, W1U 2RN
Email: info@halleonardeurope.com

In Australia, contact:
Hal Leonard Australia Pty. Ltd.
4 Lentara Court
Cheltenham, Victoria, 3192 Australia
Email: info@halleonard.com.au

2nd EDITION

Teaching *with* RESPECT

Inclusive Pedagogy for Choral Directors

BY STEPHEN SIECK

ABOUT THE AUTHOR

Dr. Stephen Sieck serves as Co-Director of Choral Studies at the Lawrence University Conservatory of Music, where he directs the Concert Choir, Viking Bass Clef Ensemble, and Viking Chorale, and teaches in the rehearsal techniques sequence for music educators. Stephen received his B.A. in music from the University of Chicago, and his M.M. and D.M.A. degrees from the University of Illinois at Urbana-Champaign. Steve's research focuses on strategies for inclusive teaching, diction pedagogy, building tenor voices healthily, and teacher wellness.

Table of Contents

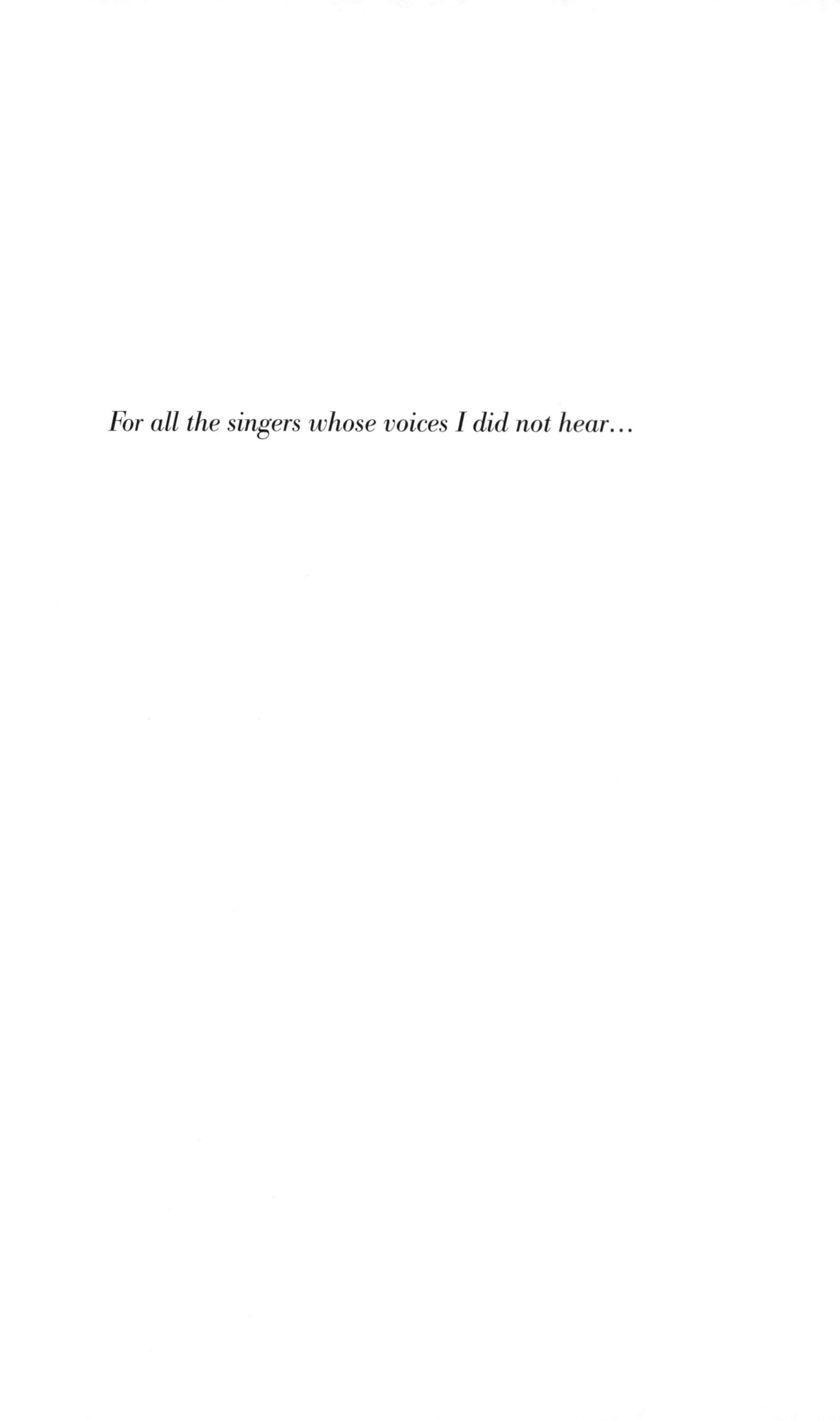

For all the singers whose voices I did not hear…

Preface to the Second Edition

Since being contacted about a second edition for *Teaching with Respect*, I have struggled for a year to find an opening sentence which best describes the space between writing the first edition in 2016 and writing the second edition in 2021. All I could come up with was, "well, that happened," to describe the storm of powerful events that make 2016 feel like a lifetime ago.

I wrote the first edition of *Teaching with Respect* in the summer of 2016, when the most exciting news was the summer Olympics in Rio de Janeiro. By the time my editor and I were parsing sentence construction of the manuscript in October, the *Access Hollywood* video was released. By August 2017, the "Unite the Right" rally in Charlottesville reminded everyone that white nationalism remained (and had never left) the fabric of American life. By October 2017, the #MeToo movement reminded us that sexual assault and misogyny remained (and had never left) the fabric of American life. Mass shootings in Las Vegas, Stoneman-Douglas High School, and Pittsburgh's Tree of Life synagogue reminded us that gun violence and anti-Semitism remained (and had never left) the fabric of American life. The murders of Philando Castille, Breonna Taylor, George Floyd, and so many others, reminded us that anti-Black violence remained (and had never left) the fabric of American life.

And then there was, and still remains at the time of this writing, the global Covid-19 pandemic. Surely, I thought, a highly contagious and deadly virus could unite our fractured society. We would band together for the clear and noble goal of saving one another's lives. But masks, and then vaccines, became political litmus tests instead of basic public health measures. And the cost of turning a virus into a political contest has been awful: hundreds of thousands of American lives lost within the first two years of the pandemic, and counting.

What, therefore, is different in this second edition?

To begin, I needed to sit with some hard realities. I referred to Nazis in the first edition in several places to serve as an easy common denominator of what we all obviously oppose. I now understand that it is not a fair assumption that all Americans identify themselves in opposition to the idea that the "White race" is superior. In fact, White supremacists are, according to the Homeland Security and Attorney General's offices,[1] America's number one terrorist threat. While "I'm a Nazi" remains a taboo thing to say in public discourse, the evidence suggests that many Americans are comfortable electing officials who use threats of White Americans being "replaced", pass laws banning any curriculum that includes an honest admission of racism throughout history, or strip voting rights in surgically precise ways to disenfranchise minoritized voters. I wrote the first edition with the sort of naïve optimism that a White man like myself is privileged to have, seeking to appeal to our better angels as music educators. While I still hold that hope, this second edition no longer assumes that we all want a thriving, diverse learning space. Now, I advocate for it.

Second, I realized that the audience had changed, and writers write for an audience. Back in 2016, discourse about culturally responsive pedagogy felt limited to a very narrow audience. I hoped to share out what I had learned (through *so much* trial and error) to an audience of mid-career choral directors who, like myself, had little prior engagement with gender studies, ethnic studies, or critical race theory. But what I came to realize was that the primary audience for this book was music education students who were assigned to read it in rehearsal methods courses. Writing about racism or sexism to the Gen X or Baby Boomer audience is a different process than writing to the GenZ audience. And, after five years of constant national discourse on these topics, there is little that I am saying in this book that should still feel "new" to readers, unless they have avoided the conversations.

Third, my personal life changed. I became a treatment-level foster parent and now adoptive father to a child who is Black and who has trauma-centered needs. Family members transitioned genders. Conversations about racism or transphobia are different when you are living in them. To borrow Rev. Dr. King Jr.'s expression, there's a "fierce urgency of now" when your family member's right to exist is being debated.

And finally, I continue to learn. The second edition includes a new section on teaching students with trauma, an updated section on working with trans voices, a more robust discussion of Universal Design for Learning and neurodiversity. I've also learned to say things more precisely. For example, I would rather say "culturally responsive" than "inclusive", since "inclusive" suggests that I am the host of this party and I've decided now to extend an invitation to everyone else (how generous!); "culturally responsive" acknowledges that all people have cultural identities and I am responsive as a teacher to and interested in my students. I've made an important change from the word "minority" (a characteristic that a person possesses) to "minoritized" (a characteristic of otherness imposed on one by another), and likewise, from "slave" to "enslaved".

I am deeply grateful for the wisdom and expertise of Keira Jett Kowal and Dr. Derrick Fox, who were generous consultants in this rewriting process. Thank you, as well, to the many folks who sent suggestions and comments along the way. I continue to welcome disagreement, which is a bedrock for democracy and for critical thinking. This book is not meant to make voters of any particular political party feel seen or feel excluded. It is meant to help us remember that we are all fallible people, working in fallible systems, teaching young people how to find their voices in community. My deepest hope is that if we can learn to listen and share our voices toward a common goal in choir, we might yet transfer some of those skills to our world.

FOREWORD

One of the operational definitions of critical thinking is the ability to change your mind on a deeply held belief. It seems perfectly appropriate to invoke this definition when you are trying to explain to someone else why *they* are wrong, but it is a lot harder to apply inwardly. I was raised in one way of doing the business of leading choirs, and I was good at it. In recent years, however, students have challenged me to think critically about the choral experience. I did, and it has changed my life. But… it took me *a lot* of time. It took months of reading other people's ideas and scholarship. I debated, I wrestled, and I processed it all at my own pace, until finally, I was ready to change my mind.

You could probably read this book in an afternoon. Perhaps you will be a better or faster critical thinker than I was. Hopefully, the arguments will appear in an easily-digested format, and you may see the point more quickly than I did. Maybe after you read this, you will be motivated to continue on your own journey of reading, debating, and processing in the months ahead. Or maybe, you will simply disagree with me.

This book is grounded in research, but my argument is fundamentally a moral one.

This book is grounded in research, but my argument is fundamentally a moral one. I can make the case that some of our singers are significantly oppressed, and even use data where appropriate, but you may argue that choral music is independent of such oppression. In this book, I start with the assumption that you value and respect everyone, and then I critically examine how the choral experience does not always provide that respect and value for everyone. I argue that we have a moral responsibility to address how we honor – or marginalize – our singers.

This book is in four sections:

- The **Prelude** addresses why a book about inclusive choral pedagogy is so urgently needed.
- In **Section 1**, we will consider the ways we can make our choral rehearsal space more inclusive.
  - *Chapter 1* helps us become better aware of our own perspective;
  - *Chapter 2* looks at some principles of inclusivity and safety;
  - *Chapter 3* helps us to better understand working with singers with diverse abilities.
- In **Section 2**, we look at the ways choir intersects with different identities, challenging us to account for marginalization and offering strategies for more inclusive practice.
  - *Chapter 4* looks at gender issues;
  - *Chapter 5* focuses on sexual identity;

- *Chapter 6* considers the intersection of choir and religion;
- *Chapter 7* examines our relationship with World Music;
- *Chapter 8* addresses choir and African-American Music.

- Finally, the **Postlude** looks at the choral experience from the perspective of audience.

I will use the first person *they* throughout this book. I was raised with she/he and her/his, so this was one of many ongoing examples of changing my thinking (see Chapter 4).

I use the words teacher, conductor, and director interchangeably in this book, but they have different connotations individually. We tend to interpret *director* and *conductor* as a top-down, "here's what you need to do" approach; whereas *teacher* can suggest a range of pedagogical approaches. On the one hand, I know some readers will identify as *conductors* who do not work directly in education, so I am careful throughout the book not to assume that we are all working in schools. On the other hand, I believe that anyone who guides and leads a choir teaches a choir, and in that sense we are all teachers. I certainly do not mean to imply in this book that to conduct a choir is to stand in absolute power and authority, delivering one-way instruction to singer-receptacles. I consider these terms – *conductor, director,* and *teacher* – as placeholders for the person who is guiding a rehearsal.

I am tremendously grateful to be in a community as supportive and thoughtful as Lawrence University. Thank you to every colleague who has helped in this endeavor, including Helen Boyd Kramer, Carla Daughtry, Phillip Swan, and many more. I would not have gotten past page two without the exceptional research assistance of Lauren Vanderlinden. I'm honored to call her a collaborator in this project. Special thanks to early readers for their terrific insights and suggestions, especially Mary Hopper, Eric Banks, Steven Paul Spears, and Karen Bruno. And there are no words to express the thanks for Anne Sieck for the countless hours of discussion and priceless wisdom she provided throughout the process.

PRELUDE
Why this Book?

WHY *THIS* BOOK?

When I was in my first year teaching 7th-12th grade, I arranged Schubert's *Die Forelle* for our middle-school choir. A parent who is Jewish contacted me to say that she would not let her daughter sing this song. I argued back, explaining that *Die Forelle* was a remarkably *un*controversial poem about a fish. When it became clear that her concern was that her daughter would never sing in *German*, I connected the dots, sighed with relief and said, "Schubert died over a century before the Third Reich, so obviously he was not part of that." It seemed simple to me: she was convicting someone who had lived in the early 1800s for an atrocity that happened in the 1940s. Art is of its time and yet universal. It seemed obvious to me that to hold the German language on trial for all of history because of World War II was ahistorical censorship.

I heard the words this parent spoke, but I failed to hear *what she was trying to communicate*. I had not lost my entire extended family to Germans. I had not grown up without grandparents and uncles and aunts, or without a homeland and culture because Germans had destroyed them. German, to me, was simply a language musicians learn because so much vocal music is set in that language. For this parent, the German language was a trigger, a *signifier*, for a culture that had oppressed her forbearers for centuries (yes, in Schubert's time, too). To put her daughter on stage to sing in German might feel like an act of historical erasure for her family, as if what had happened sixty years prior was all forgotten and forgiven. And for me to deny that there was any pain involved in this for her and her family was a sign that we were not seeing this song from the same perspective. I moved about the musical world with a privilege that she and her daughter would never feel. All these cultures, all these languages were equally fascinating to me, because none of them had ever tried to kill my family.

Now, I understand that these conversations about music and culture and marginalization will always come up. They should.

I was not ready for this conversation. I was ready to conduct in all the time signatures, to play piano and sing, to study scores and plan rehearsals, to take attendance and give quizzes. I wish I had been ready for her phone call. I might have changed the song. I might have performed the song but had a more substantive conversation with her. Now, I understand that these conversations about music and culture and marginalization will *always* come up. They should.

Most choir directors love choral music because it brings people together in community and because it expresses text so beautifully. These conversations about what we are saying and who is saying it ask us to look carefully at the texts we are expressing as a community.

WHO IS THIS BOOK *FOR*?

This book is a contribution to this other, essential responsibility for those that lead choirs.

No single book serves all audiences well. There are many choral directors like me who have existed for most of our lives in a bubble of privileges. I write from my lived experience, hoping to walk with you out of that bubble. And, I want to acknowledge that if you are reading this book from a place where others have gate-kept you, marginalized your contributions, and stereotyped and tokenized you regularly, you probably do not need to read my attempt here to explain why discriminatory pedagogy needs revisiting. I hope to know my lane.

I make two central assumptions in this book about you, the reader. First, I believe you place a high value on teaching choirs very well. Second, I believe you are willing to examine both your own behavior and the structure of institutions that you work for in order to root out sexism, racism, and bigotry. I will be frank: the evidence for this second assumption is not always apparent. But I am an optimist and I believe that people can change. I am grateful someone believed in me enough to call me into these conversations, so I pay it forward with hope.

This is a book that prompts us to ask deeper questions about the language we use, about systems of power, and about our heritage and inheritance.

If this is a book that asks us to re-examine how our choral pedagogy may not be as inclusive as it could be, shouldn't this come from an author who has experienced such marginalization? Why read the words of a White, male, heterosexual, Christian-raised, suburban professor like me? I include articles and books in the bibliography by outstanding scholars and writers who speak from their lived truth and research and encourage every conductor to explore such literature as much as you can. One of the expectations of people with privilege is that they learn to use that unearned power to do something helpful. And, I will not continue to be a passive bystander to oppression. It is people like me who have never been oppressed who need to start showing up for this work and to foster a curiosity about how we can become better directors. My task in this book is to spark that curiosity for those in our field who are not yet curious. I want to help teachers like me see that the sky will not fall and that you will not be cancelled if you step into uncomfortable new spaces.

In other words, **we must ask ourselves what kind of witness we want to be to the history that our present lives will become.** We need to stare at images like this iconic photo[1] of Dorothy Counts in 1957 as she walked to school to enroll in a North Carolina segregated (White) public high school:

Credit: Bettmann / Contributor

I imagine most of those children did not think at the time that spitting on Dorothy and throwing bricks at her father's car was a bad thing to do. I imagine it did not occur to them that the Christian faith they professed and the bricks they threw at Rev. Dr. Counts' car (he was a Presbyterian minister) were at odds. Beyond that, what we do not see are any people in the photograph supporting Dorothy. There may have been many allies that morning, and they might have felt supportive, but they stayed in their homes, safe and sound. The photograph gives stark testimony to their absence. As bystanders to this injustice, they, too, failed to treat others with respect.

The truth is that there is no urgent motivation for those of us who do not feel personally oppressed to do or change anything. Personally, I can go anywhere, do anything, and expect to be treated with respect and dignity. This is what scholars call *privilege*. I have no incentive whatsoever to challenge the status quo. The established systems of power reward people like me *a priori*. And while I have learned that pushing back at the system is not always well-received, it is still far safer for me to critique systems of power than it would be for most people.

Recently I attended an event that gave witness to a difficult and politically charged issue. As I stood on the busy street in obvious support, I was constantly concerned about all the cars passing by – how many people would honk, jeer, or throw something at me? What if we were attacked? I knew that I could always return to my home, retreating to the safety of my comfort zone. But this state of anxiety that I felt for only a relatively few moments is a constant reality for oppressed people. I wanted to return to my feeling of peace, but I began to understand that real peace happens only when everyone has that same opportunity.

There is, in short, a distinction between 'not rocking the boat' and 'peace,' and it hinges on whether or not we are all *respected.*

There is, in short, a distinction between 'not rocking the boat' and 'peace,' and it hinges on whether or not we are *all* respected. Those of us who perceive no personal incentive to make our teaching more inclusive must become the conductors who daily live out the goal of teaching with respect for all singers. As Rev. Dr. Martin Luther King Jr. so famously wrote in his "Letter from a Birmingham Jail," the greatest stumbling block to freedom was not the Ku Klux Klan leader,

> ...but the White moderate, who is more devoted to "order" than to justice; who prefers a negative peace which is the absence of tension to a positive peace which is the presence of justice; who constantly says: "I agree with you in the goal you seek, but I cannot agree with your methods of direct action"; who paternalistically believes he can set the timetable for another man's freedom... Shallow understanding from people of good will is more frustrating than absolute misunderstanding from people of ill will.[3]

Every time we select repertoire or discuss texts, we have the opportunity to become agents of justice and peace. And it is essential that those of us who suffer the least amount of daily marginalization use this opportunity to educate ourselves. If we want to teach with respect, we have to ask ourselves how we are doing our work and how it affects all of us. For people like me, life is great, and I want to keep things in this equilibrium. But there are many kinds of equilibriums, as social scientist Thomas Schelling observes: *The body of a hanged man is in equilibrium when it finally stops swinging, but nobody is going to insist that the man is all right.*[4] Just because the German language is not problematic to me does not mean that there is nothing to discuss with that concerned parent. And it cannot - and should not - fall only to the marginalized in our community to remind us that our equilibrium is not always a good one.

WHY THIS BOOK?

We want to teach with respect, compassion, and wisdom. We direct choirs that are comprised of a variety of singers, each with very different life experiences. If we are marginalizing our singers or perpetuating stereotypes, we need to know. But the burden cannot be on our singers to steer us toward a more respectful path. Rather, it is up to us to examine what we are doing that produces that oppressive feeling in our singers.

The burden cannot be on our singers to steer us toward a more respectful path.

I write this book to walk us through some of the difficult questions that all will inevitably encounter as we strive to teach with more respect. These are some of the many questions that I was surprised by, often managed poorly, inevitably encountered again, discussed with colleagues, read, debated, and have continued to learn about to this day. Indeed, most of the issues or scenarios I present in this book come from my own experience of handling them poorly. We will all want an all-encompassing guide – a simple, straight-forward answer to questions like, "what's the right term for this person?" or "how am I supposed to handle this issue?" This book offers no answer key in the back – only an approach to teaching choral music that is centered first and foremost on respecting the singers in front of us.

I believe, as I think most of us do, that choral music has the power to change the world. Yet I came to realize that I had never given much thought to *what I was trying to change it into*. During a series of very real and difficult conversations with singers in 2016, I lost many nights of sleep asking myself what it was that I was after, what tradition I was defending, and which skills was I trying to foster in choir. The answer was a surprisingly old idea: respect.

I hope, for myself and for my singers, that we respect the inherent worth and dignity of everyone. I hope we respect the composer and the poet as artists who have a say in the process. And, I hope we respect the audience as participants as they engage with the art that we have worked so diligently to prepare for them. This idea of *doing unto others as I would have them do unto me* is very old indeed.

SECTION I
Creating an Inclusive Choir

CHAPTER 1
Growing Our Perspective

Teaching choral music is hard. We wrestle with auditions, assessments, national standards, musicals, concerts, tours, conferences, and festivals. We develop curricula in music literacy, history, and theory. We teach how to sing, pronounce, tune, and make a phrase. But at the end of our term, we do not collect exams and grade them at home like our colleagues in English or Math. Instead, we put our work out onstage for everyone to see and evaluate.

There is an unspoken assumption that, in teaching choirs, we also have a pastoral role. We expect the teacher to inspire our singers to become their best selves, to foster upstanding citizens of the world. We expect choir to be a group with especially strong bonds of fellowship, where all are welcome, but where all agree on what and how we are doing everything. Our goal is to 'sing with one voice,' using as many voices as possible. We do not just teach choral music. We teach singers, and in the teaching, we shape who they will become.

This makes a difficult job even harder. Whose voice are we blending to? Which moral compass are we calling north? We know that our singers come from many different backgrounds. How do we navigate their differences in our quest for unity? I might believe in X, but some of my students believe in Y. Do I force X on them? Sacrifice my beliefs for Y? Is there a Z option?

RESPECT

I want to suggest that we as choral directors need not fear that, by acknowledging X's rights and concerns, we then endorse/become X or hate Y. I can learn to respect that female-identifying students might have different needs and concerns than I do as male-identifying without fearing that I become a woman in the process, or that I somehow endorse the end of maleness. I can learn to respect that singers that identify as Lesbian, Gay, Transgender, Bisexual, or Queer (LGTBQ+) have different needs and concerns than me without fearing that I might become gay or somehow endorse the end of heterosexuality. I can be a dog person and not hate cats. If I learn to respect the rights of people that are not me (and there are seven billion examples), I do not lose myself in this, nor do I negate my beliefs. Rather, I amplify and enrich myself, pedagogically and otherwise. Respect is not a perfectly balanced, net zero-sum equation. Respect is infinitely generous and available. And the full embodiment of respect is a basic principle that has been taught for millennia.

OLD PRINCIPLES

> Do not impose on others what you yourself do not desire. - Doctrine of the Mean 13.3 (Confucianism)

> This is the sum of duty: do not do to others what would cause pain if done to you. - Mahabharata 5:1517 (Hinduism)

> What is hateful to you, do not do to your fellow man. This is the law: all the rest is commentary. - Talmud, Shabbat 31a (Judaism)

> So in everything, do to others what you would have them do to you, for this sums up the Law and the Prophets. - Matthew 7:12 (Christianity)

> None of you [truly] believes until he wishes for his brother what he wishes for himself." - Number 13 of Imam "Al-Nawawi's Forty Hadiths," (Islam)

The *Golden Rule* is a unifying thread throughout many religions and ethical frameworks of human experience. It asks nothing more or less than the ability to imagine how another feels and to act with respect for those feelings: I do not like being punched in the face, so I ought not punch another in the face.

Respect is not a perfectly balanced, net zero-sum equation. Respect is infinitely generous and available. Treat another as you would have them treat you if your roles were reversed.

We imagine another's situation and empathize – so simple! Here's the dilemma: someone might *like* getting punched in the face; should that person punch others? Clearly not. The Platinum Rule addresses the spirit of the Golden Rule with more precise language: treat another as you would have them treat you if your roles were reversed. This captures the spirit of the rule better. Let's suppose Tim wants to throw Tammy a big birthday dinner. Tim is an omnivore who loves grilled chicken; Tammy is a vegetarian who loves grilled tofu. If Tim does for Tammy what he would want done for himself, he makes grilled chicken. But I think we would all read the spirit of the law as more clearly suggesting that Tim should make Tammy some grilled tofu. That is, Tim thinks to himself, "on my birthday I would want my favorite foods, so I will make my friend her favorite food." The danger in too narrow a reading of the *Golden Rule* is to assume that everyone likes grilled chicken.

Respect, then, is not a question of giving everyone what we ourselves want. Rather, respect is about showing everyone the kind of *dignity* that we hope to be shown. To more fully grasp this, we can turn to further moral guidance from old sources:

> There is no longer Jew or Greek, there is no longer slave or free, there is no longer male and female; for all of you are one in Christ Jesus. – the Apostle Paul, Letter to the Galatians 3:28.

Radiate boundless love towards the entire world — above, below, and across — unhindered, without ill will, without enmity. – The Buddha

Respect, then, is not a question of giving everyone what we ourselves want. Rather, respect is about showing everyone the kind of dignity that we hope to be shown.

The more we recognize and understand the taxonomies and value-laden distinguishers we use for each other, the more we can begin to quiet that mode of thinking and see our interdependent worth and dignity. But first, we will need to look honestly and deeply at the ways we teach ourselves to look.

Expanding Our Perspective

POSITIONALITY

If you stand in downtown Chicago at the intersection of Adams and Michigan, what you see will depend on which way you are facing. If you're coming from the west, you have thousands of miles of road stretching behind you; if you're coming from the east, you only have a few blocks behind you before you're in Lake Michigan. From the north, you will have just walked the Magnificent Mile; from the south, you will have seen new construction in formerly redlined neighborhoods. It matters where you came to the intersection from as well as the direction you are looking.

I come to this book as a male who identifies as heterosexual, White, and raised Christian. I grew up in a moderately affluent, diverse, well-educated suburb with strong public schools. I went to an excellent private university, married and had children, taught in 7th-12th grade private school, and did my graduate studies at a public research university. I have taught in private liberal arts colleges for more than fifteen years. Had I been raised in a wealthy home, I would be a nearly complete definition of privilege in America. I bring my background into public discussion precisely because every discussion brings its speaker's background with it, whether public or not.

I have enjoyed so many exceptional advantages that I cannot possibly claim to have arrived at this point solely by my own hard work. I come to this book from the life I have lived as an intersecting loop of identities that include male, White, Christian, heterosexual, musician, teacher, scholar, etc. In order to teach with respect, you must first acknowledge how you came to this moment as a director. Consider your intersecting loops of identities. What advantages and disadvantages have you experienced to bring you to your current position?

THE PLAYING FIELD

Most of us live by the simple premise that if we work hard enough, we will earn opportunities. All men are created equal, and all have the right to life, liberty, and the pursuit of happiness. If I succeed, it is because I earned it with my particular strengths;

if I fail, it is because I failed to earn it. What is assumed in this formulation is that the playing field is universally level – any of us can arrive at that same Chicago intersection. Do you, for example, believe that people are poor or wealthy only because of how hard they work or how well they manage money? Low or high Body-Mass Index only because of their diet? In what ways do you assume that we all exist on the same playing field?

Many, however, question how level the playing field is or ever was. In what has already become a famous quote, President Trump remarked in a New Hampshire town hall, "It has not been easy for me, and you know I started off in Brooklyn, my father gave me a small loan of a million dollars..."[5] This is a wonderful example of positional disparity. In New York real estate, one million dollars is not a lot of money, which I assume is his point. At the same time, most of us have never seen anything close to a million dollars. Moreover, President Trump's real estate success is not from the ground up, so to speak; his father, who gave him that small loan, was a successful New York real estate developer, so he enjoyed access to knowledge, skills, and opportunities that 99.9% of us have never had. It is safe to say that President Trump's playing field was not as level as a similarly ambitious real estate mogul who grew up as the daughter of a part-time electrician in Omaha. Some people inherit resources and access that others do not have, and that tilts the playing field. **We cannot all simply 'work hard' to achieve the same level of success if we are given different background experiences.**

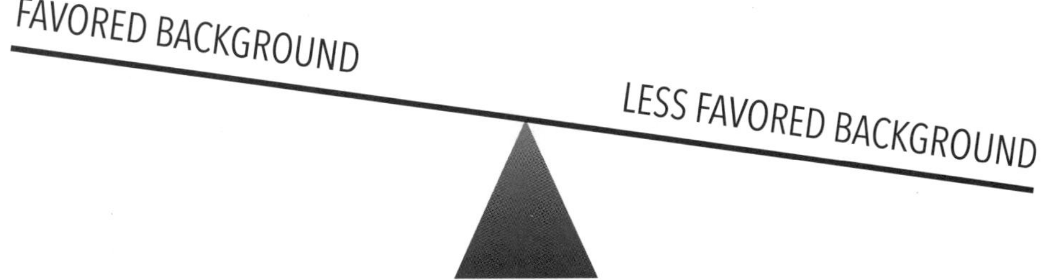

Many of us grew up wanting to play professional sports. Basketball favors those who are very, very tall, and football favors those who can develop very, very strong bodies. As I and countless others who played sports have learned, we are not all made equal in this respect. We cannot all simply work hard to achieve the same level of success if we are given different body types. **We cannot all simply 'work hard' to achieve the same level of success if we are given different body types.**

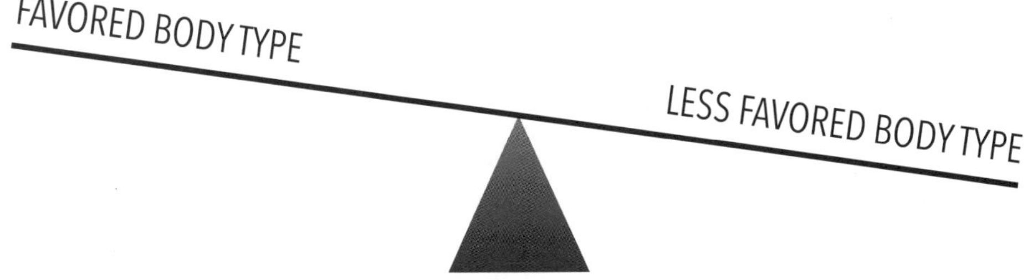

When I moved to Los Angeles after college, my plan was to perform, and, it went better than I imagined it would. I learned that a tenor who can sight-sing and sound decent is always in market demand. I remember being hired to sing the lead role for a professional operetta way before I had the technique to merit the opportunity, and I will never forget the logic of both the colleague who recommended me and the director who hired me: "you're a tenor, you look like the romantic lead (you're not obese or short), and you sound fine." (I heard this hiring logic many times in my short career, not just at this one moment.) I thought of the hundreds of sopranos in the city with master's degrees in vocal performance from major conservatories who had trained their technique to the knife's edge of artistic perfection; yet here I was getting the opportunity because I wasn't terrible and because I 'looked the part.' Not unlike a 6'10" basketball player, some people possess a constellation of basic skills and traits that others do not have (e.g., a good musician with a tenor voice versus a good musician with a soprano voice), and that tilts the playing field. We cannot all simply 'work hard' to achieve the same level of success if we are given different vocal ranges.

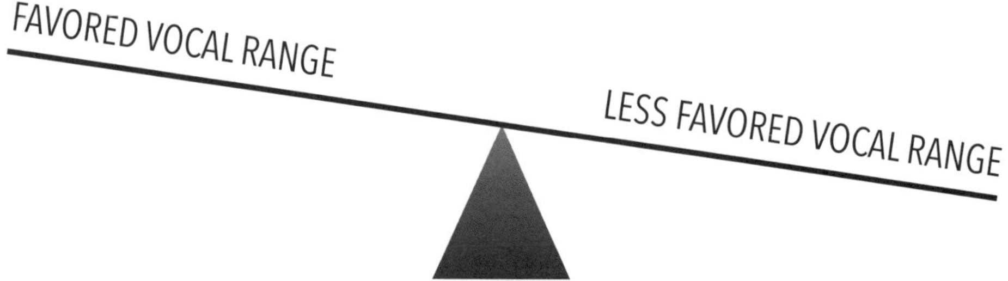

I hope that these three examples help to start a process of deconstructing the idea of the ever-flat playing field. I have worked hard as a tenor, and I do not discount that. What I do want to put forward is simply this: I did not get a professional contract from the same starting point as the soprano I sang with. She *definitely* worked harder to get there, and was by all accounts a much better singer. More importantly, getting that opportunity *changed* me, enriched my professional experience and perspective, and a similarly (or even a far more) qualified soprano did not get such a career-building experience. I entered the next playing field, graduate school, with yet another leg up, as a singer with professional experience.

In what ways do you see the playing field as tilted toward or away from you? Did you have to work your way through college, and then slowly pay off a sizeable debt over years, or did your parents cover your college tuition so that you graduated without any debt? Were you given piano lessons and access to a piano at home as a child? Did every child in your class? Were you overlooked in choir because you had a soprano voice and the choir needed altos? Take a few moments to consider real, concrete ways in which the field was decidedly not level in your life.

NO "US" WITHOUT A "THEM"

Have you ever played 20 Questions to figure out what something is? For example, first we can say that you and a tree are both alive, whereas a rock is inanimate. That's a binary split: living/not-living. Then, we can classify among living things: you belong to kingdom *Animalia* and a tree to kingdom *Plantae*. Keep going through these either/ or questions (are you warm-blooded? do you have a tail? are you a mammal? do you have thumbs?), and you will eventually arrive at 'human' as the answer.

Choral directors classify all the time in our daily lives: sopranos versus mezzo-sopranos, choral repertoire versus band repertoire, arts versus sciences, curricular versus extra-curricular. We know that a soprano is not a mezzo-soprano because they sing higher, and we know that choral music is not band music because it has words and does not have saxophones.

Further, we sharpen our identity of 'who we are' when we contrast it with an opposing definition. For example, Chicago Bulls fans might hate the Indiana Pacers – *they* are not *us*. But the interesting thing is how quickly the *they/us* can expand or contract. That same Bulls fan might have been perfectly happy to see Reggie Miller and Michael Jordan play as teammates in the Olympics because they were both Americans (*us*) taking on the world (*them*). As a tenor, I would give grief to the baritones, but would stand up for *them* against the altos (us now equals all low voices in choir), and would defend *them* all against the band kids (*us* now equals all singers in choir).

In other words, we use binaries to make taxonomies work simply and clearly, and in so doing we strengthen our position against a foreign position. There are several problems with this approach. Let's start with the changing circle of inclusion, and use a less harmless example than Bulls vs Pacers. At the turn of the 20th century, Irish immigrants like my great-grandparents came in huge waves to America to escape famine and to seek a better life. While this may come as a surprise to modern readers, the Irish were not considered part of the 'White race' at this time. They were thought of as unwelcome, poor, Papist, alcoholic, violent monkey-like degenerates - they did not belong in the dominant us. America might be a melting pot, but the Irish immigrants didn't deserve to be part of the recipe. As this political cartoon[6] from 1889 shows, the Irishman is a violent, zealous monkey who gets no part of our equal rights and citizenship as an American.

So when a US congressman in 2012 like Steve King (R-Iowa) compares Latino immigrants to the lazy kind of dog that one does not want to pick from the litter,[7] he uses a similar binary of *us/them* that was used on his own Irish ancestors a century ago to clarify that they were not us.

Indeed, the very language of distinct ethnic races is a product of the same man who brought forward the classification system for trees and humans, Carolus Linnaeus (1707-1778). Just as one would describe a Collie versus a German Shepherd, noting both their physical and psychological profiles, Linnaeus proposed these four races with characteristic attitudes:

- Americanus – red skinned, Black straight hair; stubborn, righteous
- Europeanus – light skinned, blue eyes; inventive, gentle
- Asiaticus – yellow skinned, dark eyes; haughty, greedy
- Africanus – black skinned, black frizzled hair; crafty, careless

I hope that every 21st-century reader finds this list appalling. We may dismiss this as archaic thinking from 250 years ago, but the line of thinking progresses from 19th-century Darwinian arguments about races to early 20th-century 'proof' of different racial dispositions based on skull size to 1930s eugenics to 1950s arguments against integration based on similar fake science. Though we continually seek to classify based on perceived race, the perception of race is culturally dependent. So, for example, for an American census, an Argentinian woman of European descent is not considered White – she is Latina; yet on her Argentinian census, she is White, not Black or indigenous. In other words, we define us as 'not them.' When we do that, we build a slope to the playing field, favoring us and disadvantaging them. In doing so, we lift up the voices that are on the high side of the field, and silence the voices we place on the lower side of the field.

DOMINANT NARRATIVES

When you read a book, whose voice do you imagine speaking? You would be playing the odds well to answer "a White male," simply because the overwhelming majority of the books you have read were written by White males. That brings us to an exercise in seeing privilege. Take a sheet of paper and a pencil. Draw a line down the center of the sheet of paper. On the left side, list every famous male writer you can think of. On the right side, list every famous female writer. Count how many you have listed on each side. Now turn the sheet over, and on the left side, list every famous White writer you can think of. On the right side, list every famous writer of color you can think of. Again, total both sides. Do the same exercises for composers instead of authors. Your experience with this exercise no doubt bears out the reality that we learn the writings of mostly White, male authors and composers. We will discuss the ethics of this later, but for the moment, let us begin by simply acknowledging it.

The cumulative effect of such an overwhelming tilt in the playing field is that we take as normative the dominant represented group, and consider someone outside that group to be in the category of 'other.' Even with Title IX ensuring equal access and rights to collegiate sports for men and women, we can see in the names of teams, for example, the respective basketball teams of the Tennessee Volunteers (normative, the team) and the Lady Volunteers (modifier added; we're *similar* to the team, but we're the *lady* version). In this particular case the irony is all the more striking because the Lady Vols have experienced far more success. So even though it would make more sense to say the UT Vols (our star team) and the UT Gentleman Vols (they *also* play basketball), the processing dissonance you might experience here points to the gender binary which favors male as default.

The cumulative effect of such an overwhelming tilt in the playing field is that we take as normative the dominant represented group, and consider someone outside that group to be in the category of 'other.'

To return to our conversation about races, we in America are steeped in dominant narrative language. We define White, publicly and implicitly, as "not anything else." The historical legacy of the "one-drop rule" shows up whenever we proactively label someone as 'other' who has equal claim to several ethnic identities. I think of the children of two American parents I know, one who checks the White box and one who checks the Asian/Islander box (although born in the Midwest), and I suppose their children will continue to check the Asian/Islander box, as will their children, and so on.

We define White versus what it is not; hence, all "people of color" are, by definition, minoritized, even if and when such populations create a majority of the nation. As a mental exercise, I imagine having to check the "without color" box a thousand times a year. I imagine CNN commentators discussing how Black soccer moms might pull some of the vote this way and Black working-class dads will go that way, but the White vote is locked up with the one candidate who "has a good relationship with the Whites." I imagine one White character per television drama, who is never the protagonist. The oddity of such an alternate reality is a strong sign that I am a part of a dominant narrative because we have these exact conversations about African-Americans.

I continued along these mental exercises in exploring the dominant narrative, and challenged myself to imagine for one week in my life what it would be like to interpret everyday culture as someone who does not fit into the heterosexual dominant narrative. How many songs would I sing or hear that confirm male/female love? How many times do candidates discuss 'family values' to mean my heterosexual marriage? How many movies would hinge on heterosexual plots? So I imagine an alternate reality in which my heterosexuality makes me minoritized to the dominant narrative. What if I went to choir and conducted or sung songs written for and by LGTBQ+ poets and composers? If I heard politicians debating whether or not my marriage was real? If I watched a thousand movies in which the homo-normative plot left me out? If this seems difficult to imagine, that is a good sign that we inhabit a hetero-normative narrative in which straight is treated as default, and LGTBQ+ becomes 'other.'

The cumulative effect of living outside the dominant narrative is called marginalization.

The cumulative effect of living outside the dominant narrative is called marginalization. When we put people in the category of 'other,' we put them in the margins, outside the center of the document itself. Imagine that the human experience is painted on a 10' x 10' canvas. Whichever part of that canvas we decide to focus on with our 3' x 3' frame is what we thus treat as important, normative, and central to our gaze. Whatever remains outside it is, by definition, in the margins - an outsider perspective. If everything we sing is written by men, then our frame has captured that corner of the choral canvas, and women in choir learn, by our actions and our omissions, that they are in the margins. Women are often the *object* in choral music, the thing we sing of: Mary, Nelly Bly, or Jeannie, etc. But they are usually not the *subject* – the I, the composer/voice. If everything we sing is written by White European composers, then the brief detour outside the frame is a journey to the 'foreign.' Moreover, if we put forward the best art music of White composers (Mozart, Tallis, *et al*) and our brief journeys outside the frame are to sing arrangements of spirituals for light concert entertainment, what do singers 'of color' - especially those identifying as African-American - learn? They realize that they are not only an appropriated object, but also an object of the worst crime in our nation's history?

Female composers
Black composers
Religious other
World music
Choral Music
(European, male, Christian, heterosexual)
LGBT composers

Example of unmarked dominant and marginalized other

Now I return to my positionality as a White, straight, raised-Christian male. I sing the works of men, but I only see them as composers. I sing hetero-normative texts, but I only see them as love songs. I sing of White culture, but I only see it as texts about history and aesthetics. I sing the faith that I was raised in, tunes and texts that I knew before I knew how to ride a bike. The choral music experience is, for me, the endless feast of grilled chicken that I have enjoyed so much that I have dedicated my life to it.

So let us take a moment to contemplate in the most general way what a singer might experience in choir if she identifies as female, lesbian, a person of color, and an atheist. She sings mostly the works of men, mostly hetero-normative texts, mostly of White culture, mostly of someone else's faith tradition. If she prefers tofu, she is being served a lot of grilled chicken. She would certainly describe the playing field differently than I would. Intersectionality is a term that is used to describe the multiple forces of discrimination that would all impact this singer. As legal scholar Kimberlé Crenshaw defines it, intersectionality, "is a lens through which you can see where power comes and collides, where it interlocks and intersects. It's not simply that there's a race problem here, a gender problem here, and a class or LBGTQ problem there. Many times that framework erases what happens to people who are subject to all of these things."[8] What makes this student's experience harmful in choir is often a combination of multiple forms of discrimination and marginalization.

Recognizing that the playing field is usually unequal, that there are dominant and marginalized voices, I now have a few choices as to how to respond to this knowledge. I encourage you to take a moment to consider how you might respond. Most of us tend to default to one of three destructive responses. Sometimes I think I have used all three within a given week!

1. *If everything marginalizes someone, is there anything we can sing?* Yes, of course there is. Here I threaten to filibuster the conversation by saying that a critical examination of choral repertoire and pedagogy will draw away the respect accorded to "great works." I threaten to cancel the whole enterprise of music-making because I am upset or confused that someone experiences this art so differently than I do. By acknowledging that some people get marginalized a lot, it does not follow that therefore everything marginalizes everyone. Remember, respect is not net zero-sum. If I teach and perform choral music from a traditionally marginalized community, I do not disrespect the traditional canon. Respect is infinitely expansive. Mozart does not stop being great repertoire by being carefully examined, and does not lose his greatness if I also include other compositional voices. That is, I can sing Mozart, and I can and *should* also learn and sing music of composers from historically marginalized identities.
2. *The repertory of choral music is what it is* (mostly White, male, Christian, and hetero-normative), *so either get on board with it or pick another class.* This has the satisfying allure of removing any of my responsibility to do something, but in fact, there is a great deal I could do. I could look a little harder through the repertoire, and I will find works I did not know existed. I could, with some proportion of the research and resources than I put into studying the traditional choral canon, study other repertoire with thoughtful care. Otherwise, I demand everyone think as I do, regardless of their position.
3. *Declare the traditional canon irredeemably biased and poisoned, and only do works that satisfy my worldview.* Whereas in the second option I too easily absolve myself of the work of finding new repertoire, in this option I too easily absolve myself of the work to critically re-examine the canon. Instead of seeing that all works carry with them both the author's position and mine, the performer's and the audience's, I reclaim the entire artistic process for myself into a series of personal credos. Since I will never find the perfect line-up of composer, ensemble, and audience that share exactly my personal moral code, I reduce art to my own manifesto.

I do not believe in easy solutions that absolve us of the work of teaching with respect. If we say there are no problems in canonic choral music, we continue to silence the voices of the *many* people who have been marginalized throughout history. If we say the canon is irredeemable, we silence some of the greatest music ever written. No, we must work at this. **We must come to understand why and how**

our choral experience meets different singers differently. We must honor the power of our repertoire and our teaching to build a better world and give to all singers the respect they deserve.

I have now come to a clear understanding that, out of respect for the humans I teach and direct, I wish to see the world more clearly through their eyes. I wish to provide a choral experience that gives every singer a voice. To do this the best I can, I first need to create a more welcoming space for all singers (Chapters 2 and 3). Then I can walk through some identity intersections and consider how each lens shapes the choral experience (Chapters 4-8). What can we learn about considering the intersection of gender, or sexual identity, or ethnicity, or religious identity and the choral experience? In which ways do we empower or marginalize our singers with our words, our repertoire, and our actions?

CHAPTER 2
Creating Room for All Singers

In this chapter we examine some of the concepts and structures that can help us better understand how our singers might feel more included. When we think of teaching with respect, the word *respect* connotes the act of being thoughtful, of esteeming another. Let's explore the many ways in which the choral experience can put respect at risk, and then consider constructive possibilities to make choir truly inclusive.

Section I:
UNDERSTANDING WHO WE ARE, AND WHO OUR SINGERS ARE

Do you remember the first day you walked into a choral rehearsal room? What were your expectations, your hopes, and your fears? How well did you know yourself? What did you expect from your choral director? What did you expect from your peers? For many of us, our first choral experience was so long ago that it can be easy to forget how much we have evolved in the intervening years. In this section, we will explore how we *and* the singers approach the choral experience from a variety of perspectives.

AGE AND EXPERIENCE

I work with very advanced collegiate singers. It is not uncommon for me to teach a 21- year old whose voice is superior to mine. I am okay with this - actually, I am *delighted* by this! It means I have the privilege of rehearsing advanced music at a fast pace with beautiful singing.

My students, however, often present as being so mature that I forget that they are still adolescents. Speaking generally, they have not bought or sold a house, married or divorced, had children or miscarriages, worked in an office 50 hours per week, or any number of other experiences that fellow directors have lived. They have probably only know the experience of being a student in school. Most of my students are still in the process of learning who they are, to say nothing of learning how to sight-read in 6/8 meter. We want them to understand what we are teaching and why, but their sense of context is limited. I cannot un-live the experiences that gave me more perspective and wisdom, and neither can they pre-live those experiences to meet my expectations.

If they seem young to me sometimes, that is a reflection of the gap between their normal, age-appropriate behavior and their abnormal, age-precocious musical ability. We will consider throughout most of the book how our singers' experiences often have a perspective and wisdom in ways that we ourselves might not experience. But for this moment, I encourage us to remember that most singers are working from a much smaller set of life experiences than their directors.

One of the great advantages of adulthood is choice. If I decide tomorrow that I hate conducting choirs, I can choose to start a different career. If I do not like how I am teaching, I can change my approach, mid-term or even mid-rehearsal! My students also have choices, of course, but not these kinds of freedoms. They may choose choir, but they cannot modify my behavior the way I modify theirs. They need the school experience in order to progress in the direction they want to go, but they do not have the same power I have to shape that experience. It is helpful for me to remember that the singers I work with are both much younger and possess less ability to steer the course of their day than I do. These are two salient aspects of the kind of power I enjoy which they do not.

POWER GAP

One of the hallmarks of a choral director versus a math teacher, for instance, is how strong our personal relationships become with our singers. Sure, we can fix notes and shape vowels, but what really makes the choral experience profound is the emotional connection of humans working together in putting text to collective voice. Since we need them to be courageous, emotionally vulnerable singers who can sing with deep honesty, we often strike an implicit bargain. We will relinquish our teacher role as "authority in the room" in exchange for emotional accessibility. That is, we joke, we hug, we know a *lot* about their emotional dramas, we provide a shoulder to cry on – in short, we position ourselves as wiser, older friends.

However, we *also* act like instructors. We audition to determine whether or not they sing in which choir, we give grades, cast solos, write recommendations, and otherwise exercise the authority with which we have been charged. In short, we have the luxury of toggling between buddy and maestro because the power has always been in our hands. I am not saying that if we espouse a constructivist, singer-centered approach, we are abdicating our responsibility, or that a responsible leader is emotionally unavailable. What I am saying is that the implicit, understood power dynamic favors us. Our singers find themselves, then, in a potentially confusing situation of navigating whether they are speaking to us as an ally who is there for them in a supportive and non-judgmental way, or as a conductor who determines the bar for quality, or as a teacher who educates, or as a faculty member who guides their future career decisions.

Have you ever had a singer speak to you as if you were complete equals about, say, how to teach choir? It is *very* disquieting, and that disorientation gives voice to the unspoken rule that this singer has transgressed a boundary: authority rests with us. We may choose when to promote our authority and when to downplay it, but we never assume the structure has changed. The advantage here is that when we want to lead, we do not need to put forth much effort to invoke it; the challenge is that when the choir is not healthily led, we have to step up to our part as the most powerful person in the room. And most often, the choir is not led well when we view all these singers collectively as *the choir*.

ME AND 'THE CHOIR'

A choir is more than the sum of its parts, and it has many parts. When someone asks us how work is going, we usually give a response like this: "Choir X is going pretty well; Choir Y is going far better than I expected; Choir Z, though, I'm just losing my mind about that group." In this language, there's *me*, and there's *the choir*, the monolithic sum of those parts. We recognize that the issue with Choir Z might be that there are about four or five singers who are behaving poorly, but the net result is that "Choir Z has a behavior problem." In truth, a handful of singers in Choir Z are not meeting our expectations - and each of them may have dramatically different reasons for this - while dozens of singers in Choir Z are doing great work.

It is easy to treat fifty singers as a monolithic entity, and very hard to treat fifty singers as fifty humans. 'the choir' is not a personality – it's the aggregate behavior of multiple personalities who bring multiple positions and perspectives to the group.

I share this observation because it is crucial in creating room for all singers. It is easy to treat fifty singers as a monolithic entity, and very hard to treat fifty singers as fifty humans. Musically we do not want to hear fifty different vowels or rhythmic subdivisions or dynamics – we want one vowel, one sense of rhythmic subdivision, one dynamic. But we must acknowledge that the musical result comes from fifty very different people who have very different needs. One of the first steps toward a more respectful pedagogy is to remember that 'the choir' is not a personality - it's the aggregate behavior of multiple personalities who bring multiple positions and perspectives to the group. How should we make space for all of these different positions and perspectives? We are teaching singers who are younger than us, who we expect to be emotionally available, over whom we exercise power, and each of whom has a different voice within this unified ensemble. The more we come to know and understand our singers' individual experiences and journeys, the more complicated and beautiful and real our teaching becomes.

Section II:
OUR WORDS MATTER

I still remember being reprimanded by Mrs. Phillips in kindergarten for sitting on the counter, but I don't remember how she taught us to read. I remember being chastised by Mrs. Reher in fourth grade for shooting a rubber band, but I don't remember who my friends were in that classroom. I remember Darnell making fun of my teeth in fifth grade, but I don't remember anything about our friendship. I remember audition lines for the role I was not cast for in high school, but I cannot even remember the *name* of the play I had a lead in that same year. As it turns out, such a curiously selective memory is normal. We store our hurts and attacks deep in the brain, processing them in the limbic system as part of an evolutionary adaptation that presumably kept us from going back to watering holes where dangerous predators roamed or trading with people who double-crossed us. The spiritually unfortunate side of this adaptation is that the gracious and kind things we hear and opportunities we enjoy have a habit of passing by us. In this section, we come to a fuller understanding of our responsibility as respectful teachers to create a space in which singers can be their fullest selves.

A SAFE SPACE TO BE BRAVE

Some of us struggle to understand how and why the term 'safe space' is used. Some of us read the term 'safe space' to connote a place where one is shielded from physical violence. For example, a refugee might move to another country, and we would call their new homeland a safe space from the war. Many of us read the term 'safe space' to connote a place where LGTBQ+ singers can feel comfortable being themselves without fear of judgment or persecution. Teachers will recall the stickers put on doors in the 1990s or 2000s declaring one's office a 'safe space' with precisely this meaning: I accept and affirm you as a person with rights and dignity in the face of an outside climate of discrimination.

In recent years, the term 'safe space' has expanded. The term now implies a space in which all positions and experiences are respected and no one feels physically, emotionally, or psychologically threatened or judged.

> A Safe Space is a place where anyone can relax and be able to fully express, without fear of being made to feel uncomfortable, unwelcome, or unsafe on account of biological sex, race/ethnicity, sexual orientation, gender identity or expression, cultural background, religious affiliation, age, or physical or mental ability. A place where the rules guard each person's self-respect and dignity and strongly encourage everyone to respect others.[9] (from The *Safe Space Network)*.

I encourage you to process this definition for a few moments. The term *Safe Space* is no longer limited to providing refuge to those who feel persecuted. Rather, this broader definition protects against someone being "made to feel uncomfortable, unwelcome, or unsafe" because of any number of identity intersections.

Some readers will express concern with this broader definition. Where does grit fit in this? How does one learn and grow if one is never uncomfortable? Haven't we all developed thicker skin by hearing a few unwelcome personal insults? Into what imaginary kind and gentle world do our singers think they will go?

No part of great teaching requires insults.

This is an important conversation and these are important questions. I will offer one reading for now, and we will continually come back to this issue throughout the book. Let me propose that another way to read this broader definition as a choir director is simply: don't put down singers to teach. Hold your singers to the highest musical standards. Expect the best work from them. Be honest when they make mistakes, and teach them how to achieve. But no part of great teaching requires insults.

Here is an example from a recent rehearsal that could go either way. The sopranos sang a high A that was sufficiently behind the beat and out of tune to need correction.

> Safe-space version: *"Sopranos, let's look at that page turn again. It sounds like the high A caught you by surprise. Let's go back to the last two measures of the previous page; can you take in the kind of breath that sets up a vibrant and easy A there? Also, write that note in at the end of the page so you see it coming. That way it'll be rhythmically much tighter."*
>
> I identified the two issues (vocally unprepared for the airflow needed; visually unprepared for the page-turn) and offered corrective strategies to sing it better.
>
> Unsafe-space version: *"Yikes, you sound like cats getting a bath! Do us all a favor: if you don't have a good high A or can't count, don't sing it."*
>
> I identified the problems (sort of) as something to do with timbre and something to do with rhythm. Then I demeaned 'the sopranos' as a group and shamed their lack of self-awareness of their poor skills.

In this broader definition, a safe space is not a rehearsal in which 'any perspective on intonation is valid' or 'each of us finds our own sense of rhythm.' Rather, the choir room is a space where every singer feels safe being an ambitious musician without having to worry about personal insults and marginalizing comments.

This example shows a fairly obvious dichotomy, but it is not always so clear. In this example above, the conductor is actively abusive. As I hope to demonstrate throughout this book, we can also be passive adopters of a broader, less perceptible paradigmatic level of creating less safe spaces. As we saw in Chapter One, being in a choir that sings almost exclusively Euro/American male hetero-normative poets and composers can be an experience that does not make every singer feel welcomed. We will meet this issue again, but for now, let us remember that we are teaching singers who are expected to be emotionally vulernable enough to share their affective truth about a song or poem in rehearsal and also sing completely unified. They will need first and foremost a space in which to thrive.

And perhaps "safe" is not the right word to set up a thriving learning community. What we are really hoping to create is what educators Brian Arao and Kristi Clemens call a Brave Space. They assert that authentic learning often challenges students' sense of familiarity, and the anxiety or discomfort this creates is not compatible with the definition of 'safe.' If, for example, we want to have a conversation about something as emotionally difficult as institutional racism in America as related to singing a Spiritual, there are very few, if any, 'safe' positions. Participants who identify as White may feel "a sense of guilt and hopelessness," while participants who identify as Black "may, in fact, react with incredulity to the very notion of safety, for history and experience has demonstrated clearly to them that to name their oppression, and the perpetrators thereof, is a profoundly unsafe activity."[10] However, if we can frame the choir room as a place where we can be brave, we can grow and challenge and be challenged in a respectful, humanizing way.

If we can frame the choir room as a place where we can be brave, we can grow and challenge and be challenged in a respectful, humanizing way.

TRIGGER WARNINGS

If you are not yet familiar with this term, a *trigger warning* is simply a note of caution that an upcoming remark or text or other material may be upsetting. Merriam-Webster defines it as: "a statement cautioning that content (as in a text, video, or class) may be disturbing or upsetting."[11] The concept of a 'trigger' originated in psychological studies with war veterans. A car backfiring may trigger a veteran's Post-Traumatic Stress Disorder, for instance. The sound cues the soldier to relive the emotional stress of being attacked in a combat zone. Victims of such intense traumas learn to develop coping strategies, and the trigger warning allows those victims the opportunity to put the strategy in place before experiencing the content.

I did not know what trigger warnings were until I failed to provide one when some of my singers very much needed one. A guest artist was presenting a recital that intended to raise awareness and funds for victims of sexual violence and had emailed me to ask if I could promote the performance to my ensembles. I wanted to support her project so I read her paragraph out loud at the end of rehearsal ("Tonight you can hear a lecture recital that brings awareness to victims of rape and abuse…"), dismissed the choir, and patted myself on the back for being an ally to my friend. A student met me after class, chided me for not providing a trigger warning, and then left, upset.

I had multiple reactions in swift succession:

a) I was confused about this new term;

b) I was annoyed that I was somehow supposed to know about this new procedure (when were we supposed to get the memo?);

c) I felt that no good deed goes unpunished;

d) I questioned what this student hoped would happen after college, when customers, colleagues, and bosses from all walks of life burst their bubble of hyper-thoughtful liberal arts college students and professors;

e) Finally, I resolved that life is tough, no one-line warning makes the pain of abuse go away, and students today lack the grit we had in college to manage our struggles.

I share these not because I still advocate these immediate reactions, but because I hear some version of these reactions in the ongoing debate about the purposes of trigger warnings. As with the debate on safe spaces, I am unequipped to offer a definitive answer that resolves all questions and concerns. I can only share these few reflections and strategies that help us to become more respectful teachers:

First, I think we should *acknowledge the limits of our ability* to appropriately manage triggers. Since we understand that a choir is not an 'it' but a collection of many different people, we are limited in our ability to imagine every possible stressor. No one on either side of the debate seeks a perfectly sanitized climate, and we would do well to remember that we will never achieve one.

Second, we must understand that what is not a trigger for us can be one for others. I might make a casual joke during warm-ups about how I ate so much right before rehearsal that I cannot take a good singing breath. For 80% of the choir, it's a throw-away joke, a way to lighten the mood and an innocent transition as they came from taking midterms into rehearsal. But for 20% of the choir who are actively struggling with an eating disorder or are recovering from one, they now return to that horrible space in which food/body is a torturous issue.

Third, those of us who have the hardest time grasping the value of a trigger warning should *take a moment to reflect on our life's blessings*. I have not been in a firefight in Fallujah. I have not been a victim of sexual assault. I was not in Manhattan on September 11, 2001. My family did not physically abuse me. I was not called a racial slur a thousand times. I have not gone nights without food, lived in foster care, lived through divorce, lost parents, or been admitted to psychiatric care. I have the tremendous *luxury* of not needing trigger warnings, because everything for me is just the content (words, music, etc) without the profoundly painful context. I do not mean to suggest that I have not ever suffered deeply, felt depression or anxiety, or been hurt by others, physically or otherwise. I cannot imagine living on this earth without encountering some slings and arrows. But I draw a distinction between the bumps and bruises of life (which do hurt a great deal), and the trauma of abuse.

Fourth, even those of us who have enjoyed such a remarkably fortunate life can see that we have been sensitive to this for longer than we might think. *Knowing when not to say something is a social cue* that we pick up in childhood. We sixth-graders felt that we had both invented and perfected jokes about each other's mothers, but we also understood not to tell them around the boy whose mom just passed away. Sixth-graders can often lack interpersonal kindness (see also: making fun of each other's mothers as a primary form of entertainment), but even we understood that it's "not appropriate" around that kid. It wasn't impossible for us to grasp that his mind was swirling with grief, and we did not need to amplify that with another reminder that we had mothers to make fun of and he didn't. As we grow up, we begin to understand that there are more and more people like him who carry grief for a lost mother, and soon our mom jokes fade away from our conversational repertoire as inappropriate.

Fifth, even if we have lived a remarkably good life, *we all have our own triggers*, and should reflect on them as well. I experienced a vocal injury in graduate school, just at the precipice of starting a career as a singer. It took me the better part of five years to admit that something was wrong with my voice, seek a diagnosis, participate in speech therapy, and grieve that small but real change in my hoped-for life. It took much longer to learn not to resent students who failed to appreciate the blessings of their pristine vocal folds. Every time I talk with a student who has been diagnosed with a vocal injury, I relive the emotional wound of my diagnosis. Though the grieving process gets easier with time, I cannot hear about a vocal injury and not re-experience that grief. I obviously put this in a much lower category of trauma than, for example, physical abuse from a parent, to be sure. Still, while I can hear about plane crashes or famines or floods and feel a generalized sense of pity and empathy, when someone talks about vocal damage, I re-live it. What is your personal trigger? How do you hope others will handle that topic when you are present?

I challenge myself to ask what it would be like if my life included a different, more powerful trauma. I remember singing *The Drunken Sailor* in elementary school. I'm still not clear on what the pedagogical value of this sea chantey was, but I know we were a little confused by it. In hindsight, I know now that some of my peers lived a daily nightmare of having an alcoholic parent. What to us was an adult problem (how to handle a drunk colleague) which made as little sense as most things in school (but had a nice tune), was a constant poke in the defining wound of their young lives for some students.

When 'the choir' transcends being an 'it' and becomes a group of singers with their own stories, we see a rich and haunting collection of powerful life experiences, each in some process of grief or pain. Choir can help heal these wounds; but choir can also inadvertently open them.

If this line of thought leads us to suspect an impending argument for censorship against all repertoire that isn't constantly pleasant to everyone on the planet, fear not. Yet, I hear those two thoughts rising in our minds:

1. Well, if *everything* reminds someone of *something* bad, what can be performed?
2. Isn't art *supposed* to be problematic?

By acknowledging *why* trigger warnings exist, we can focus less on which songs are acceptable or *how* art provokes, and instead pay attention to how we handle difficult topics. When we acknowledge that teaching the Brahms *Ein deutsches Requiem* will feel differently to someone who has lost their mother, we approach that repertoire selection and instruction with more empathy, compassion, and respect. We see that this work has different emotional connotation for different singers, and we do not presume that our experience is everyone's. We leave space for this to be difficult. We can have the class take some slow breaths, notice their feet connecting with the floor, notice smells and colors. We can employ Social-Emotional Learning strategies to help everyone feel calm and grounded in these discussions.

Moreover, **trigger warnings are not intended to censor our repertoire curriculum, but are a consideration when guiding the discussions that flow from curriculum.** As the origin of the trigger warning is in PTSD therapy, we understand that we invoke them to remove painful surprises. That is, we use a trigger warning when our conversation goes to the *otherwise-unprepared* hurt places, not as a daily activity about the songs we always sing. To come back to the example I began with, I do not even remember what my choir was singing the day I announced the upcoming concert about sexual abuse, but I know that abuse had nothing to do with it. I also knew that members of the choir were sexual-abuse victims. In hindsight, had I been able to say a preemptive word or two that would allow those students a moment to employ their recovery strategies, it would have cost me nothing and made a great difference in their lives. These small adaptations go a long way in creating a safer, more accessible space for all singers.

TEACHING STUDENTS WITH TRAUMA

Our discussion of trigger warnings points us to a broader reality. Some of our singers have endured, or are currently enduring, profound trauma. Let us first begin by defining the word "trauma", since the word has a lot of popular usage as well. Here is a definition from the American Psychological Association: "trauma is an emotional response to a terrible event like an accident, rape or natural disaster. Immediately after the event, shock and denial are typical. Longer term reactions include unpredictable emotions, flashbacks, strained relationships and even physical symptoms like headaches or nausea. While these feelings are normal, some people have difficulty moving on with their lives."[12] Social worker and educational consultant Jennifer Bashant defines trauma as, "an experience that overwhelms one's ability to cope, changes the wiring of the brain, and has an impact on both learning and behavior."[13] Hence the clinical use of the word 'trauma' needs to be separated from casual use of the word, as in "they cancelled my favorite tv show and it's, like, *trauma*." Trauma a word that describes an experience that overwhelms and *changes* the person experiencing it.

Researchers Vincent Felitti, Robert Anda, Nadine Burke Harris, and others demonstrated the connection between traumatic adverse childhood experiences (known as ACEs) and significant risks to health and wellness. It is worth taking a moment here to look together at the ACEs screening test.[14] For each question, count 1 point if you answer yes.

Before your 18th birthday:

#1. Did a parent or other adult in the household often or very often… a) Swear at you, insult you, put you down, or humiliate you? or b) Act in a way that made you afraid that you might be physically hurt?

#2. Did a parent or other adult in the household often or very often… a) Push, grab, slap, or throw something at you? or b) Ever hit you so hard that you had marks or were injured?

#3. Did an adult or person at least 5 years older than you ever... a) Touch or fondle you or have you touch their body in a sexual way? or b) Attempt or actually have oral, anal, or vaginal intercourse with you?

#4. Did you often or very often feel that ... a) No one in your family loved you or thought you were important or special? or b) Your family didn't look out for each other, feel close to each other, or support each other?

#5. Did you often or very often feel that ... a) You didn't have enough to eat, had to wear dirty clothes, and had no one to protect you? or b) Your parents were too drunk or high to take care of you or take you to the doctor if you needed it?

#6. Were your parents ever separated or divorced?

#7. Was your mother or stepmother: a) Often or very often pushed, grabbed, slapped or had something thrown at her? or b) Sometimes, often, or very often kicked, bitten, hit with a fist, or hit with something hard? or c) Ever repeatedly hit over at least a few minutes or threatened with a gun or knife?

#8. Did you live with anyone who was a problem drinker or alcoholic, or who used street drugs?

#9. Was a household member depressed or mentally ill, or did a household member attempt suicide?

#10. Did a household member go to prison?

I took this test as part of a foster-care training seminar, and realized at the end of the test that, to my surprise, I scored zero. Most children I have fostered have scored at least 6, that I am aware of. That left a lasting impression with me.

What do we know about outcomes for children based on ACEs results? First, most people have at least 1. Second, 50% of children's ACEs scores happen by age 3. Third, one in six adults report having more than four on the ACEs.[15]

Most powerfully, children with high ACEs scores have:

- A 20-year drop in life expectancy. You read that right. A *20-year* drop in life expectancy.
- 7.4 times the likelihood of alcoholism and 12.2 times the likelihood to attempt suicide if they have 4 or more on the ACEs.
- 3 times the likelihood of repeating a grade with 3 or more on the ACEs.[16]

Trauma changes the brain, and a lot of trauma changes the brain a lot. Of course, there is much we can do to heal, but let us never assume that all singers come into rehearsal with the same basic sense of safety, trust, focus, and resilience.

How widespread is trauma for children? How many students in our teaching day are we talking about with high ACEs scores? A 2007 study by Copeland et al found that "more than two thirds of children reported at least 1 traumatic event by 16 years of age, with 13.4% of those children developing some PTS [Post-Traumatic Stress] symptoms."[17] Almost a quarter of children in America live with a single parent.[18] One out of fifty children in America have a parent in prison.[19] In 2019, over 672,000 children spent time in foster care, and the average duration in care is a year and a half.[20] Approximately 1 in 30 children experience homelessness.[21] In short, it is almost inconceivable that we as choral directors are not teaching multiple singers who are presently navigating significant traumas.

Let us consider the challenge of teaching singers in trauma from the lens of Maslow's hierarchy of needs.[22]

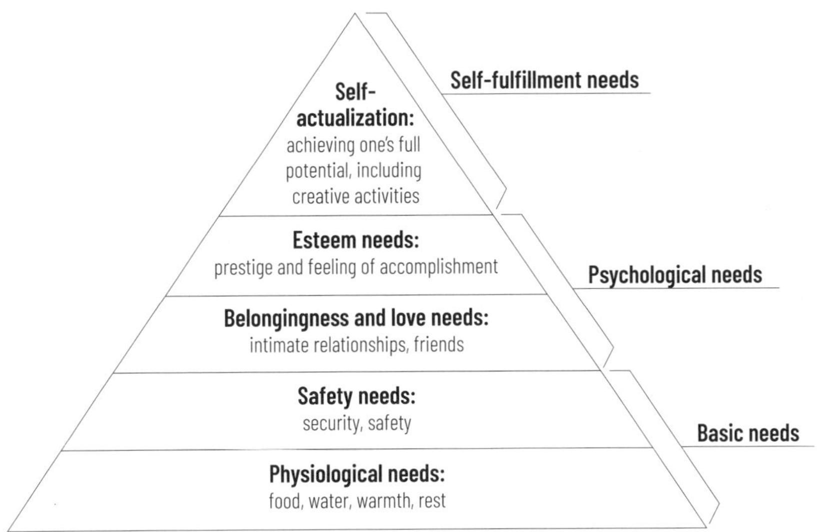

Our lessons often focus, with good intention, on helping students self-actualize and become the best they can be. We usually create the learning space for self-actualization by fostering a sense of belonging in the room (we know one another's names, we celebrate one another's birthdays) and cultivating self-esteem (we work hard and earn a sense of value and recognition from our practice). But if a singer's panic prevents sleeping at night, or they are determining how to hide the food stamps from Mom so she doesn't sell them for drugs, or they are strategizing how to mitigate the next attack from Mom's new boyfriend, they are not going to sight-read or name key signatures or memorize page five with the same efficacy as their neighbor in the section.

The reality is that a singer in trauma may have a different brain chemistry. In basic terms, the amygdala, within the limbic system of the brain, communicates what to do urgently in a crisis: fight, flee, or freeze. If you've nearly avoided a car accident or jumped in fright at a garden hose that you mistook for a snake, you recognize the rush of immediate adrenaline and cortisol to handle the crisis. Children in trauma tend to stay in a prolonged phase of amygdala response.[23] They are living in a state of panic and survival, and not without cause. The problem is that learning only occurs when the learner is calm enough to engage the prefrontal cortex so they can plan, evaluate, discern, and imagine.

What can we do as teachers? To be clear, you and I are *not* psychiatrists and are not charged with healing our singers with significant trauma. But by knowing that our choral space includes singers with trauma, we can examine our lesson-planning, our routines, and our expectations so that singers develop a sense of safety, connection, and trust in this space. To support this work, Bashant offers several ideas that we can implement effectively. First, many of us have inherited a disciplinary model of, "here are my expectations – meet them or get out". For a student who has learned with good reason to distrust adults and who entered the classroom in fight/flight/freeze mode, this is a recipe for a blow-up. Instead, Bashant recommends focusing on intrinsic motivation, which happens when: "1) the student can experience mastery of the expectation, 2) the student is given some degree of autonomy regarding their learning, and 3) the student understands the purpose of the given expectation and is able to understand the relevance to their own life".[24]

Second, Bashant suggests that teachers re-examine their gut response to difficult behavior. Our default response is likely some version of "what is wrong with you?" Bashant recommends replacing that internal script with "what has happened to you?"[25] Do you feel how that verb change pivots us to empathy? 'What has happened to you' allows us to see that behavior is a form of communication. When a student blurts out "I hate this song" or sits like a statue when everyone else is warming up, they are communicating, "I am not feeling safe and connected right now". When we see the behavior as a way to communicate "something has happened / is happening to me", we are moved to curiosity and empathy.

Third, Bashant reminds us that our "number one priority when a student is exhibiting challenging behavior is to help them become regulated".[26] That is different than "asserting control", which, again, is not going to go well when the student is already in fight/flight mode. In other words, take the student on in a power-challenge only if you want the student to fight you or run out of the room. Instead, we need to de-escalate the situation. Slow down the speed in the room, reduce the volume and frequency of words, and bring the emotional thermometer down. As I say to my music education students, the classroom is already full of children, so what is needed in that moment is an *adult* response – measured, calm, and learning-centered. That is hard, especially when a student pushes our specific buttons. My wife is a special education teacher who is regularly slapped, bitten, and punched by children, and she has developed what I would consider to be a super-human ability to interrupt her own amygdala response so that she can bring her students back to calm. To be clear, she is immediate in responding, such as: "no, slapping is not safe; you can say, 'Mrs. Sieck, I would like a turn'." As Bashant observes, when teaching children in trauma, "what really needs to happen is the child needs to feel safe, both physically and emotionally, so that the parasympathetic nervous system can engage and effectively calm the body."[27] One of our most important and lasting roles as teachers is to create the calm and safety in the room for singers to learn this life skill.

I want to take a moment in this discussion to share the lived experience as someone who has parented nine children in foster care. Even after hundreds of hours of training and two decades of parenting, I still find it challenging to wrap my head around the range of behaviors. Children in trauma can: break a teacher's nose; pull the fire alarm; run off the school bus and hide under it at a red light; wipe feces on walls; spray disinfectant in another student's face; wish for or attempt suicide; wield a knife at another child; sexually proposition and attempt sexual acts with other children; steal and destroy other children's favorite items; break doors, walls, and windows; and so much more. And, children in trauma can also: snuggle up for bedtime; be amazing movie night companions; beat adults in games of Uno; sing hymns at church; go on long bike-rides; stay up after bedtime to continue reading a nail-biter of a story;

and so much more. And most days, children in trauma will do something from both lists. With my biological children, I too often took for granted how stable their lives were, and fussed about "typical" parenting concerns, like remembering to turn in a permission slip or turning the phone off at bedtime. With foster children in my care, I have continually struggled to wrap my head around the severity of their range of behaviors. Some days a reading lesson will be an easy 15-minute item, and some days a reading lesson will involve a chair being thrown and a book being destroyed. What made today's reason lesson so much worse than yesterday's? Sometimes it is a function of the foster-parenting adage that the child feels safe enough with you to truly fall apart and process their trauma. Sometimes it is a function of a brain panicking over something you and I probably would not panic over, like misreading a word. Or, that story reminds the child of something their biological mom did or did not do. Or, this is the same time of the year and the same weather as the time their father abandoned them. Or, I was upset about something at work, and the child, who has hyper-vigilance for adult emotions (a survival adaptation for traumatic childhood), picked up on my anger and flipped into fight-flight. The reality is that children with a lot of trauma are harder to teach. But I know three things as both a teacher and a parent: 1) it's always "what happened to you?", never "what's wrong with you?", 2) they can get a lot better when the environment is safe, and 3) it takes a long time.

Section III:
ACCESSIBILITY AND ACCOMMODATIONS

As with other topics in this chapter, I think of accessibility as a window into the ways in which we welcome or exclude our singers, the ways in which we empower our community or marginalize the 'other.' Chapter Three explores this topic in depth. Here, we examine briefly how our awareness of different singers' needs and abilities creates a respectful and welcoming space.

Those of us who direct church or community choirs often work with older singers who cannot stand for extended periods of time. Most directors allow the choirs with older singers to sit often, and view this as simple act of kindness and practicality. Imagine the alternative: "look, I don't care if you're 80 and had two hip replacements – this choir *stands*!" We are not watering down our musical standards to acknowledge that singers might need to sit more often.

It has been my experience that my older singers who cannot stand are not seeking to cut corners or to work less hard. They might even prefer to have their younger legs and spines, standing comfortably and without pain. No one has the sense that these singers are being lazy or playing us; we simply make the accommodation as a basic courtesy. In fact, organizations such as churches work hard to find the best language that is inclusive and respectful of both the tradition of standing and the accommodation for those that cannot: "please stand as you are able" or "please rise in body or spirit" are commonly used options. We are grateful for our elder members, and we do everything we can to include them.

I have found that we choir directors are far less likely to extend such compassion to younger singers. I suspect there are several reasons for this opposition:

a) We educators are in the business of training students how to sing well. One sings well by standing with great posture. We can do some rehearsing in chairs, of course, but great singing is a physical act that requires full body engagement. The first week or two on risers may be uncomfortable, but once we build those standing muscles, we free ourselves up for great singing. If the first time we stand on risers for any length of time is the concert, we are not ready for the concert.

b) *We're* the old ones in the room, not them, and we stand for hours; they only need to stand for 45 minutes. If anyone in this room deserves a seat, it's the middle-aged teacher, not the 17-year-old, right?

c) We can sometimes feel as if students are endlessly asking for shortcuts, and our teaching experience shows us that pushing students past what they think they can do is often rewarding.

These are all sensible arguments, and I have used them all many times.

The error here is that I have reverted to a 'me versus *the choir*' instead of a 'me and *these singers*' mindset. Collectively, yes, the choir has younger, healthier muscles and tendons than the director; individually, no. Collectively, yes, the choir sings better when it stands; individually, no. Here's a simple mental exercise: let us imagine that some of our singers on these risers are experiencing menstrual cramps, with several students suffering diagnosed premenstrual syndrome that produces debilitating cramps. Will these singers learn how to better cope with this by the time they enter adulthood? Yes, probably. But they might not have all the right strategies and medications yet. Will they feel comfortable telling their middle-aged male conductor that they would prefer to sit today for this reason? Not usually, and moreover, that shifts the burden of accommodation onto the adolescent student in pain, not on the professional educator. It costs me nothing if we sit in chairs and sing well versus standing in great suffering. So it is not my responsibility *per se* to get them to wake up to the profession's demands; it is my job to teach them how to sing choral music, and this small accommodation gets us past *'why can't you just deal with it'* and move toward music-making. I chose this example because it is directly relatable to many singers. Consider other ways this could apply: migraines, vertigo, asthma, allergies, and more.

When I try to empathize by assuming a singer's pain is like a pain I know, I get myself in trouble. It is unprofessional for us to take on the role of physician or psychiatrist. I would rather focus on being a choral conductor.

When I try to empathize by assuming a singer's pain is like a pain I know, I get myself in trouble. I do not get migraines, so, like many others, my first reaction to a student's migraine as a teacher was something like, "take an ibuprofen and get over it already!" But I have now worked with enough migraine-suffering colleagues to know that a migraine is not like a headache, and if I think they're the same, that means I'm lucky to have never had a migraine. With life experience and education, we learn that *being stuck in a rut* is not the same as depression, that *fierce attention to details* is not the same as Obsessive-Compulsive Disorder, that *being wiggly* is not the same as Attention Deficit Hyperactivity Disorder. I can't empathize with everyone directly, but I can learn to respect their needs.

My explicit goal here is to help us to free ourselves from the exhausting burden of being more than choral directors. If I question the validity of a singer's migraine or ADHD, I assume a degree of authority over medical diagnoses that I simply do not have. It is unprofessional for us to take on the role of physician or psychiatrist. I would rather focus on being a choral conductor.

What would ever possess us to do this? I have two theories. First, we will all encounter singers who are manipulative and misuse real medical conditions that they do not have. They will use migraines as a lie for missing choir. They will use the term depression and never turn in assignments. And there are few things people like less than being duped. We might know in some part of our brain that we're talking about a very, very small population of our singers. But we also know that we do not want to be duped again.

Second, choral music is a 'people profession.' If our career aspiration was to make music become better tuned, we'd tune pianos. We see how a singer's self can radiate into the singing and music-making. We see our singers as whole people, and when they are not thriving – whether through the real suffering of something like depression, or simply a more benign 'stuck in a rut' – we want to get involved and help fix them. So we extrapolate from our own experiences and offer suggestions.

I propose that we can create a healthier, more vibrant and inclusive choral community by focusing our energy on the intersection of people and music. We can and should help those who we are concerned about connect with professionals who can help. If we have a singer who says they are suffering from migraines, let's pass that information on to the student's counselor/advisor. We can share that we want every singer in our choir to thrive, and that we are concerned because this work isn't getting turned in or that many rehearsals are being missed. We want to help in whatever ways we can. We can share that we have been burned before by singers that have abused our trust, and have learned that the best way to support a student with migraines is to make sure that people who can help (e.g., counselors, physicians,) are made aware of the singer's issues and can, likewise, let us directors know how best to proceed.

I propose that we spend less time after work being frustrated by singers we think we can cure from their personal/psychological issues and more time at work connecting those singers to people who can help them with those issues.

I propose that we spend less time after work being frustrated by singers we think we can cure from their personal/psychological issues and more time at work connecting those singers to people who can help them with those issues. And, we can admit that it took us a long time to get to the healthy place we are now in, and that such health is a project that we continually work at. We can show the kind of patience that we needed when we were younger. Let us come to see our singers more as people-in-process (ever working toward a stronger sense of whole) and less as people-in-product (broken or whole).

Section IV:
TALENT VS. GROWTH

There are two reasons why I ended up as a choral director instead of the NFL defensive tackle I desperately wanted to be in fourth grade. The first and most obvious answer is that a defensive tackle is usually about 6'2" and 290 pounds, and those are two qualifications I am incapable of achieving. The second, more pervasive answer is that I was told a thousand times that I was not talented in sports and told a thousand times that I was talented in music. People are not always rational actors, but we tend to follow the path of positive feedback.

In the former case, there were fixed attributes that I could not achieve – that degree of height and size. We can each name dozens of fixed physical attributes in ourselves that are unchangeable - our eye color or skeletal frame, for example. . Especially for children who become passionate about sports, these fixed attributes of height or weight mean a great deal at an impressionable age, and we tend to extrapolate that such fixed or innate characteristics apply to more than just our bodies.

In the latter case of being told that I was talented in music, admirers praised an innate quality that I possessed, a gift for playing piano that I received the way Lebron James received height. With reflection, I think each of us conductors can construct a similar narrative in which we knew that we had something special in music (and also other things we should not do). Such a gift filled us with the confidence to take on increasingly difficult music, a duty to persevere through long, tedious hours of practice, and a stewardship-like obligation to see the training through so that we could share our gift with others. Knowing that we had a gift for music, we pushed through music theory classes, private lessons, conducting classes, and all the other appropriate rigors of training.

As it turns out, people who practice effectively and passionately at something for many years with thoughtful mentorship become exceptionally good at it.

It turns out that talent is not as simple as we thought. You may have already seen the studies or heard about the magic *ten-thousand hours*. As it turns out, people who practice effectively and passionately at something for many years with thoughtful mentorship become exceptionally good at it. Anders Ericsson et al first reported this with a groundbreaking study on deliberate practice.[28] They surveyed the faculty at a German music conservatory and asked them to identify which students were the most talented and likely to succeed in the profession as violinists. The students identified as most talented were the students who had practiced the most hours (10,000 hours, give or take), while the ones that seemed to lack the talent had practiced the least hours (4,000 hours or so). There are *many* outstanding books and articles on this subject, so I will simply summarize here.

I am interested in exploring our personal reactions to the idea that talent is a constructed myth. *What about me?* Have I not demonstrated the validity of my talent in my life's work? Absolutely, we have affirmed our skill at music by becoming the musicians we are today. But we are not the musicians today that we were as children. Someone taught us to read music. Someone taught us how to sing well. Someone taught us how to conduct, how to plan a rehearsal, how to lead a group. We did not succeed at these skills with the same proficiency ten or twenty years ago as we succeed today. Rather, we improved with continued and reflective practice. Consider your college voice lessons, your conducting classes, your piano lessons: do you not recall learning certain skills, being chastised for poor work, practicing many hours, and finally getting better? Or, was everything flawless from day one?

Believing that we are talented might carry us through years of hard work, but it risks erasing the memory of the work.

Believing that we are talented might carry us through years of hard work, but it risks erasing the memory of the work. When I was in sixth grade and messing around at the piano, I was told I had musical talent. The idea was planted, the spark ignited. When I started singing in ensembles in high school, I was told I did not have vocal talent. When I started studying voice lessons in college, I was told I did not have vocal talent. Ten years after I started singing in ensembles, I worked in professional choirs, and people told me I was a talented choral singer. Ten years after I started studying voice privately, I sang professionally, and people told me I was a talented singer. I am very comfortable admitting that the talent myth got me through the ten years of focused practice that take someone from novice to professional. Such an admission does not make me sing less professionally. It makes me appreciate the value of practice. And that is a tremendous relief to me as a teacher.

What would it look like if we taught a roomful of singers that had talent? We would assume that every singer had a natural aptitude or inclination toward music. We would assume that every singer was capable of learning to read scores, hear intervals, develop great vocal habits, and learn to sing well together. We would no doubt recognize that we could not bring to full fruition all of their talents in a year or two, but we would work as grateful stewards to this remarkable ensemble. When they stumbled, we would challenge ourselves to modify our pedagogy to better educate and inspire them. When they 'checked out,' we would reflect on our pacing. When they struggled to sing in tune, we would scan our technical background to review breathing, placement, and other vocal skills. In short, we would do everything in our power to make manifest this great gift in our ensemble.

What would it look like if we taught a class that was a mixture of singers, only a select few of which had talent? We would need to sort out the sheep from the goats, first of all. We would want everyone in the room to be musically literate, but we would not want everyone to be an equally active participant, and we might even ask some goats to "just mouth the words" on some songs. We would need the goats to, as much as possible, stay out of the way of the sheep, so that they did not hold back such talent from its potential progress. Better yet, we would decide to sort out our singers into different groups based on their talent, so that there was a super-talented group, some moderately talented groups, and a group for goats.

Let's play out both scenarios. In the first program, every singer is pushed to grow and practice and learn. The teachers put on themselves the burden of designing the best education and the best rehearsal process to grow the potential in each singer. Freed from pre-determined limits, every singer grows and performs increasingly better every year. They stay in choir, seeing their progress over the years. They become lovers of music and advocates for the arts.

In the sheep and goats program, the teachers serve as gate-keepers and talent scouts who help identify who has *it* and who does not. On this bell-curve, a small group of chosen talent ascends to glory, while a large middle of the pack waits in nervous hope for being selected one day, and the wrong side of the curve drops choir and all future musical endeavors.

Since I dislike thinking in binaries, especially ones painted as lopsided as this, let us consider the matter from a few other perspectives. First, when we call talent a myth, do we suggest that there is no such thing as a top group versus a beginning group in our programs, no such thing as singers who perform better than others? Of course not. Our own experience shows us over and over the scenario in which Student A can sing beautifully, sight-read, count, shape phrases, etc., whereas Student B does not even match pitch...yet. It will be hard to find an appropriate learning pace in class if they are in the same group. When we see talent as a myth, though, we remove the idea that there is some innate, fixed characteristic in Student A (that encompasses sight-reading, vocal technique, etc.) that is lacking in Student B. Rather, I would wager that Student A grew up with music around the house, had a solid general music curriculum, took private lessons, sang in children's choir, etc., whereas Student B did not.

In other words, Student B is not a great singer… *yet*. As Carol Dweck contends in her paradigm-shifting work *Mindset*, Student B has not *yet* learned how to sing like Student A. Student B can and will (with the right strategies and practice) become a singer, but is not there yet. Student B will need the kind of ensemble experience that teaches the skills that Student A has already mastered – skills like breathing, vocal production, counting, hearing intervals, shaping vowels, etc. Student A will need the kind of ensemble that assumes those skills as prerequisites and pushes them to higher-level musical decisions. We do not need to throw away the tiered-ensemble structure in our choral program; we just need clarity on what each group is aiming to achieve, and to let go of the fixed limits and assignations.

We teach what we perceive, so let us see in
each of our students the potential for future excellence.

If we are to teach our singers with respect, then we must see in each singer the capability of becoming great through excellent teaching and steady practice. Let us see each singer's present ability as a reflection of how much time and expertise has been invested in them before today, not as a referendum on their 'it' factor. Education studies warn us of the troubling danger of pre-casting our students for failure or success. Indeed, this is known as the Pygmalion Effect, based on Robert Rosenthal's Stanford University research. Rosenthal led elementary school teachers to believe they were teaching "gifted students", so the teachers taught the (actually normal) students in such a way that the class made the kind of significant growth associated with gifted learners. We teach what we perceive, so let us see in each of our students the potential for future excellence.[29]

This is not just a feel-good sentiment – this is a call for social justice. Let me look at the world from my own home to bring this to better clarity. My children grew up with two very musical parents who always sang to them, played them music, and took them to musical events. When they outgrew musical toys, we purchased instruments for them to study, paid for private lessons with excellent teachers, sent them to summer music camps, and coached them in the skills of effective practicing every day. If my child mentions a student in the back of the section who doesn't play well, I can't help but think that this other player has had, at age 15, literally thousands of hours fewer of musical experiences, plays on a poor instrument that the school rents to her, and has never had private lesson instruction.

I pray that my childrens' teachers recognize that the 'gift' they have is that of musical privilege. They were born into a set of musical experiences that their peers did not get. I pray that my childrens' teachers see their proficiency not as a confirmation of an innate talent (which, too, dishonors the years of practice they have put into their instruments), but as yet more confirmation that music is a skill that is nurtured through teaching. When we focus on finding a sheep among goats, we help the privileged ascend still higher, and demote the under-privileged still lower. And when choirs exist to screen out, we sign our own death warrant as a viable and relevant art that speaks to humanity.

CHAPTER 3
Teaching Singers with Diverse Abilities

When choral directors think about teaching singers with disabilities, what often jumps to mind are people with profound disabilities, such as those with significant intellectual impairments or physical restrictions. The reality is that most of us work every day with singers with a broad range of abilities and needs. As discussed in Chapter 2, many choral directors lead community or church choirs having older singers, some of whom cannot stand for extended periods of time, safely negotiate stairs, and struggle to read the music notation or text.

These singers with disabilities need adaptations or modifications, and choir directors typically make those adjustments automatically. For individuals who cannot stand for long periods, we incorporate extended seated rehearsal time. For singers with mobility issues, we make the processional optional. For singers with vision impairments, we create large-print copies of the score. Making these adaptations is a skill so integral to our leadership that we may not be aware of how frequently we are making them.

Although we all have a range of strategies for addressing the needs of our singers, we may still find ourselves confronted with individuals whose needs fall outside the realm of our experience. For those of us who went through our schooling before the passage of the Individuals with Disabilities Education Act in 1990, we might never have personally participated in mainstreamed classes with students with special needs. Most music teachers in the field today took a required course with a title like "Educating All Learners" or "Teaching Exceptional Students," and that helps. But our *choral* experience in high school and college has likely been profoundly segregated from intentional integration with students with special needs. We may have some basic framework of understanding that different singers learn differently and may need different accommodations. But if we are to teach all our singers with the respect that we would want if we were in their shoes, we need to build a deeper awareness and have more strategies available for them.

ABLE-ISM

To begin, we need to search ourselves for discriminatory habits of mind. Many of us grew up with the mindset that to have a disability was to be less valuable or a burden to others. This mindset is "able-ism", which is defined as:

> ...the practices and dominant attitudes in society that devalue and limit the potential of persons with disabilities; a set of practices and beliefs that assign inferior value (worth) to people who have developmental, emotional, physical or psychiatric disabilities.[30]

An able-ist mentality normalizes the huge range of human ability into one set standard, and then identifies those that do not or cannot fit that standard as aberrant. An able-ist mentality would assume that students who have fine motor difficulties should not be able to sign up for an art class because "they would never be able to draw well." In this situation, the focus on the student's potential for mastery trumps any other benefits from the experience, including the value of self-determination and choice, aesthetic expression, and high teacher expectations.

An able-ist mentality normalizes the huge range of human ability into one set standard, and then identifies those that do not or cannot fit that standard as aberrant.

A choral director who has shed the able-ist mindset will see that their singers will come to them with a wide range of abilities, needs, and experiences. Some of them already know how to sight-read, some will learn to sight-read, and others may learn over a much longer time than you anticipate. Some will understand the concepts but fail to demonstrate them, and some may never sight-read. If they are in your choir room, you have the opportunity to treat all your singers like fully human beings.

This approach can be especially hard to adopt for musicians. We have spent our lives using the language of talent, identifying the select few who will shine where everyone else falls short. While we celebrate some singers we have fostered to excellence, in the same mind-set, we discard as many, if not more, as not having 'it.' Moreover, the choral experience is a group endeavor; our choral excellence requires the best collection of talent we can assemble. In this mindset, it is very easy to see how students who might 'ruin' the choral experience would be prevented from participating.

An *anti-able-ist* choral director does not forgo the drive for excellence. An advanced choir that places a premium on sight-reading might not be the right curricular fit for all students. To teach in the most respectful way possible, however, directors must go beyond *tolerating* students with disabilities and move toward looking for ways that those students can participate meaningfully in the choral program.

THE WORDS WE USE

Teachers know that the words they use matter and, therefore, many struggle with what to call our students who have atypical abilities and needs. We might worry that we are going to say 'the wrong term' and be shamed in 'gotcha' culture. In order to engage in truly respectful teaching, we must understand the distinction between *political correctness* and respectful language. Political correctness is a term we invoke when we feel that our words are censored, but do not understand *why* they are being censored. A teacher who does not understand this distinction might, for example, be told to stop referring to his a student with one inappropriate term but then might call that student a different inappropriate term as a replacement, or learn to use the appropriate term though they are clearly thinking of the student from the mindset of the inappropriate term. We conductors need strategies for determining the most respectful way to refer to our singers.

Political correctness is a term we invoke when we feel that our words are censored, but do not understand why *they are being censored.*

If we are looking for the politically correct way to talk about people who do things differently than we expect - as in "what's the acceptable way to say [insert offensive term] these days?" - we are starting from the wrong place. "Handicapped" might be less offensive than some older terms for mobility impairment, but it still describes someone by their difference: "Bill can't get around on his two feet; he's handicapped." Normal (fully valued) people walk; Bill is abnormal (not quite as valued).

One way to approach "how we should talk about this?" is to lead with *people first.* We start by acknowledging Bill as fully valued, a man with hopes and dreams, a past and a future. People-first language would sound like, "Bill is a person who is disabled." Better yet, we can leave the limiting factor (disabled) out of the conversation unless and until it is relevant. Bill is a person. If there's a question or concern about whether he can get onstage by himself, we would say, "Bill uses a wheelchair for mobility." There are real and important contexts in which we absolutely must address the special needs of some of our singers. There is no need to tiptoe around those details in that context ("how will Bill get onstage?"). But the solution to worrying about political correctness is to start by seeing all our singers as valued humans. I encourage you to think about how you use language to describe your students. I will use "students with diverse abilities" here, but most educational documents still use "students with disabilities" – people-first, but focusing on their disability.

When we lead with a descriptor like "Bill is a disabled student," we may implicitly narrow the broad array of qualities that make Bill who he is, and offer instead a medical diagnosis. Everyone at my house wears glasses, but I am very glad we are not introduced as "the visually-impaired Siecks." Unless we are applying to the Air Force, 20/20 vision is not relevant. Pedagogue Susan Gabel suggests that we reframe our mode of thinking through our language, offering instead the expression *ability diversity*:

> "…I use ability diversity to refer to the range of cognitive, physical, emotional, and perhaps even behavioral ways humans interact with and live in the world. My implicit argument is that ability diversity should be considered among other diversities (e.g., race, ethnicity, gender, sexual orientation, culture, etc.), whereas disability should be considered as a status of oppression or identity that usually stigmatizes an individual but that preferably involves consent."[31]

Diverse abilities, as a term, allow us to discuss both students who struggle and those with unusually strong abilities (giftedness), or those whose development is asynchronous (such as a student with strong math skills who struggles with social interactions). It also allows us to remove the judgment or shame that so frequently used to be heaped on anyone who was perceived as 'flawed.' While our educational system may continue to refer to students with disabilities, we can refer to ability diversity as a sign of our respect for all singers.

Having said this, it is important to note that there is also a strong argument against person-first language. For example, many in the Autistic community have pushed back against the expression, "Steve is a person with autism" and prefer "Steve is autistic". One of the concerns with person-first language is that it stigmatizes or treats a person's difference as undesirable when it is not. Person-first language presents the person and the attribute as (desirably) separate. If Steve has cancer, we don't say Steve is cancerous; we say that Steve is a person who is undergoing treatment for cancer, or Steve is a person battling cancer, because cancer is a deadly disease that Steve does not want. In this example, Steve has existed without cancer and hopes to exist without cancer in the future. In this way, person-first language can pathologize someone's difference. Autism is not cancer, and it is not something to pathologize. Moreover, having a learning, physical, or neurological difference is typically a lifetime experience. As a friend of mine who identifies herself as disabled said, "to say that I'm 'Jane with a disability' suggests that there was ever a version of Jane that didn't have this disability. I've always been Jane, and I've always been disabled."

So where does that leave us? We return to our Platinum rule, to treat people the way they want to be treated. Create a space where singers can identify themselves the way they want to be identified, and honor their choices. Additionally, check your own biases: *why* is this person's difference coming up in your mind? Is it relevant to teaching and learning today? Why is this descriptor important to your train of thought?

THE LAW

There are three key dates in education law that we need to know. In 1975 Congress passed the Education for All Handicapped Children Act, which required schools to *teach* students who were identified as having special needs. Prior to that law, approximately 1 in 5 of those students received accommodations in public education.[32] In other words, after 1975, public schools could no longer turn away students with diverse abilities.

In 1990 Congress passed the Individuals with Disabilities Education Act (IDEA). Its stated goals were:

> a) To the maximum extent appropriate, children with disabilities, including children in public or private institutions or other care facilities, are educated with children who are nondisabled; and
>
> b) Special classes, separate schooling, or other removal of children with disabilities from the regular educational environment occurs only if the nature or severity of the disability is such that education in regular classes with the use of supplementary aids and services cannot be achieved satisfactorily.[33]

This was the birth of "mainstreaming," namely, the idea that children with disabilities would be educated with their peers as much as possible. Whereas Math and English classes tend to track students by perceived aptitude, choir was seen as an ideal way for students with diverse abilities to share in the social-educational goals of ensemble music-making. Most readers who teach in public schools presently work with multiple students with diverse abilities.

In 2004, several revisions were added to IDEA to connect its programs to No Child Left Behind Act, including a provision guarding against overrepresentation of specific communities. Congressional findings demonstrated that children from minoritized communities, especially African-Americans, were being put in special education overwhelmingly more frequently than other children, especially in predominantly-White schools. I encourage every reader to reflect on this. We who want to show the same respect to every student need to be aware of this legacy of institutional racism in our own schools.

In 2015 Congress passed the Every Child Succeeds Act, which further ensured access for students in special education to general education, Universal Design for Learning, evidence-based interventions, and more robust bullying-intervention and interrogation of overuse of discipline practices such as restraint and seclusion.

INCLUSION

As an application of the mainstreaming principle, federal law requires schools to include students with diverse abilities to the maximum extent possible, creating the least restrictive environment. Depending on the student, this can vary a great deal. Some might read the implied goal as a fully inclusive education, by which we mean this:

> *Full inclusion, full integration, unified system,* and *inclusive education* are terms used to describe a popular policy/practice in which all students with disabilities, regardless of the nature or the severity of the disability and need for related services, receive their total education within the regular education classroom in their home school.[34]

As such, complete integration is not something that meets the actual needs and goals of every student with diverse abilities, and many students receive an education with partial inclusion:

> *Partial inclusion* (sometimes called "mainstreaming") refers to the practice of educating students with special needs in the general education classrooms for some portion of their day, while they spend the other portion of the day receiving instruction in a special education classroom or resource room.[35]

And for some students, participating in classes with 20-30 peers is overwhelming and inhibits their educational goals. Hence, a third option is a self-contained classroom, which

> ...focuses on the idea of smaller groups, a more close-knit environment, and one-on-one attention, which can help children with special needs feel safe while fostering creativity and learning. These groups typically consist of 5 to 10 students and are run by a special education teacher and para-educator, who takes instruction from the primary teacher. They can cater to a specific group of children who all have the same disability or learning needs, or can be a mixed group with unique abilities. This alternative form of classroom setting provides support and structure for children whose educational needs are not met by a general education.[36]

In short, it depends a great deal on what each student and family need for the best possible education outcomes. The Learning Disabilities Association of America, for example, clearly advocates *against* full inclusion as a mandate, noting that

> ...the regular education classroom is not the appropriate placement for a number of students with learning disabilities who may need alternative instructional environments, teaching strategies, and/or materials that cannot or will not be provided within the context of a regular classroom placement.[37]

It is important that we understand our legal mandate to create the 'least restrictive environment' for our singers.

While the choral conductor at a public school does not make such decisions, it is important that we understand our legal mandate to create the 'least restrictive environment' for our singers, and our role in helping parents and educators determine the optimum degree of that inclusion.

IEPs

Most teachers in public schools equate teaching students with special needs with Individualized Education Plans, or IEPs. The Individualized Education Program was first introduced in the 1975 EAHC Act, and serves as a written statement and guideline for every child with a disability. It must include:

> A statement of the child's present levels of academic achievement and functional performance
>
> A statement of measurable annual goals, including academic and functional goals designed to:
>
> - meet the child's needs that result from the child's disability to enable the child to be involved in and make progress in the general education curriculum; and
> - meet each of the child's other educational needs that result from the child's disability.

> For children with disabilities who take alternate assessments aligned to alternate achievement standards, a description of benchmarks or short-term objectives of:
>
> - how the child's progress toward meeting the annual goals described in 34 CFR 300.320(a)(2) will be measured; and
> - when periodic reports on the progress the child is making toward meeting the annual goals (such as through the use of quarterly or other periodic reports, concurrent with the issuance of report cards) will be provided.
>
> A statement of the special education and related services and supplementary aids and services, based on peer-reviewed research to the extent practicable, to be provided to the child, or on behalf of the child;
>
> A statement of any individual appropriate accommodations that are necessary to measure the academic achievement and functional performance of the child on State and district-wide assessments.[38]

As every special education teacher knows, IEPs take a *long* time to put together. Special education teachers involved with these students need to gather data throughout the year in order to provide required evidence to measure goals and progress. The "IEP meeting" involving all related professionals and the family takes coordination, time, and careful attention.

IEPs are, appropriately, kept as confidential as possible. However, as an educational professional directly involved with that student, you as choral director have the right and obligation to read through and discuss the IEP with the team of teachers, administrators, and family. The full document can be overwhelming and/or confusing to many teachers. Our primary focus as choral educators is to get as clear a sense as possible from the special educator and the IEP about the student's present level of function (what they can do), goals that are relevant to this class (e.g., behavioral, executive functioning, social, reading), and appropriate modifications/supports (will there be an aide? will the student need a binder or visual schedule? a technological adaptive device?). Your team will help you create the best learning environment for each student. It is important to note that, despite all the legal requirements for supporting all learners, the reality in many schools is quite different. Yes, a student may qualify for speech-language services, but the speech-language pathologist may also have an extraordinarily big caseload, and therefore cannot meet the IEP requirements for contact hours with the student. The system in most schools simply does not provide the services needed for all students. While you as a choral educator cannot necessarily fix the system, please know that you may be one of the only teachers who sees your student in their wholeness and cares about their success.

Our primary focus as choral educators is to get as clear a sense as possible from the special educator and the IEP about the student's present level of function, goals that are relevant to this class, and appropriate modifications/supports.

YOUR TEACHING TEAM

The choral educator should never feel alone when teaching a student who requires special accommodations as a reflection of their diverse abilities. Indeed, conductors are members of a strong team of education professionals who collectively help the student meet their educational goals. That team usually includes a special education instructor who serves as the coordinator or point-person for the student. In many cases, with students who have profound needs, a paraprofessional educator will travel with and help the student. A student may also work with: a speech/language pathologist, who helps with issues of communication (effective vocal usage, diction, communication with pictures -PECS, etc), an occupational therapist, who helps the student navigate daily tasks (e.g. holding a pencil, playing an instrument), and a physical therapist, who helps the student with movement/muscular issues.

As choral conductors, we should therefore never feel like we are alone or making it up as we go along.

As choral conductors, we should therefore *never* feel like we are alone or making it up as we go along. As educators, we do have the right and responsibility to read through the IEP for each of our students who has one so that we understand where they are, what their goals are, and what accommodations they need. Collaboration meetings are discussed below, but I want to emphasize here that it is not our role to understand every possible disability or to have a need for an additional degree in special education. We have colleagues who do this full-time. It *is* our role, however, to work with our colleagues to help every singer thrive while in our choir.

YOUR MINDSET ABOUT BEHAVIOR

Our team can support us, but it is up to us to examine our approach for respecting every singer. One of the most important mindsets we hold as educators is to assume that our singers are doing the best they can at any point in time. I do not mean that the choir's work on any given rehearsal is their best *possible* work—there would be no room for teaching! I mean to suggest that our singers, like ourselves or our parents or our spouses, are doing the best that they know how to do at present. Until we guide them to create a more rounded vowel or to cut off precisely on beat four, they will not improve, because they do not know what they do not yet know. It may take a variety of creative pedagogical approaches to get their collective final 't' on beat four, but that is the sort of challenge we live for.

We have all had that moment when an ensemble seems determined not to learn something. They insist on chewing a final 'r' sound in a British anthem, or the basses seem to be intentionally singing the soprano part down an octave instead of their own part. We start to think, "they're doing this to *spite* me!" Usually, when I figure out where I skipped the needed scaffolding in their learning, the issue begins to resolve.

Students with specific cognitive or behavioral disorders are also doing the best they can, but it is often harder to see. Precisely because many students with such disorders have communication difficulties, they may have a harder time letting us know what is on their mind, what they are struggling with, and what they are concerned about. Precisely because they have a documented learning or processing disorder, what might take another student one or two rehearsals to learn might take them twenty or thirty rehearsals. If they could learn in one or two rehearsals or communicate effectively, they would not have been given a diagnosis for a disorder. Sometimes learning a song 100 times slower than one's peers is the best one can do. Our role as teachers is to focus on how our teaching facilitates their learning; it is okay that it takes a longer time for some singers.

Our role as teachers is to focus on how our teaching facilitates their learning; it is okay that it takes a longer time for some singers.

Sometimes a student with a behavioral disorder might have a sudden outburst or make an inappropriate comment or otherwise disrupt rehearsal. Taken in the abstract, these behaviors are rude, and a teacher might feel offended or angry. It is therefore essential that we make a mental distinction between voluntary and involuntary behavior. If I shout in the middle of rehearsal, it is voluntary, and I'm just being a jerk. If a student with Tourette's Syndrome shouts in the middle of rehearsal, it is involuntary, and they are doing the best they can.

Rather, we might look at a singer's behavior as a form of communication. A negative behavior can often stem from a desire to *participate* in choir – that desire may trigger anxiety, which triggers the behavior. Often with students who do not communicate easily, the behavior provides a glimpse into the internal feeling. Directing our language to that student as a response to their attempt to communicate – "I'm excited to be here, too!" – can be more effective than simply trying to shut down the (largely uncontrollable) behavior – "Brayden, be quiet!"

I encourage you to think back on all of your various private music instructors for piano, voice lessons, conducting classes, etc. Did you work with a teacher whose primary mode of instruction was what *not* to do (don't rush the eighth notes, don't tighten your shoulder, don't scoop the consonant, etc.)? Did you work with a teacher whose primary mode of instruction was, instead, what *to* do (this passage likes to go quickly, so let's think about adding an internal off-beat track on beats two and four; this passage is nerve-wracking, so let's mark in the score to roll our shoulders and breathe deeply right before we get here; remember that the consonant 'v' is voiced, so let's imagine it starting right on the same note as the rest of the word, etc.)? In these examples, the first teacher identifies a problem and says, "don't do that". The second teacher identifies the same problem, but offers suggestions that the student can do to improve.

All of us—singers and directors, teachers and students—would rather be given feedback on what we should be doing rather than on what we need to stop doing. If a teacher shouts to a student, "keep your hands to yourself!" for touching someone, there are probably 100 similar chastisements heading that student's way today. If the teacher instead reminds the student that we need both hands on our books so we can read them better, the class will likely run more smoothly.

When we work with students with diverse abilities, we must develop – ahead of time – strategies and suggestions for what we want to suggest for them when they do engage in the behaviors that they will predictably engage in.

We know that some of our singers are going to demonstrate disruptive behaviors. We *know* this. Even if we have no students with an IEP in our ensembles, the chances are excellent that we will see disruptive behavior – I've witnessed it in professional choirs! What language do we choose to use to address this? "Tenors, please listen to the altos and basses here so you know where your part fits in" gives the tenors a pedagogically useful task; "tenors, shut up!" does not. Likewise, when we work with students with diverse abilities, we must develop – *ahead of time* – strategies and suggestions for what we want to suggest for them when they do engage in the behaviors that they will predictably engage in.

With good teaching strategies, we can circumvent some stressors that would otherwise trigger poor behavior. As Bryan Price notes:

> Many students with emotional disturbances also have difficulty sitting still for long or even short periods. Provide many opportunities for movement in the classroom, including dancing, hand motions, or the use of manipulatives.[39]

Of course, not only does movement help those students with special needs; it also helps every student. I wouldn't want to stand still for 45 minutes either!

The other advantage to providing students with positive guidance instead of negative shut-downs is that it fully values each student. Our choral rehearsal space is meant to be a place of creativity. Kimberly McCord notes this point of tension for students with special needs who are still trying to figure out how to negotiate their world:

> …Instead of learning to think for themselves, many children with disabilities learn that the key to success in the classroom depends most of the time on finding the right answer and using the right social skills, including the right way to be expressive. Children with disabilities are rewarded for conformity rather than for creativity.[40]

Neither McCord nor anyone else is advocating a devil-may-care discipline plan. Rather, it is useful to consider how much of our rehearsal dynamic is geared toward absolute conformity, and where or how each singer's creativity is manifested.

When we consider the educator's mindset about singer behavior, it is worth remembering that we treat people we like differently than we treat people we dislike. One of the most impactful professors in my wife's special education degree reminded her class regularly that learning to like every student can be hard work, but it must be done. When we think, for example, about students who manifest severely autistic behaviors and are non-communicative, we are reminded that some students are unable to share with us in the ways we expect from others, and that makes relationship-building harder.

Ryan and Amy Hourigan note that, "Children with autism often struggle with many aspects of everyday life that cause them to retreat into their comfort zone."[41] Some strategies including calling students 'friends,' as in 'my friend Jayden'; finding *something* in their behavior that you like and building out from there (e.g., "you're so good at putting your coat on!"), giving words to their non-verbal communications (e.g., if a child throws a toy, "you're upset that it's time to clean up!"), and trusting that there is a fully thinking human inside that silence who is taking everything in, but has not yet figured out how to share it.

A final thought about behavior in rehearsal with students with special needs. As I said, I'm no fan of a disruptive classroom without a discipline plan. Choir is for learning to sing together to the best of our capabilities, and we cannot do that if there is no sense of order. But we needn't be too concerned that a student's vocal tic 'ruined our work.' If a professional choir is recording an album and someone groans or shouts in the middle of a rest, then yes, that take is ruined, and at some significant cost. But we're not conducting The Robert Shaw Chorale - we're teaching, and sometimes when we teach, a student behaves in a way that they cannot control. I hope we are able to admit that a) we weren't sounding like The Robert Shaw Chorale anyway, b) that the student was not doing this voluntarily, and c) that behavior does not need to stop our learning process.

YOUR PLAN

You've planned your repertoire, your concert attire, your tour, and your rehearsal. Have you planned for how you will teach your singers who require special accommodations? Whether you spend zero hours preparing for these students and then many hours later to 'deal with them,' or you spend many hours planning proactively, you will probably spend the same amount of time either way, but you will have better results and enjoy your job more if you front-load it. You will have a much clearer sense of who you will be teaching and how your team will be prepared. Here are a few suggestions for how to prepare.

Whether you spend zero hours preparing for these students and then many hours later to 'deal with them,' or you spend many hours planning proactively, you will probably spend the same amount of time either way, but you will have better results and enjoy your job more if you front-load it.

Unless you have a singer who is newly diagnosed or undiagnosed, your students will be coming to you from colleagues who have taught them before and who can guide you on how each student with special needs will thrive. You will want to hear how the student learns best, what might set them off, what might help them return to appropriate behavior.

> An important part of your consultation with other teachers, parents, and administrators is to uncover the learning processes used in other classes. Questions you want to ask may include the following:
>
> 1) Does the student respond to visual or aural teaching?
>
> 2) Does routine comfort the child?
>
> 3) Are there sensitivities that may impede their learning (e.g. loud sound)?
>
> 4) What is the current cognitive level of the child?
>
> Answers to these questions will give you a foundation from which to start your individualization or accommodation of instruction.[42] [note, the author refers to children, but these questions are appropriate for all singers with behavioral disorders]

The special educator, paraprofessional, and previous teachers will be invaluable in gathering the information you need.

Take time to review the IEP with your team to fully understand the accommodations required. If the student has a reading disability, you will need to strategize who will make recordings of the student's part, and how those get distributed, for example. If the student needs to be able to leave occasionally, you will want to remember that in your seating chart and put them nearer to an exit. If the student is supposed to come to class with a paraprofessional, you will want to know and hold the school to that responsibility. This is not necessarily a process that we as choral conductors think of as 'our job,' but it is actually our legal obligation, in addition to being a manifestation of the respect we show our singers.

Your student's parents have lived with this student for years, they have been to all the doctors, and they have navigated years of other teachers and educational frameworks. Your expertise is in choral music; their expertise, as well as the deepest love in their life, is their child.

Of course, there are people who know the student even *better* than your colleagues. As Margaret Fitzgerald writes, "the link between you and other educators is necessary, but it's vital that you collaborate with a student's parents."[43] Your student's parents have lived with this student for years, they have been to all the doctors, and they have navigated years of other teachers and educational frameworks. Your expertise is in choral music; their expertise, as well as the deepest love in their life, is their child. Fitzgerald writes about how she felt in her very first IEP meeting with teachers for her son, Matthew:

> …I needed everyone there to understand and acknowledge that I sent them the "very best Matt" I could each day. Thank goodness the teachers raised the comfort level for me at that meeting. They used humor, spoke to me kindly, and demonstrated honest concern and affection for Matt. I realized it was important for me to feel that they actually liked him.[44]

As a parent of two children who thrived in public schools, I nearly wept when I read her story. I had never thought about what it would be like to go to a meeting at school to discuss and strategize around my child's deficiencies. Then I began to foster children with severe trauma, and I learned how much it meant to hear some small word of support for my child's success (asset-based language) even when the main reason for the phone call was to let me know about a violent episode that required school resource officer intervention. In Fitzgerald's essay, these teachers had taken to heart the idea of liking every student, and it won immeasurable goodwill with his mother. And this is why Fitzgerald suggests: "When something good happens with a child in class, please remember to take the opportunity to share it with the parents. You will never know the effect you might have on that child and the entire family."[45]

After you and your team review IEPs for students who will be in your choirs, leave time to contact each parent. This front-loading of time pays off. Frame the conversation from the goals of establishing rapport, comfort, and common goals for the student. Focus on what the student can do and likes to do, not on their deficits. Learn the student's triggers, redirections, and comforting mechanisms. Establish an open line of communication, and follow through by sending regular updates, focusing on those moments or skills in which the student is doing well.

If you are able to make contact prior to the start of the year, **spend time building relationships and strategies** with every singer with diverse abilities. Get a sense for how the singer does or does not communicate. Recognize, for example, that some students on the autism spectrum may view the music room as a potential nightmare of intense lights and sounds. As Ryan and Amy Hourigan suggest, arrange to have that student come into the room when no rehearsals are happening to desensitize that space.

> We have also found that children on the spectrum may be sensitive to situations or environment. For example, a large, loud music room with lots of people may be the last place that a student on the spectrum wants to be. He or she may need to start class in the hallway (with supervision) and work his or her way into the room. He or she may need to wear noise-reducing headphones at first.[46]

The more comfortable the student feels in the space, the more the student will learn and the less the student will disrupt. This proactive relationship-building is important for a variety of diverse abilities. If a singer has vision impairment, you can collectively discuss the layout of the room and preferred standing and seating locations. If a singer has mobility limitations, you can collectively discuss strategies and accommodations. When we build these relationships, we create an inclusive and respectful relationship with every singer.

As noted above, if students could reliably control their reactions, they would not be diagnosed with an "emotional and behavioral disorder." In conversations with your team, you will get a clear sense of what a student's triggers might be, and what helps with them. But you will need to **establish a very clear behavior plan and intervention strategy** with your team and the parents ahead of time. You do not want to be inventing one when you are in the middle of your first rehearsal with the guest brass quintet for the concert on Friday.

If you mainstream students with special needs into your ensemble, they will stand next to other students. **Be proactive and discerning in who you assign as peer helpers.** Judith Jellison did a careful study of the on- and off-task participation of 'typical' students next to students with disabilities in elementary general music classrooms. She writes:

> Data [from her study] show that most of the typical students were more on-task when they were located away from either of their two peers with disabilities and that individual students were more on-task when seated close to Ann (the student with mild disabilities) than when seated close to Thomas (the student with severe disabilities). Importantly, some students showed an ability to remain on-task irrespective of their placement (close to or away from Ann or Thomas).[47]

That is, standing next to a student with severe disabilities may impede the education of some adjacent students, and those positions should not be taken lightly. Yet, some students demonstrate a keen ability to stay focused either way, and those students should be peer guides. Jellison also observed that, "students were often excessive and inappropriate in their helping… [this] resulted in a high percentage of off-task for typical students and systematic learning opportunities"[48] for those students with disabilities. Look for students who can help, but otherwise can stay focused on your class as much as possible. This way, the student with special needs is paired with someone who respects them enough to let them learn their own way (and continues to learn themselves). A genuine friend of your ability-diverse student is the ideal match most of the time.

As we look at who stands where, we should also look at **how we configure our rooms**. Bryan Price offers three excellent suggestions that make the choir room more effective and inclusive. First, "facing students toward the corner of the room directs their attention to a single focus point" and helps students who are easily distracted. Second, directors need to be sure to place students who have difficulty maintaining appropriate behavior "clearly in the director's line of vision" so that we can stay attentive to their needs. Finally, he suggests that such students might be placed "in an area that provides for a quick exit or entrance"[49] so that if they come to class late or need to leave early, they do not disrupt the class.

All of these strategies help our singers, but **if we do not effectively manage our transitions from one activity to the next, we cause unnecessary anxiety in some of our students.** Many singers with emotional and behavioral issues experience intense anxiety around transitions from one activity to the next, or from a change from an expected experience to a new one. The more predictable the routine, the more comfortable such a singer will feel in your rehearsal space.

Predictability does not mean using only one mode of pedagogy or one rehearsal plan every day! It means that there is a sense of routine about coming into the space (the risers are up, the folders are in this slot), about how the rehearsal starts (we stretch, we warm up, etc), and about the flow of rehearsal. If you always rehearse in the choir room from behind the piano you are also playing, and then one day you're suddenly in the auditorium and on the podium, that could be an anxiety-producing transition. It helps students (both those with special needs and those without) to name what the rehearsal will involve, both on the board and verbally. Ryan and Amy Hourigan offer this suggestion:

> ...We want to keep children busy so we tend to plan lots of small activities within our music classes. This can be a challenge for children on the spectrum... Anticipate these transitions by using verbal and nonverbal cues as well as visual representations.[50]

Of course, as we think about our usual concert week, there is predictably a big transition when we go into the auditorium, turn the lights up, and see hundreds of audience members. Pryce asserts:

> ...many students can practice well in their class and with confidence but may have difficulties in front of an audience... such anxiety issues are often absent from a child's snapshot IEP... It is therefore important to have conversations with the student's case manager/special educator.[51]

He also suggests having run-throughs for special guests, like a colleague or the principal, so that the teacher can observe how students with anxiety handle this stress. In short, we can teach rehearsals with a quick pace and covering a lot of musical material very creatively – we are simply aiming to reduce the amount of surprises.

PLAN WITH UDL IN MIND

UDL stands for Universal Design for Learning. It is a pedagogical framework that has emerged in the 2000s as an effective model for inclusive teaching. It is defined as:

> a set of principles for curriculum development that give all individuals equal opportunities to learn. UDL provides a blueprint for creating instructional goals, methods, materials, and assessments that work for everyone--not a single, one-size-fits-all solution, but rather flexible approaches that can be customized and adjusted for individual needs.[52]

Indeed, it is clear to any conductor that there has never been 'one method' to build an excellent choir. As we flip this around to our students, then, we recognize that different students will need different approaches, tools, and outputs to learn.

HERE ARE THE GUIDELINES[53] FOR UDL:

- Multiple means of **engagement** to foster purposeful, motivated learners
- Multiple means of **representation** to foster resourceful, knowledgeable learners
- Multiple means of **action** and **expression** to foster strategic, goal-directed learners

How does this translate to our choral rehearsal?

- **Engagement** refers to how students stay motivated to learn, how we stimulate interest. For most of us, the primary (even sole) motivator is the public concert. Perhaps we have programmed one song that the choir begs to sing every day, that we use almost like a bargaining chip. What other ways do we motivate?
- **Representation** refers to how students gather information. For most of us, we want the choral score to be the primary referent, but we also play the music at the piano, in individual parts or collectively, as well as use recordings or conduct (these are all different ways of taking in the music). How do we help students who need more time to learn the music? A website with the lyrics posted, or part-recordings, or visual symbols would be further examples.
- **Action** and **expression** refers to how students organize, express, and act their thoughts and understanding. In choir, that means singing! If we have a music theory component, how do we allow a student who cannot read or write to express their understanding? If a student has a difficult time discerning pitch differences, how do we assess them?

I believe that this pedagogical framework is as valid for my conservatory ensembles as it is for early childhood special education classes. We are, all of us, teaching groups of people with multiple ways of processing the world. As conductors committed to teaching all our singers with respect, we can look at the ways we design our classrooms, rehearsals, assessments, and concert programs, and find as many ways as possible to engage all learners in the joy of choir.

As we flip this around to our students, then, we recognize that different students will need different approaches, tools, and outputs to learn. Neuroscience now regularly shows that the concept of a 'typical' learner is misleading and inaccurate. The word 'neurodiversity' should be understood the same way we use 'biodiversity' – not to suggest that there is a large population of "normal" and a small outlier population of "abnormal", but as a wide spectrum. If we imagine that there is a typical learner, then we teach for a typical learning modality, and then we offer specific remediation or enrichment for special learners. Or, if we think that there are three kinds of learners – kinesthetic, visual, and auditory – we design lessons designed to help specific students learn with their specific modality. But the "learning styles" approach has been widely debunked. As Paul A. Howard-Jones writes, "the implicit assumption [for 'learning styles'] seems to be that, because different regions of the cortex have crucial roles in visual, auditory and sensory processing, learners should receive information in visual, auditory or kinesthetic forms according to which part of their brain works better. The brain's interconnectivity makes such an assumption unsound, and reviews of educational literature and controlled laboratory studies fail to support this approach to teaching."[54] What has been shown in UDL research is that students do best when they have multiple motivations to learn and persist, multiple ways to see/process/engage the material, and multiple ways to express their learning.

Using CAST.org's UDL framework, here are some examples of how we can reconceive of our teaching/learning environment:

Multiple Means of Engagement

Recruiting Interest:

- Getting to know students' cultural background and preferred music at home.
- Offering a range of songs, based on this information, that advance ensemble singing, aligning with specific NAfME standards
- Video-conference with alumni about what they learned in choir and how it has helped them.
- Clear conversations on how to participate safely.

Sustaining Effort and Persistence:

- Explicit written and verbal discussion of the immediate and long-term learning goal for every song and concert.
- Clarify and show the distinction between sufficient, advanced, and exceptional work (in reading, singing, tuning, listening, contributing, etc)
- Group discussions to make explicit what healthy group work looks like. Clarify roles, and how to ask for help from one another. Use rubrics.
- Teacher- and student-led, frequent, timely feedback from rehearsal that teaches/connects/transfers.

Self-Regulation

- At beginning, throughout, and at end of term, discuss with each student how they are doing, and which strategies they will use to maintain engagement.
- Share out strategies that students use to keep focus and energy throughout the term/project.
- Provide daily check-ins about how we are feeling, what we need today, where we are in our projects.

Multiple Means of Representation

Options for Perception

All music learning should include:

- Scores
- Historical/cultural/linguistic background information (with access to text-to-speech)
- Videos (with access to subtitles)
- Recordings (with score, with part-only, with rhythm, with diction, etc)

Options for Language and Symbols

- Pre-teach (or give access to pre-teaching) new rhythms, intervals, chords with hand-outs, teacher or student modeling of new motives or rhythms
- Draw from prior knowledge in past songs learned, classes in other subjects (e.g. students in French 4 co-leading the text for the Fauré)

Options for Comprehension

- Consider rotating the "pre-teaching" responsibility among students ("Lili, your assignment will be to remind us how to pronounce pages 4-5, drawing from your knowledge in French 4")
- Demonstrate with media as often as possible, e.g. how to mark the score, or how to turn a page quietly, or how to interpret 4/2

Multiple Means of Action and Expression

Options for Physical Action

- Evidence of Learning submitted through a variety of choices (written essay/journal, mp3, video, one-on-one or small-group meeting, recording with mobile phones, octet or quartet performances, etc)

Options for Expression and Communication

- Assignments and teaching need to be visual, aural, on the board, on Canvas, etc. Color code for Evidence of Learning vs memorization date vs performance date vs sectional, etc
- Demonstrate performance proficiency in specific skills – clapping rhythm, speaking the French, singing the alto part on [nu], singing the part in French, singing in two parts, singing in all four parts

Options for Executive Functioning

- Always clarify the learning goal.
- Always clarify what a successful completion of the project will look like, with rubrics, examples, etc.
- Build in regular check-ins and scaffolding for longer projects: either one-on-one meetings, or Canvas/Office check-ins, or 90 second group check-ins ("let's break up into groups of 4-5 to talk about where we are in our project…")

SECTION II
Choir, Identity and Marginalization

CHAPTER 4
Choir and Gender

If we want to teach all singers with respect, we need to reflect on the ways we discuss our singers and the settings in which we frame their choral experience. When we acknowledge that the playing field is rarely equal, that our positionality matters, and that our words and our systems may disenfranchise singers, we begin the hard work of inclusive pedagogy. In this chapter, we look at ways in which our structures and language about gender can exclude or include all singers in choirs.

WHAT DO WE MEAN BY *GENDER*?

In order to talk about how the choral experience intersects with gender, we need to examine what we mean by the word *gender*. For some of us, this question feels so obvious that we may have never thought about it. We believe that we have either XX or XY on our 23rd chromosome; hence, we have either a female or male reproductive system; ergo we behave like either a woman or man. We perceive that our behavior flows from our biology, which we perceive to be fixed. Below, I will argue that gender is not a binary, that gender identity and expression are not always the same, and that our language of "men and women" is insufficient and exclusionary. For the moment, I want to meet the reader at this perspective, and gradually explore the complexities of gender.

Gender studies is a discipline that investigates these questions more deeply. Judith Butler's important work, *Gender Trouble*, for example, suggests that we learn to *perform* the expectations of our gender as we grow up, just as we learn to speak a language. If I am consistently dressed in blue and my sister is dressed in pink, I learn that blue is a boy's color and pink is a girl's color (even though the reverse was true a century ago). If I am signed up for baseball and my sister is signed up for dance, I learn that sports are for boys and dancing is for girls. As Wendy Cealy Harrison puts it, we get better at performing our gender by practice:

> [W]e learn how to behave and then, like learning to ride a bicycle, we forget that we once wobbled and found the whole thing improbable and impossible, and it all comes naturally.[55]

Put simply, gender studies scholars argue that boys don't know a *priori* that blue is a better color than pink or that baseball is better than dance until it is *practiced* into them. Moreover, we all participate in such practice constantly. Gender studies seeks to question what precisely we are practicing and how it affects different people differently.

I encourage you to take a moment to reflect on those experiences in your life in which your performance of gender was celebrated. Do you recall moments when you were praised for being such a 'strong man' or a 'sweet girl'? Do you remember times when you were praised for 'dealing with it like a man' (no emotional reaction) or 'having a woman's intuition' (anticipating someone's feelings)? Do these memories help you see how your gender identity relates to your expected behavior?

Now I encourage you to reflect on those experiences in your life in which your performance of gender was questioned. For my part, I loved dancing and chose to study dance in middle and high school. I was keenly aware that this was perceived as abnormal for heterosexual men, and I was often reminded of it. (It turns out that dance is excellent training for conducting, though!) In what ways has your life experience revealed these performance expectations? In which ways do you see your choral experience confirming these behavioral expectations? In which ways are your singers held to these standards as well? What do these standards tell our students about themselves and their sense of self and worth?

GENDER AND POWER

Scholars in gender studies are keenly interested in how our gender roles reflect power. In what ways do we construct our system to favor or oppress some people and not others? In essence, when we look at how we favor or oppress others, we get to the heart of respect - the Golden Rule. When we stop to consider our (often subconscious) practices and ask whom we are favoring and whom we are oppressing, we heighten our respect for all. As Kathy Davis, Mary Evans, and Judith Lorber write in their introduction to the *Handbook of Gender and Women's Studies*, our divisions by gender

> ...not only permeate the individual's sense of self, families, and intimate relationships, but also structure work, politics, law, education, medicine, the military, religions, and culture. Gender is a system of power in that it privileges some men and disadvantages most women. Gender is constructed and maintained by both the dominants and the oppressed because both ascribe to its values in personality and identity formation and in appropriate masculine and feminine behavior. Gender is hegemonic in that many of its foundational assumptions and ubiquitous processes are invisible, unquestioned, and unexamined.[56]

As we draw out that last sentence, we can question, examine, and make visible those foundational assumptions of who we think our singers are and how they should behave. In the spirit of teaching with greater respect, let us look openly at how we teach our singers through the lens of gender.

WHO GETS THE RESPECT?

Let's start with a thought experiment. Do you have more women than men singing in your choral program? Would you describe the overall ability level of your women to be higher than the overall ability of your men in the program? Would you describe those men in your top SATB ensemble as generally being less advanced than the women? Given that your women are probably more advanced and that there are more of them to select from, would you describe the women's choir as your top choir? If not, why not?

Especially for those of us in the educational setting of teaching early through late adolescence (middle school through college/university), we usually work with far more women than men in choir. Kenneth Elpus demonstrated in 2015 that the ratio of 70% female/30% male choral participation in schools has not changed during the last 30 years.[57] But rarely do we translate these numbers into a program that features an exceptionally high performing women's ensemble and a good, developmentally appropriate mixed-voice ensemble.

Patricia O'Toole brought this point to our collective attention as choral directors in 1998. She spurred important change in her *Choral Journal* article about neglecting women in our choral programs. She writes:

> Women's choirs generally fall to the bottom of the choral hierarchy for various reasons. First, some listeners do not prefer the timbre of women's voices—a dislike internalized, even by some women. Furthermore, female singers learn early that mixed-voice choirs receive more attention than women's choirs. Mixed-voice choirs tour, record, and are usually the last to perform on concerts, a position that suggests their dominance. Most directors construct their choral programs with the mixed-voice choir as the advanced ensemble, and this limits the participation of women to the number of available male singers. Directors then place the excess women in a women's choir, which students often perceived as the dumping ground for leftover and less talented female singers. Being assigned to a women's choir, then, is a direct comment on a women's (in)ability.[58]

To be in the women's choir, then, is to be in the less-prestigious ensemble. Sherry Ortner observes:

> [G]ender is itself centrally a prestige system—a system of discourses and practice that constructs male and female not only in terms of differential roles and meanings but also in terms of differential *value*, differential *prestige*.[59]

This fits a patriarchal model of society, in which a male-privileging culture determines that ensembles with men in them are worthy of more prestige than those with only women.

Some readers may question whether patriarchy exists, so let's take a moment to define patriarchy. The literal definition is simply a social system controlled by or giving preference to men. Using our metaphor of a 10' by 10' canvas, patriarchy frames our lives through the male side of the canvas. When we refer to gender as a prestige system, we say that power comes with being male or being with males; we focus on that half of the canvas. When we in America have had 46 male presidents and zero female presidents, when women's sports receive less than 5% of television sports coverage,[60] when 80% of the Senate and House of Representatives are men,[61] and when women with advanced degrees are paid 74% of what men with those same degrees are paid (a pay-gap not explained by different training/careers[62]), we are looking at patriarchy and prestige systems.

How is patriarchy manifested in the choral experience? Jill Wilson expanded on O'Toole's perspective of neglecting/disenfranchising women in choir with a qualitative study of women's choir perceptions in 2012. Do our high school females pick up these cues? Absolutely. According to Dr. Wilson:

> Most female students reported that they would prefer to sing in a mixed choir. Those stating a preference for singing in a treble clef ensemble stipulated that it be an auditioned ensemble. Two common responses included their appreciation for a) the sound that only a mixed choir can create and b) the quality and perceived higher level of difficulty of mixed chorus literature. Many expressed a desire to sing with males despite their perceived lower skill level and lesser work ethic.[63]

Let's pause here to lift out two key points. First, the women being interviewed perceive music with male voices to be intrinsically better, and second, that they acknowledge that the males in choir are less skilled and less motivated. There's a cognitive dissonance here. How can a choir that includes men be both the more-desirable option and simultaneously the less-advanced option? Wilson continues:

> A strong majority of the students who were interviewed viewed singing in a mixed choir as being more prestigious than singing in a treble clef ensemble. Choral educators both create and reinforce this view by making the mixed ensemble the most select in their programs. No one named treble-clef choir as being seen as the most prestigious ensemble. Students saw the treble clef-choir as gaining status, but still viewed it as a 'stepping stone' to being selected for participation in the mixed choir. Members got upset if they did not 'get into' the mixed choir. One conductor explained by saying, "They feel like it's stepping back, a 'slap in the face,' to have to sing in women's choir again after being in a mixed ensemble.

We see this paradigm in the way we design our choral programs, in our scholarship, and in our own singers' experience in choir.

It is not that I cannot find great compositions for treble voices;
it's just that it is easier to find compositions for mixed voices.

I lived in this mode of thinking for decades. One of my primary arguments for this status quo has been that the historical choral repertoire is richest for the SATB ensemble, thus the SATB ensemble needs to be the top group in order to perform this treasure trove of music. This may be true, but it is also a circular argument. That is, when I say, "Composers (in a patriarchal system) preferred to write for ensembles with men (and indeed often *exclusively* men, with counter-tenors and treble boys), so that is where the best music is found," I defend the bias by supporting its legacy of compositions. Put differently, if composers in racist societies wrote racist music for centuries, I would not be necessarily right to program exclusively their (racist) music just because that is what was written. It is not that I cannot find great compositions for treble voices; it's just that it is easier to find compositions for mixed voices.

My second reason has always been that it sounds better to hear mixed voices. The agrugment goes that, since it is more aesthetically pleasing to hear a fuller spectrum of frequencies, people want to be in a group that has that more than a group that does not. This is a relativistic argument. Aesthetic pleasure is not an essential, inherent quality in the same way that biology is. The human body will always crave salt; this is ingrained in us. Craving an SSAATTBB score is a learned behavior; it is taught to us. We are *taught* what to describe as beautiful, and what to describe as ugly; we are taught which kinds of choral music sound more beautiful and which kinds do not. Indeed, many of us regularly switch between different aesthetic models of beauty: country/folk singer Alison Kraus would fail her conservatory voice juries because her tone is too aspirate; Placido Domingo would be kicked out of choir for not blending; Beyoncé would be in trouble for adding notes to the National Anthem in choir; Ian Bostridge would be disappointing for *not* adding notes to the solo in jazz choir. We learn to embrace cultural norms of aesthetic success by genre.

The truth is that most of us learn what it means for a choir to sound great by having SATB choirs (and their repertoire) taught to us: the Robert Shaw Chorale, Conspirare, the Tallis Scholars, Voces8, etc. If we had a choral history sequence in college that taught us from Hildegard through Ospedali through Brahms' Frauenchor through Jocelyn Hagen, and spent one day addressing "the interesting tradition of Viennese masses for SATB choirs," and we grew up listening to Anonymous 4, Elektra, Vox Femina, Mirabai, and other professional women's choirs, we might have a different take on the relative aesthetic value of a treble ensemble.

My third point is the most well-intentioned, and that is to question why we have fewer men singing in choir in the first place and therefore seek to bring more singers to the art. We will explore this question below. For now, in the context of this question of why SATB choirs are given the most prestige, I would say that we are perhaps trying to solve the wrong issue by needing one choir to be the more prestigious, irrespective of gender issues. I assume this has to do with the standard flow chart and motivation of the choral program, as in, "work your way up the program so that you can make our top group one day." This presents two pedagogical concerns: first, that we have to have a clear winner (a binary of good/not-as-good); and second, that the purpose of singing in the less-advanced groups is fundamentally aspirational. We do not frame our World Literature class as a leftover section for those who did not make the cut for AP English Literature. We see these as courses that students take to develop proficiency and comprehension in literature. I give my 'beginner' choir the repertoire that they can manage with their present skill sets, and my 'advanced' choir the repertoire that they can manage with their present skill sets, but I expect both ensembles to perform at their highest level.

As we take stock of our preference for SATB ensembles, we need to look honestly and deeply at what drives these preferences. I do not mean to suggest that SATB ensembles should be demoted to second-class, that all adolescent women are by default more advanced than their male colleagues, or that we should not be working to develop a stronger culture of male choral participation. I only ask that we look with clear eyes at what lesson we are teaching adolescent women when we create an ensemble for treble voices that is, by structural design, inferior to the SATB ensemble.

I only ask that we look with clear eyes at what lesson we are teaching our women when we create an ensemble for them that is, by structural design, inferior to our SATB ensemble.

How do your singers perceive themselves in your choral structure? If you direct single-gender choirs, how do they see their status in the program? What language do they use for the SATB ensemble's repertoire and status versus TTBB and SSAA ensembles' repertoire and status?

WHAT WE CHOOSE

If we acknowledge that our female singers in a typical choral framework are not treated with the same respect and prestige, we must also acknowledge that this is not a new problem, nor does it come from nowhere. One glaring inequality in choral music education is the significant imbalance in composer gender identity. Most of the historical repertoire we know and study was written by men. The patriarchal argument would say that if women were as good as composing as men, the repertoire throughout history would be relatively balanced by composer gender identity, and thus the relative dearth of great female composers and repertoire in the western art music canon would suggest that it is not something in which women excel.

In response to this line of reasoning as it related to literature, Virginia Woolf produced a famous thought experiment in her important work, *A Room of One's Own*, in which she imagined that William Shakespeare had a sister, Judith, who possessed an equal amount of intelligence, creativity, and potential. As their lives progress in the clearly patriarchal turn-of the-17th-century English culture, William joins a theatre company and performs and writes with great success, while Judith is forced into marriage and child-rearing, or a desolate life of trying to support herself in performance amid a culture that would not tolerate independent women. Woolf notes: "Imaginatively, she is of the highest importance; practically, she is completely insignificant."[64] In response to the patriarchal argument, Woolf offers a powerful critique in which she asks how women were ever supposed to write at the same level as men if they were systemically oppressed and cut off from the same education and employment opportunities. If we today in choral music have a smaller canon of music for treble choirs or music by women, we have to ask how often in the western tradition have we seen music for or by women's voices given the opportunity to thrive.

While America's anti-discrimination laws have improved since Woolf's essay in 1929 England, the legacy of such discrimination haunts our canon. Through the tireless work of advocates, governments in America and England eventually ceded to women such basic rights as voting and having a bank account in the 20th century, but no present law can retroactively create a space for women to be thriving composers or conductors in past centuries. Woolf's critique is just as valid for those of us who study the historical western art music canon. As Ruth Solie observes in her study of mid-20th-century writer Sophie Drinker's text *Music and Women*:

> [C]ultures as a whole must answer for the failure of female talent to appear in substantial quantity, for, as she says of a later period of history, "what was yielded to an individual woman of genius or charm was not yielded to women collectively and as a right."[65]

That is, Nannerl Mozart, Fanny Mendelssohn, and Clara Wieck-Schumann had to be *overwhelmingly* excellent in order to achieve any level of recognition in the canon, and even then we know them primarily in relation to their brother or spouse with the famous name. Composers of our time have stepped forward with outstanding compositional voices, including Gwyneth Walker, Alice Parker, Libby Larsen, Joan Szymko, Abbie Betinis, Andrea Ramsey, Rosephane Powell, Jocelyn Hagen, Dale Trumbore, and so many more. But if you were asked to name five significant female choral composers pre-1950, how would you do? Do you believe that women prior to our time had neither the inclination nor ability to be creative artists? Or that this opportunity was thwarted for female composers? If it is the latter, we as teachers who respect all people cannot continue to endorse such a model.

So how do our women in choir today situate themselves with such a lopsided canon? Sandra Snow offers this perspective in *Conducting Women's Choirs*:

> Singing words penned largely by men and music composed primarily by men has constituted the bulk of the Western European canon, a canon that arguably is shifting but retaining potent hegemony. Because women were silenced for so long in both sacred and secular spaces, treble voicing has emerged as a rich body of repertoire only in recent years. Many composers now writing for women are women and male composers who are more often choosing to set poems by women... Neither texts nor musics are neutral, because they are conceived in culturally specific and situational settings. Singers' interactions with such text and music, likewise, cannot be a neutral or value-free experience.[66]

Dr. Snow shines a light on our curricular choices, for indeed our repertoire is our academic curriculum just as much as the books being studied are our English department's curriculum. What we choose is never neutral, for it carries with it both an endorsement and an omission. It endorses the work presented by saying "this is something worthy of our study for the entire concert cycle – let us dive into this with all our depth of resources." It omits any other composition that could take its place in the concert program. So when we choose a curriculum for women in our choir, and few to none of the composers or poets are female, what do our singers learn? How do they situate themselves in the choral experience?

Moreover, we cannot sing a text without having some sort of reaction to it. There is a great difference between an ensemble of young women singing the text *Now I become myself* and *Three little maids from school are we* – and I say this as someone who has taught both songs to women's choruses. Snow adds:

> The message that serious music is White, male, and formal stands alongside the reality that women have, likewise, been slower to achieve notoriety as performers and conductors in the Western European tradition… Programming musics by women composers can have a powerful effect by opening world-views, challenging old assumptions, and providing a model for women to emulate.[67]

If I am to teach my singers with respect, I want them to fall in love with the art of choral singing the way I did. It is worth exploring how we expect our singers to make that deep connection to the choral art if the repertoire we explore never speaks to them.

WHAT WE MODEL

Take a moment to make a guess for the percentages of teachers who are women at the Pre-K/Kindergarten, Elementary/Middle, High School, and Post-Secondary (College/University) levels. As you reflect on your own life experience, do you see any trend? What might this trend have taught you about leadership as you grew up and learned to perform gender? The Bureau of Labor Statistics offers this data for the percentage of teachers who are women in 2013:

> Pre-K/K: 97.8%; Elementary/Middle: 81%; High School: 56.7%;
> Post-Secondary: 50.2%[68].

As we go through the schooling experience, we experience a gradual transition from almost entirely female teachers to an equal ratio of male to female teachers as we get older and the subject matter advances. What effects do you imagine we might experience from this?

Let's look at some data from 2001 about choral directors specifically. As Kimberly VanWeelden reports:

> Occupational gender trends in regards to choral music revealed females (n=15,472) outnumbered males (n=7,341) by a margin of two to one (MENC, 2001). However, when teaching levels were separated, results indicated the majority of pre-school (85%), elementary (79%), junior high/middle (66%), and secondary (56%) school teachers were female while male teachers became most prominent in post-secondary (55%) grades (MENC 2001).[69]

So, here again, in our music classes, we are far more likely to have female teachers when we are younger and slightly more likely to have male teachers in college. VanWeelden wanted a richer perspective on the assignment of post-secondary choral ensembles, so she surveyed thousands of colleges and universities to get a clearer picture:

- Males directed 65% of choirs, females 20%, with 15% of choirs unspecified.[70]

In programs that included a "Director of Choral Activities," 83% of those positions were held by men.

- Women's choirs were directed by women 72% of the time (28% directed by men), and 35% of female conductors conducted only a women's choir.

She observes:

> Research has found men attain upper level positions of power and leadership because they are perceived to possess the necessary masculine characteristics needed for these jobs (Powell, 1988; Powell & Butterfield, 1979, 1989). While there is little evidence to indicate that females in leadership positions function differently than males in similar circumstances (Jacobsen & Effertz, 1974; Wentworth and Anderson, 1984), research has shown that many people believe men are better leaders than women regardless of leadership performance (Dobbins & Platz, 1986; Rosen & Jerdee, 1978).[71]

I see from this that I am not the only one in America to have had female music teachers in elementary and middle school, and male choral directors in high school and college. In fact, my experience was the norm. What I learned from this was that if I liked choral music as a male, I should teach high school or college, and those are the positions I've held in my career. If we are to teach with respect, we must acknowledge that the legacy of gender discrimination is continually inherited in our repertoire choices, our teaching models, and our choral program structures.

If we are to teach with respect, we must acknowledge that the legacy of gender discrimination is continually inherited in our repertoire choices, our teaching models, and our choral program structures.

While men have tended toward positions of leadership within the choral field, notably fewer males go into choral music in the first place. As teachers concerned about including all singers, we need to confront the ways in which boys may feel excluded from or shunned by the choral experience. Dr. Wilson's study revealed some of the most compelling factors, through the observations of high school girls:

> When asked why they thought there are so few boys in choir, many students cited singing as a feminine activity and pointed to how singing is viewed by our society. The terms 'girly' and 'gay' were used often. Peer pressure was frequently cited as a reason not to sing. Kate discussed the "rules we have in society that dictate what men and women are supposed to do. Guys are

supposed to be athletic and strong and stuff like that. It [choir] is more of a girls' thing." Sam explained, "Singing is seen as effeminate. It has a 'female vibe.' I don't know why. A lot of guys don't like to sing 'cause it's not a manly thing, I guess, or something like that. You know how teenagers are."

While we continue to progress as music educators in our inclusive efforts, still, many of us remember that it was an uphill social battle to be in choir, as these students attest. In our efforts to teach with inclusivity, we must ask ourselves what we are modeling when we see simultaneously fewer males in the teaching field and yet we marginalize the voices of women in the structure and repertoire we teach.

WHAT OUR REPERTOIRE TEACHES OUR SINGERS

Let us step back now and examine how we might teach all our students with respect. Let us begin with a closer look at our curriculum, since the repertoire we rehearse is the core of our teaching. Hilary Apfelstadt challenged us to do this in 1998, observing:

> [I]n the past it seemed that the majority of women's contemporary choral music, in particular, was what I call "butterflies and rainbows" music, mostly moderate to slow tempo, melodically pleasant settings of rather vapid texts. It was as though women's choirs should exist on a steady diet of light, pleasant music or love songs and the like. Those of us who conduct women's choirs, from high school age through adult levels, know that the sameness of such music is boring. In my experience, women seek more substance than this, substance that can be found only in high quality music.[72]

Those of us who direct treble choirs know all too well what Dr. Apfelstadt means by *butterflies and rainbows*, and composers still fill the catalogues with *pleasantness*. How many of us have started to sketch out a treble-choir concert set, looked at it, and realized everything was slow and lyrical? Finding a strong or driving composition for treble choirs is difficult, and it speaks to the unspoken assumption, given voice through repertoire, that women should be sweet and pleasant.

Perhaps even more troubling, the repertoire for treble choir rarely speaks as women who engage the world. Rather, women in choir too often sing as objects in a man's world. As Kathleen Gallagher observes in *The Everyday Classroom as Problematic*, "Daily, in public education, girls are asked to locate themselves inside a canon which has constructed them as 'other,' as object of study rather than subject."[73] Look again at a popular song like *Somewhere Over the Rainbow*. At what point in this story does Dorothy strike you as empowered? The beloved Serbian folksong *Niska Banja* translates to more than "let's go to the bath and kiss;" rather, it's closer to "I will get her; I will love her; and I will leave her," and the "I" is a male voice. What are our young women supposed to make of this text? At an age when women are discovering their sexuality, how many times are they asked to sing about purity? And, ironically, if they consistently sing in praise of virginity, why do they also sing so many lullabies? How often do women in choir speak from their own life experiences?

Fortunately, we are seeing more and more compositions that do address our singers' agency. Gwyneth Walker's setting of *Now I Become Myself* (poem by Mary Sarton) is an outstanding text of self-realization. Susan Borwick's *And Ain't I a Woman!* speaks from the too-long omitted voices of Black women. Abbie Betinis has written multiple masterpieces containing rhythmic vitality for advanced treble choirs, including *From Beyond the Caravan* and *Chant for Great Compassion*. Carol Barnett's *Song of Perfect Propriety* (poem by Dorothy Parker) is a wonderful example of a choral composition for treble choir that mirrors the sort of humorous, aggressive song that we program twice per concert for our male choirs. Sandra Snow curates the "In High Voice" series and Doreen Rao curates the CME series for Boosey & Hawkes, both of which are excellent. Emily Crocker, Andrea Ramsey, Judith Clurman, and so many others are active in creating this repertoire. The ACDA Women's Choir Commission Consortium, among others, is an active participant in this project of writing a new chapter in the repertory for our treble choirs.

What do our choices teach us about young men in choir? We have songs that say 'it's great to be here with you, fellow men,' such as *Vive l'Amour* and *Brothers, Sing On!* We have the slow, lyrical religious songs, such as the Biebl *Ave Maria* and the Chesnokov *Spaseniye Soldelal*. We have folksongs (*Loch Lomond, Shenandoah, Tshotsholoza*), spirituals (*Ride the Chariot, Joshua Fit the Battle*), Renaissance motets (e.g. Josquin's *Absolom, Fili Mi*), Romantic part-songs (Schubert and Schumann), and everything in between. Indeed, it is perhaps more insightful to discuss what men sing that women do not sing. Sea chanteys, for example, are staples of the bass clef choir repertoire, but we have few equivalent songs for treble choirs.

In spite of the broader range of repertoire, Joshua Palkki notes that men's choirs too often focus on re-affirming male stereotypes. That is, they tend to sing caricatured versions of masculinity that pigeon-hole the entire spectrum of male experience into the stereotypical manly hero (broad-shouldered and strong, a lady's man who loves to drink and joke around with his fellas, and conquer). Palkki advocates that we reconsider such programming: "a balanced program for a bass-clef choir should mirror the spectrum of masculinities that may accurately reflect the lived experiences of male singers."[74]

These texts for gendered choirs speak to the implicit behavioral expectations we have for adolescent men and women, as Dr. Wilson points out in her review of gender roles in music:

> Males and females are prepared to assume different roles in our society with boys and girls being rewarded for different behaviors starting early in life. Koza (1994) reports that girls are often taught to be "sweet, passive, nice and meek" while males are sometimes socialized to use disruptive behavior in order to get attention (p. 75). Additionally, girls are conditioned to "get along better, have more self-control, and be neater and more helpful than boys" (Bank, 2007, p. 544). Males are expected to be powerful, strong, aggressive and logical while

females are expected to be nurturing, cooperative and emotional (Herndon and Ziegler, 1990).

From this framework, it makes sense that our women's choir would sing O *Pastorelle, Addio* or *Lake Isle of Innisfree* while our men's choir sings *Drunken Sailor* and *Brothers, Sing On!* Curriculum is never neutral.

STRATEGIES FOR INCLUSIVE TEACHING

Here are some of the ways we can teach with more inclusivity and respect.

Behaviors, Not Traits

How do you want your singers to behave in your ensemble? Which behaviors are acceptable, and which are unacceptable? If we establish our expectations, we hold all our singers to these rules, while making appropriate accommodations for special needs. We do not dismiss inappropriate behavior in our males as 'just being guys,' or expect wildly different behavior from our females because 'they know better.' We make a thousand differentiated instructional decisions based on vocal issues, of course, but we do not hold one group to totally different standards. We must learn to recognize when we are describing a singer's trait, such as tenor or senior, and when we are describing a behavior, such as marking the score or breathing well. When we conflate a trait like man with a behavior like 'horse-play,' we lower the expectation for male students and create an implicit, higher bar for female students.

Acknowledging Unconscious Bias

There is a terrifying amount of evidence that, even those of us who think we teach all students equally, in fact, do not. We tend to call on males more frequently, and tend to correct and explain over females more frequently. We tend to expect certain failures or successes in one section that we do not in another, such as expecting a very high sight-singing ability in altos and a lower ability in basses. The first thing we can do is catalogue and identify our behaviors by taping ourselves in rehearsal and then watching it with a friend. We will usually be surprised at the frequency with which we demonstrate these behaviors.

The first thing we can do is catalogue and identify our behaviors by taping ourselves in rehearsal and then watching it with a friend.

Instructional Language

Do we ask all singers to help set up the risers, or just 'a few strong men'? Do we make gendered comments about tone, as in "altos, put some hair on your chest for that low A!" If I had a dollar for every time a choir director made a joke about tenors not being as manly as basses, I would be rich. We want to create a vital and humorous space in rehearsal, and we tell jokes to do that and create special bonds with each section. But so often our language, whether used for humor or simply instruction, enforces and strengthens the stereotypes that we as teachers wish to break down in our quest for teaching with respect.

Appearance

Do we ask our students to wear concert attire? If so, what choices do the singers have with the attire selection? Do all women have to wear the same dress? Do men who sing soprano have to wear that dress? We can reframe this by asking what the values and purposes of concert attire are first, and then sort out the logistics from there. If the purpose of the concert attire is to provide a visual sense of unity, does that necessitate the exact same dress for all women, or can that be accomplished by having the exact same color (e.g. all black)?

Naming the Issue

If we elect to perform a work that presents clearly patriarchal or gender-biased views, we can show our singers the respect they deserve by honestly and thoughtfully naming the problematic text and addressing it. For example, when choirs perform Josef Haydn's masterwork, *The Creation*, singers will often note the gender power issue when Eve says to Adam, "O thou, for whom I am! My help, my shield, my all! Thy will is law to me," (which, to be clear, is not from Genesis, but from Dryden/Van Swieten). If we do not acknowledge that this text presents a possible conflict with our value of equal respect for all (in that, in this portrait, woman is made to be completely subservient to man), we set this composition forth unquestioningly as curriculum and therefore as acceptable. But by naming it and acknowledging it, we enter into a space of fruitful discussion about Enlightenment constructions of gender and power, and help singers foster connections with other political quests for representation in the 1790s in Europe and America, and perhaps with other musical works in the 1790s as well.

I do not believe that an increased attention to representations of gender and power in choral literature necessitates a wholesale censorship of the western art music canon. I do believe that a more inclusive pedagogy of that canon, however, requires an ability to see such representations and to *acknowledge* them with our singers. As we begin to see how gender is taught and performed, we more clearly see our responsibility in perpetuating or liberating our singers from limiting and power-imbalanced roles. As we learn that our repertoire is never neutrally selected, we can challenge ourselves to put forward curriculum that gives voice to a broader array of human experiences than the privileged European male voice. In so doing, we do not kick Mozart and Bach out of the tent; rather, we discover just how big a tent the choral experience can be.

Ensemble Names

I encourage directors to consider either continuing to naming ensembles by gender (men's and women's) – and thereby taking *any* singer who shares that gender – or to start naming ensembles by their ranges: bass-clef ensembles (TTBB) and treble-clef ensembles (SSAA). This is a more inclusive approach for trans and nonbinary singers, as we will see in the next section.

TRANSGENDER SINGERS

Perhaps no facet of civil and political discourse has changed as significantly in the last few years as the rights of trans+ (transgender, non-binary, agender, gender-fluid) students. The rapid ascent of trans publicity and storylines, legislative protections, and educational policies has been significant progress for students who had, until recently, barely been recognized as existent in most school settings. Here is a quick view of Google searches on the term *transgender* from 2004-2016:

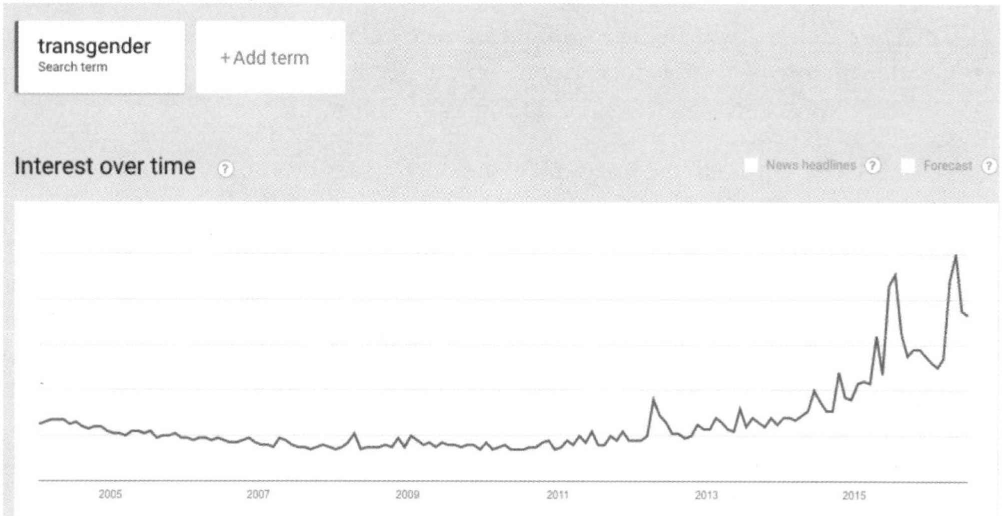

Clearly there is an increased interest in transgender issues.

While most teachers express support for all students, many feel insufficiently prepared to navigate the conversations around trans students, such as concert attire, voice-part placement, or terminology. And the data shows that being present and respectful to trans students matters greatly. Kosciw et al analyzed high school climate survey data and showed that 43% of students who are gender-variant have felt unsafe at school, and yet 97% of students felt supported by at least one staff member. We can and should be there for students. Palkki and Sauerland suggest that we begin this by building in curricula in "gender-complex pedagogy" in our music education classes for future teachers, as a recurring thread that runs from introductory courses through methods courses to student-teaching seminar courses.[76] LGBTQ+ students need to know that we are aware of and in support of the spectrum of identities they bring to our classroom. As Palkki and Caldwell note in their massive survey of student experiences, "the overwhelming message from the open-ended responses was that the singers wanted choral conductor-teachers to acknowledge and/or discuss these matters in the choral classroom. Because gender identity and sexuality are traits that are not visible, participants believed that if choral educators did not discuss these matters in a culture and schools that are heteronormative and cisgender-centric, that they were not open and accepting."[77] Additionally, Palkki and Caldwell found that students want to know if a composer is "non-hetero-normative" and make anti-bullying policies explicit, both in the classroom and online.[78] First, let's return to the idea of gender, which was presented earlier as an either-or binary.

A productive conversation with directors who work with trans singers begins with some clarifying terminology. Many teachers feel supportive of their trans singers, but worry about which words to use. Music educators and conductors can find a fantastic list of resources at galachoruses.org/resource-center/singers/transgender-voices.

Here are some helpful terms:

- **Sex assigned at birth** – Essentially, what the doctor wrote on your birth certificate. This may include male, female, or intersex (see below).
- **Gender Identity** – Your gender, as you experience it.
- **Gender Expression** – Your gender, as you express it in the world.

For me, these terms all line up as male: the doctor said I was male, I am male, and I express myself in the world as male. But that is one of many possibilities. I could have been assigned male at birth, be female or non-binary or gender-fluid, and yet express myself in the world as male. Or I could have been assigned male at birth, be female or agender or nonbinary, and express myself as female or agender or nonbinary. In other words, you may teach singers who were assigned one gender at birth, perform as in that gender to the world, but are in fact a different gender identity.

- **Cisgender** – Using the Latin prefix "Cis", meaning "on the same side of," *cisgender* (or *cis*) refers to people who share the same biological sex and gender identity. For example, I identify as cis-male.
- **Transgender** – Using the Latin prefix "Trans," meaning "on the other side of," *transgender* (or *trans*) refers to people whose gender differs from the assigned sex at birth. If someone was born with a biological male body but identifies as female, she might describe herself as trans, or trans-female, transfem, or MTF (see below).
- **Trans, or trans+** - a broader term that encompasses gender identities such as transgender, agender, non-binary, two-spirit, genderqueer, gender-fluid.
- **Transsexual** – Not a word that is used anymore.
- **Intersex** – Refers to people who have physical characteristics that do not fit typical male/female dichotomies. The term 'hermaphrodite' had been used in the past, but is no longer appropriate.
- **FTM** and **MTF** – Some transgender people may identify themselves this way. The first letter stands for the birth-assigned gender (F for female, M for male), the T stands for "to", and the third letter for the chosen gender. Hence, FTM would mean "Female-to-Male," as in, "I was assigned the gender female at birth, but I am a male." However, it should be noted that this is primarily a medical term, and carries with it the harmful implication that a trans man was ever female.
- **Gender-fluid** or **Gender-queer** – refers to people who do not define themselves in a male/female dichotomy.
- **Nonbinary** – refers to a person who does not define themselves in the binary of male/female
- **Transition** – refers to the process of changing one's gender expression.

- **Dead-naming** – refers to the harmful practice of calling a person by their assigned-gender name, not their gender-identified name. So, if a student had been given the name Joshua at birth, and, having identified as trans and chosen the name Janice, was still called Joshua, that would be dead-naming. In effect, by not acknowledging this person's new name, the speaker simultaneously fails to acknowledge the student by their name and also "outs" the student as trans.

WORKING WITH TRANSGENDER VOICES - PART I: SECOND CHANCES

Throughout my career as a singer and conductor, I have worked with one basic paradigm of voice section placement in auditions. In this mode, I would:

- Explore the ends of the singer's range to gain a basic sense of voice type.
- Explore the passaggio to hear the natural vocal turn-over.
- Listen for ease/comfort in different ranges to find the ideal tessitura.

Throughout this process, especially with the adolescents that I teach, I am less interested in what singers *think* their voices are, and more interested in what the singers' voices are telling me they need for vocal health and success. A student might identify as an alto, but only because they prefer to press chest voice, hiding an exquisite soprano voice, for example. My role as an educator is to help the student build a complete instrument, so whether *they* thinks they are an alto or not is not typically a concern for me.

It was in this audition-mode frame of mind that I made mistakes with the first transgender student I met. Rose (I changed the name here) came in for choir auditions, and to my eye and ear, I saw a man, in male clothing, build, and voice. I thought Rose was an unconventional name, but I was bleary from the previous 30 auditions that day, assigned Rose to the tenor section, and moved on. Rose wrote me later that day and expressed how hurt she had felt that she would be lumped in with the men when she was female. Her message made it clear that she was withdrawing from choral participation forever. I sat there in equal parts angry at her for assuming that I would intuit Rose's transgender identity without any conversation, and ashamed that I had been such an automaton during auditions that I didn't have a better conversation with her right away.

I'm grateful that life provided me with a second chance. The next year, Tim (again, I've changed the name) emailed me before his audition, introduced himself, and said that he was interested in choir, but needed me to know that he was FTM trans, and that I would be hearing a treble voice. I still conducted the vocal range tests as usual, but this time, I did something I'd never previously done in an audition: I *asked* Tim where *he* wanted to sing. Tim chose to sing with the tenors. Instead of me saying, "that's silly – you have a lovely soprano voice," we talked about the pros and cons. Tim's voice would add much needed buoyancy to the tenor section, which typically struggled with finding light tone. But, and I was clear about this proactively, some of the lower notes in a tenor part would be too low. So I talked with Tim about octave displacement for those notes, just as I would with early changing cis-male voices; I showed him a few vocal exercises that would help him release and strengthen the lowest register of his voice; and I asked him to keep me in the loop about how it went. Tim was a strong contributor to choir that year. When it came time for the next year's audition, Tim chose to sing in the alto section, where his voice shined.

It is hard to put into words the kind of preternatural maturity and grace that a student like Tim brings to a director who has never worked with trans singers before. Part of me writes this book so that students like Tim do not have to keep being the educators to us choral directors. It is hard enough to navigate transitioning to one's true gender identity in an often hostile world; to ask of these singers that they also prepare their first encounter with their choral directors for the comfort of the teacher is too much. Rose's experience is far more common and deeply harmful. I did not seek to deny her – it just was not on my radar until it was too late. My positive relationship with Tim produced two long-term benefits; first, Tim was a great musician to have in choir, and second, more trans students joined choir after they were able to see - through Tim - that this was a safe space for music-making.

WORKING WITH TRANSGENDER STUDENTS - PART II: RECOMMENDATIONS

I believe our first responsibility in all choir auditions is to get to know the voice in front of us. I still stand by the basic range-discerning procedures I outlined above, since I cannot steward a voice I do not know. Now, however, I pay more careful attention to ways in which a singer may have a vocal range that does not fit my preconceptions in a cis-normative paradigm. Using the name Rose, was, in hindsight, clear communication. One respectful way to gain clarity is to introduce yourself in the audition with your pronouns ("Hi, I'm Dr. Sieck, and my pronouns are he/him/his), and ask singers to introduce themselves. Please note that 'preferred pronouns' is a common but insufficient expression. "He/Him/His" *are* my pronouns – they're not just my preferred pronouns. If you respond to the question, "where's Steve?" with "she went this way", it is not just that I would *prefer* that you use "he"; you are misgendering me.

It is important to remember that trans students may be in a painful situation where they can use their name and pronouns in the choir room but need to use their legal name and pronouns in concerts, where family members who do not support their child's gender identity attend. During the audition/intake process with students, if a student specifies a 'preferred name' that differs substantively from their legal name in the registration system, be sure to follow up with that student to ask when and where it is appropriate to use which name.

Now, in auditions, I like to check in with every student about where they want to sing. Trans singers are not a monolith, and it would be inaccurate to assume that every trans singer wants to sing in the clef traditionally associated with their gender identity. As Joshua Palkki notes, "some trans singers may revel in the fact that their voice does not match society's notions of how their voice 'should' sound. Some trans people, however, consider the voice a vital way that they 'do' their gender in society."[79] Vocal dysphoria is a term used to describe the intense feeling of mismatch and discomfort in one's own vocal timbre, just as body dysphoria is a term used to describe the mismatch and discomfort with one's body. For some (not all) trans singers, being placed in the section associated with their assigned sex at birth is a profoundly harmful decision.

Let's examine some of the possible strategies with trans voices:

A trans+ singer who was assigned-male-at-birth may (or may not) choose to take estrogen as part of the transition. If that singer experienced the effects of testosterone during adolescence, their vocal folds will have lengthened and thickened (creating a lower sound) irreversibly, even with estrogen treatment. There are some strategies that voice professionals can use to help the singer use a higher tone. By engaging the crico-thyroid muscle in 'head voice', post-testosterone trans voices can stretch and thin the vocal mechanism to produce good 4th and 5th octave tones. I recommend starting singers on lip-trills in the 4th and 5th octaves, and then adding descending penta-scales on [u] and [i] from the 5th octave down. After several months of this strengthening work, the singer can use more power and agility etudes. Depending on the singer's vocal registration events, it may be easier to sing Alto I than Alto II. Alto II often hovers on the thyro-arytenoid to crico-thyroid passaggio (C-E4), and it may be easier for the voice to stay more consistent when it is reliably above that 'passaggio' than when it has to come through it often. That singer may or may not wear a waist trainer, which enhances the 'hour-glass' curve of the body, which may affect breath.

A trans+ singer who was assigned-female-at-birth may (or may not) choose to take testosterone as part of the transition. In cis-male puberty, testosterone thickens the vocal folds while the entire laryngeal structure itself increases in size significantly. Testosterone injections will thicken the vocal folds, but not lengthen the laryngeal structure, so the pitch of the voice will drop over 6-12 months, but the timbre and resonance may vary slightly from cis-male vocal change. The newly lowered voice will still need the strategies we employ with early adolescent cis-male voice change to navigate the expanded range (See Freer, Leck, et al), and will undergo periods of instability, especially in the first year. In the event that the singer is not receiving hormone treatments, there is no equivalent 'expanded range' technique for lower register in assigned-female-at-birth voices comparable to counter-tenor for assigned-male-at-birth voices. I encourage guided exercises in open belt register, sustained buzzing in lower register (consider a nasalized [o] on B♭3 for 20 seconds, e.g.), and, as with working with basses trying access low notes, give careful attention to the free and relaxed laryngeal position (avoid the larynx pushing down, though). Without the thickening of folds through hormone treatment, most assigned-female-at-birth voices will cease comfortable production around F3, though some can reach as low as C3. Hence a trans male singer may need accommodations when singing Tenor I to transpose the lowest notes. The singer may or may not choose to wear a chest binder, which reduces the appearance of breasts, and may significantly impact their ability to breathe and maintain optimum vocal function.

One thing I have picked up from my lived experience as a teacher and from multiple presentations with fellow music educators is our collective fear of 'messing up'. We acknowledge that the concert will be imperfect, we acknowledge that we are going to mix up student names regularly at the start of the year, we acknowledge that we are going to fall short in our playing of a tricky piano accompaniment or our modeling of a French text, but we are specifically terrified of messing up a trans student's name or their pronouns. I understand that fear. As Jackson Hearns and Kremer note, "even within transgender communities, peers, colleagues, and friends accidentally misgender or dead-name others, and acknowledge the learning process with compassion and patience… When well-meaning mistakes arise, it is appropriate to apologize, make the correction, and move on. It is inappropriate to dwell on and belabor the mistake, forcing the person about whom the mistake was made to take emotional care of their conversation partner."[80] If you regularly misgender or dead-name a student, though, take note. As Kelly George notes, "if you're struggling with it, there's something going on. You're still connecting your expectations in your head of gender to your language and to that person. You have not yet separated the gender expectations from what you see. You have to pull apart visual perception and identity, and probably also what you hear and how that manifests as gender expectations."[81]

Finally, I want to share a personal story. When I wrote the first edition in 2016, working with trans singers was a professional focus. I tried to follow Maya Angelou's guidance: "do the best you can until you know better. Then when you know better, do better". I was grateful to the students in the stories shared above for teaching me that I could do better, and I tried. A few years later, I learned that one of my children was trans. On the one hand, I was so grateful that my work in inclusive pedagogy had prepared me to know the appropriate vocabulary and to understand gender as a social construct. On the other hand, I realized how little I understood what it is like to be trans. My child went from class to class every day with teachers and students dead-naming them, and tried to pay attention in class while experiencing body- and vocal-dysmorphia.

We were lucky in every respect. Our child was amazing at clarifying what they were experiencing, what their name and pronouns were, when and why they were ready for what kind of treatment, and so forth. We had supportive doctors, friends, and extended family. And yet, even if you have every advantage, it is hard to transition to your true gender. Consider the journey it takes to get one's driver's license. It starts with getting the name-change approval from your local court, which then needs to be submitted to the local newspaper for public record. Then you will need a new birth certificate from whichever county in whichever state you were born in. Then you need a new social security card with the right name and gender. Now you can finally go to the DMV with the right paperwork to take your driving exam. Even if a teen in transition has the loving support of parents, transitioning is expensive and unimaginably laborious. Meanwhile there are phone calls with the IT department at the high school to beg/cajole/threaten so that the learning system (Canvas, for example) updates the child's name and pronouns so that teachers stop dead-naming them. Every interaction with a server at a restaurant or a cashier at a store is a tense moment of "will they misgender my child?" or "how can I insert my child's pronouns into this conversation before the other person says something?" Finding clothes for your child that are appropriately gendered and also fit becomes a difficult task. Some part of the parental journey is also grief; not grief because your child is trans, but simply the process of letting go of the name and gender of the child you were raising. And, in the end, you know that the child you are raising is so much happier, so much more themself, so much more comfortable in their skin, and ready to take on the world. And so you send your child off to school in the morning and pray that Canvas displays the right name and pronouns, that other students who knew the student in their birth-assigned gender/name in elementary school will remember to use your child's true name and pronouns, that they can go to a bathroom without cause for concern, and that they find teachers who see your child for the amazing human being that they are.

CHAPTER 5
Choir and Sexual Identity

Some of the most active civil rights discussions of our time have centered on issues of same-sex rights. We see this in the military's shift from dishonorably discharging gay soldiers to "Don't Ask, Don't Tell" to recruiting openly gay soldiers. We see this in television program shifts from stereotyped caricatures in "Three's Company" to more nuanced characters in "Grey's Anatomy" and "Orange is the New Black.". We see this in civil law, from the Stonewall uprising in 1969 to the 2015 Supreme Court ruling in Obergefell v. Hodges in which same-sex marriages were ruled constitutionally protected. These important shifts in rights and representations may too easily suggest that sexual identity is no longer a topic that sparks disagreement. That is to say, the federal law may have made it abundantly clear now that discrimination based on sexual identity is prohibited, but we are not in a "post-sexual identity" society by any means.

Here are two quotes from people in positions of authority weighing in on homosexuality. See if you can spot which is from 1970 and which is from 2004:

- This is a very serious matter, because it is our children who are the prize for [the homosexual] community. They are specifically targeting our children.
- As far as I'm concerned, granting a parade permit to a group of homosexuals to parade down Hollywood Boulevard would be the same as giving a permit to march to a group of thieves and murderers.

The first quote is from Senator Michele Bachmann, on the gay community and same-sex marriage, appearing as guest on radio program "Prophetic Views Behind the News," hosted by Jan Markell, KKMS 980-AM, March 20, 2004. Here, Senator Bachmann assumes that homosexuality is a deviant behavior that manifests in pedophilia. The second comes from Los Angeles Police Department Chief Ed Davis in 1970, though it should be mentioned that Davis later changed his views. As Mitchell Morris writes in *Calling Names; Taking Names*, "the historical record suggests that often such love dared not speak its name not only because of the risk of persecution, but also because usually it didn't have anything to call itself other than a string of pejoratives."[82] Before we begin a thoughtful look on how we can teach all our singers with respect, we need to recognize that many of our singers have been labeled as predatory, immoral, dysfunctional deviants hundreds of times before they ever come into our rehearsal space.

In this chapter, we will look at issues of heteronormativity and how that affects directors and singers. We will examine our repertoire and our teaching practices, and identify ways to be more respectful and inclusive.

ACKNOWLEDGING HETERONORMATIVITY

Heteronormativity is a word that combines two concepts: *heterosexuality*, as in "being sexually attracted to the opposite sex," and *normativity*, as in "what we understand as normal, default, the unmarked category." Heteronormativity is the term we use to describe a model in which opposite-sex relationships are assumed, and same-sex relationships are distinct, other, marked, or set apart from the norm. We learn this in nearly every movie we see, in every story we read, in every song we sing, and, until very recently, in every law in the courts.

Heteronormativity is the term we use to describe a model in which opposite-sex relationships are assumed, and same-sex relationships are distinct, other, marked, or set apart from the norm.

Readers who identify as homosexual will find this to be immediately obvious, but some heterosexual readers may find this confusing. Here's a simple experiment. Take a piece of paper and a pencil. Turn on the television. On one side of the paper, make a check-mark every time heterosexuality is affirmed in advertisements, television plots, movie promotions, and songs. On the other side, make a check-mark every time homosexuality is affirmed. Stop when you get the point. We - and our singers - live in a culture that constantly reinforces how normal it is to be heterosexual, even though millions are not, including many of our singers.

The academic field known as *queer studies* has called out such heteronormativity. Scholars in queer studies have asked us to question how we know what we know about our world and ourselves. We use the term *epistemology* to mean studying how we gain knowledge. As Eve Sedgwick observes in her landmark work, *Epistemology of the Closet*, only very recently have we come to understand ourselves sexually exclusively by "the gender of the object choice" – who it is that we are attracted to. This narrow defining process has remained as "the dimension denoted by the now ubiquitous category of *sexual orientation*."[83] Many adolescents do not understand themselves in these binary categories of "normal/heterosexual" or "other/gay" yet. When we as directors attach a normative sexual orientation of heterosexuality to all people, we push those students who are not sure into the category of 'other,' a closet that they must then choose to come out of on their own terms, against a tide of heteronormativity.

While we may have removed some of the stigma of that coming-out process which previous generations faced, the normative or default expectation continues, and this puts our singers who identify as LGTBQ+ in the 'other' category. This is not how I would want to be treated, and so as a conductor committed to teaching with respect, I have a responsibility to examine which kind of culture I create in the choir rehearsal. And let us be clear: there is societal violence against LGBTQ+ people and walking back of civil rights. This is not a human rights issue that is 'resolved.'

In the move away from a strict hetero/homo binary (unmarked/marked, normal/other), the term "queer" re-emerged as a way to both reclaim an insult and break open the either/or. *Queer* as a term may break down the simple unmarked/marked dichotomy, but it doesn't immediately translate to observable progress within the daily life of music-making. Patricia O'Toole writes that music education is "not comfortable with discussions of sexuality and musicing, and actively silences identity positions based on sexuality." She notes that LGTBQ+ choruses have had to create their own music publisher (Yelton Rhodes Press) "because mainstream publishers will not carry this music for supposedly ethical and economic reasons." Consequently, "gay teens who find their way into choirs are confronted by stifling politics and little support for emerging and difficult identities."[84] How can we reconcile the heteronormativity of our choral tradition and O'Toole's call to re-think how we teach?

As we look to understand heteronormativity in the music rehearsal more clearly, I *highly* recommend Louis Bergonzi's article "Sexual Orientation and Music Education: Continuing a Tradition" (*Music Educators Journal*, 96:2, Dec. 2009). Bergonzi lists, in powerful detail, *many* of the ways in which heterosexual singers and directors enjoy a favored status. He highlights his discrimination in the simple things like being able to talk about prom, making overnight room assignments for tour, and keeping photos of your spouse on your desk. He notes that, for heterosexual students, "all the love songs you hear on the radio, sing, or play in an ensemble are about a kind of love you know and understand. The annual spring musical is, in almost all cases, going to involve a romantic subplot about a kind of love that resembles yours."[85] Bergonzi concludes:

> Sexual orientation in music education is not a new phenomenon. Isn't it time to consider the beneficial presence of individuals - musicians, colleagues, and students - whose emotional, romantic, and physical attractions are to other human beings who happen to be of the same sex? Isn't it time for us to acknowledge the ways we reinforce heterosexuality and the heterosexual lifestyle, and to examine how homophobia and heterocentrism bias our curricular content and the lives and work of LGBT music teachers? Isn't it time we eliminate heterosexuality's privileged place in our profession?[86]

How can we best meet Bergonzi's call to eliminate heterosexuality's privileged place? What strategies can we use in our choir room to teach all singers with respect?

STRATEGIES FOR INCLUSIVE PEDAGOGY WITH LGTBQ+ SINGERS

Purposeful Ambiguity

Many of the songs we sing are about love, and this calls our adolescent singers in particular to a sharp focus on their sexuality. For students who are 'out' or are questioning, a love song reminds them on a daily basis that they are not conforming, so I try to be purposefully ambiguous about gender when I teach a love song. For example, I once conducted a setting of Shakespeare's Sonnet 18 (*Shall I compare thee…*) and consistently referred to the object of the poet's affection as his *beloved*. It would have been easy for me to talk about the addressee as "her"; by using *beloved*, I made a choice to leave the gender unassigned. The singers could each fill in a gender in their own minds if they wanted to. There is evidence to suggest Shakespeare wrote it for a *man* he loved, so I made a conscious choice to not guide our conversations with the assumption that his audience was female.

Creating Space

Some songs are unambiguously heteronormative, clearly describing a man and a woman in love. The oft-performed *Lass from the Low Country*, for instance, expresses a poor woman's unrequited love for a rich nobleman. As good teachers, we want to talk about the text, of course, and we want our singers to relate to what they are saying. We can create space for LGTBQ+ singers by acknowledging that this song assumes a heterosexual relationship, but that each of us has to make the song relevant in our own space. We can focus on the feeling of unrequited love, which most people felt at some point. Moreover, the interesting textual challenge in this song is not the dichotomy between her and him as genders, but between rich and poor as classes; thus the conversation is more fruitful if the singers do exegetical work on power differences, not gender differences.

Be a Listener, Not an Investigator

I have a personal teaching philosophy of being deeply uninterested in the romantic lives of my singers. I do not need to know who is dating whom. Every time I have asked, I have ended up with my foot in my mouth one way or another. We want to foster a close-knit family in our choir, and it would seem normal to lift up this couple's three-month anniversary or to find out who is going to prom with whom – it would send a message that we care. But it also sends a powerful message to students who are not in a relationship, or to students who would like to be in a relationship but are afraid of being 'out.' If a singer wants to share their identity or relationship status with me, I am supportive. But I try not to be inquisitive. I do have a responsibility to be attentive to concerns about safety or abuse, but I distinguish that from asking singers about their romantic lives simply out of a desire to be relatable.

Help Singers Understand that LGTBQ+ Authors and Composers Exist

We already program LGTBQ+ composers and poets, frequently. Here's a very much incomplete list of writers whose texts we sing whose identities do not fit tidily in the heterosexual category: Albee, Auden, Butler, Byron, Donne, Lorca, (Langston) Hughes, Michelangelo, Milton, Sarton, Shakespeare, Teasdale, Walker, Whitman; and composers: Barber, Bernstein, Britten, Copland, Corigliano, Grainger, Pinkham, Poulenc, Quilter, Rorem, Sondheim, and so many more. I do not endorse a pedagogy of simply naming that identity to participate in a "Representation Bingo", as in "this composer is gay" or "this composer is Black." That only confirms an 'other-ing' process. Weaving in that composer's identity naturally in teaching conversation, though, helps students feel seen. Moreover, I encourage us to give voice to a wide range of composers and writers, and to be the kind of conductors and teachers who are aware that the creators whose music they are performing did not fit into the heteronormative paradigm.

Be Aware of Stereotyping and Fight It

I have a high tenor voice and I studied dance, so I cannot begin to count the number of times it was assumed I was gay because those were apparently gay attributes. The activities and interests we pursue and the people we are attracted to do not always fit in tidy columns. We shouldn't put the choreography assignment onto the 'gayest' man in choir; we should assign that to the person most qualified in choreography. Sexuality is a thread in the fabric of our identity, not a magnetic pole.

Learn to Identify Uncomfortable Situations on the Stage

Many choral directors serve in a leadership role for musical theatre productions. For some of us, these productions are delightful stories that feature a compelling love story and some memorable songs. But as I look back on productions I led, e.g. *Brigadoon*, or *Guys and Dolls*, the heteronormativity of the plots now leap out at me. What if the situation were reversed, and I was myself (heterosexual) in a homonormative play? Could I imagine being me at sixteen and having to kiss another young man because the script called for it? What kind of space or accommodation or guidance would I need to make that less uncomfortable? How many students who were LGTBQ+ have I put in a similarly uncomfortable situation in my career? I do not advocate changing the script, and if the kiss is an obvious plot point, the characters need to kiss. I do, however, advocate that we create space for this to be acknowledged. Professional actors regularly engage in a range of physical and emotional behaviors onstage that do not reflect themselves – that's what acting is, in many respects. But adolescents are neither adults nor professionals, and it is worth reminding those of us who teach adolescents that they may need help working through these situations.

Look at Your Repertoire from Different Perspectives

I recently reviewed the music I have programmed in the past and realized that I had not done a good job of being inclusive in my concerts. I know that many of my singers identify as LGTBQ+. But the musical world I was trained in focused on heteronormative texts, and I never processed the cognitive dissonance or marginalization my singers might have experienced until that review. I will still program works that have heteronormative texts. But I also want to make sure that I am finding works to teach that were created by or represent LGBTQ+ voices.

Recognize the Distinction Between a More Inclusive Repertoire and Advocacy

A school concert does not need to offer the same program as the nearby Gay Chorus. The GALA chorus repertoire emerged with advocacy front and center, and many of those great scores are meant to encourage policy changes. We can perform LGTBQ+ works without turning a spring choir concert into a political event. It should be noted that the heterosexual songs we sing are also, in a sense, advocacy for heteronormativity. Every song we sing like Haydn's "Harmony in Marriage" advocates for heterosexuality. In all cases, there has to be a curricular reason for why we are singing this that is well beyond taking a political stance (for or against something).

Be Attentive to Your Teaching Language

As choral directors we hope that our singers pay attention to what we say to them. Sometimes I find myself saying so many things in rehearsal that I am hard pressed to pay attention to my own words! We need to remember that our singers may tune out our seventeenth correction of a good [a] vowel or our nineteenth reminder about all-state auditions, but they will all remember a hurtful comment. We process personal attacks in the limbic region of the brain, and store those memories far differently than our normal daily experiences. How many of us have seen teachers use phrases such as 'like a girl' to describe a head-voice predominant tenor sound (with the accompanying weak-wrist hand gesture to clarify they do not mean this to be heteronormative)? How many of us have seen directors cajole altos to be more 'butch'? Those words felt inappropriate to me in a general way, but they did not register in my limbic system as personal attacks. I cannot begin to imagine how my LGTBQ+ peers processed those words. According to the Center for Disease Control, 7th-12th grade LGTBQ+ students are "more than twice as likely to have attempted suicide as their heterosexual peers."[87] However, LBTQ+ youth who reported having at least one accepting adult were 40% less likely to report a suicide attempt in the last year.[88] Your authentic care for your students matters. As conductors committed to teaching all our singers with respect, we must be attentive to the words we use (and the words we sing), so that all our singers know they are valued.

CHAPTER 6
Choir and Religion

> Every person's concept of God is too small. Through humility we can begin to get into true perspective the infinity of God. This is the humble approach. It is also in humility that we learn from each other, for it makes us open to each other and ready to see things from the other's point of view and share ours with him freely. It is by humility that we avoid the sins of pride and intolerance and avoid all religious strife.
>
> —Sir John Templeton[89]

IMPORTANT ISSUES ARE DIFFICULT TO DISCUSS

It seems like any time the issue of sacred music is brought up, several directors raise their hands in exhaustion and say, "I gave up years ago – I only program secular music now." Others will recount stories of a fussy parent or meddling administrator. Some will remember a student who gave what felt like a disproportionate amount of grief over one song. In our quest to build community through choral music, it seems to many like religion - a human experience that seems *most* predisposed to fostering love - turns out to be divisive and toxic.

Religious traditions address these foundational questions of our existence. We should never forget their importance.

Talking about religion is difficult in the choral experience, and it should be. We are discussing questions of the highest importance about epistemology (how we know what we know), philosophy, and purpose in our lives. Religious traditions address these foundational questions of our existence. We should never forget their importance.

We aspire to live in a pluralistic democracy. American story-telling about itself usually makes the claim that we are a nation that not only tolerates, but also fosters multiple viewpoints. Our political discourse often invokes our three-word mission statement, *e pluribus unum* – "out of many, one." We make this claim and set it in direct distinction from, say, a theocracy, in which we define our national identity through one specific religion, or a totalitarian government, in which the state-sponsored viewpoint is the only tolerable viewpoint.And we hold this aspiration with the simultaneous reality that America has always been a nation with an unmarked, default religion of Christianity.

Hence, our conversations about religion in choir will be difficult. When we embrace that we are, by design, fostering multiple viewpoints, we embrace that a roomful of singers will, hopefully, have multiple viewpoints on these most important foundational questions of human existence. They will disagree with each other and with you. Understandably, administrators may desire the least conflict-laden path. Parents will want their viewpoint respected (even if their viewpoint specifically disrespects another). And this is all okay, perhaps even a good thing. If we ever perceive that we have unanimity on all these existential questions, then the many singers who in truth do not share our viewpoint are being silenced, and we stop being the nation that drafted *e pluribus unum*.

SPIRITUALITY VERSUS RELIGION

One of our most important teaching responsibilities is to distinguish between what we mean by spiritual concepts and what we mean by religious concepts. Spirituality is arguably the harder to define. Let us start with two good attempts:

> ...seeking personal authenticity, genuineness, and wholeness; transcending one's locus of centricity; developing a greater sense of connectedness to self and others through relationships and community; deriving meaning, purpose, and direction in life; being open to exploring a relationship with a higher power that transcends human existence and human knowing, and valuing the sacred. [..] certain terms surface regularly: "transcendence," "interconnectedness," "authenticity," "self-awareness," and "wholeness."[90]

and,

> [S]pirituality is not about religion, though it does include religion. Spirituality is about our sense of who we are and our beliefs about why we are here, the meaning and purpose that we see in our work and our life, and our sense of connectedness to each other and to the world around us. It deals with the sphere of values and beliefs, things that we put first and let go last.[91]

Spirituality speaks to the feelings we want to associate with the choral experience: connectedness, deeper awareness of ourselves and those around us, a grounded authenticity, and wholeness. Religion speaks to an organized system of beliefs and practices, through which one hopes to have a spiritual experience. A growing population of Americans identify as 'spiritual, not religious' as an indicator that they value connectedness and transcendence but do not value a specific system of beliefs and practices like attending a synagogue or church. Those of us who work in music ministry seek to create spiritual experiences through the music that is written for our systems of practices, our religion. For those of us who teach in public education, it is important to recognize that the spiritual experience we want our singers to feel in a well-performed motet can be 'interconnected' or 'transcendent,' but it cannot be religious.

Finally, Joshua Jacobson notes that our language about the sacred/secular divide may in itself be misleading. He says: "think about it – on the concert stage, are we performing "sacred music" or "musical settings of sacred texts"? We can have a "spiritual experience" in a secular concert; it can be a "peak experience" – but is it a religious experience?"[92] Sacred implies a worshipping community, whereas spiritual implies a sense of transcendence.

MUSIC AND THE SACRED

Choral music and spiritual experiences go hand in hand. For both religious people and for choral singers, a beautiful choral performance enters into that "thin space" between our world and the holy, to borrow the Celtic expression. In most of the major religious traditions of our world, singing plays a prominent role in worship. The muezzin who calls Muslims to prayer, the cantor that leads the Jewish service, the gospel choir that leads the AME Baptist service, the Buddhist monks who chant mantras for healing, the chancel choir that performs a cantata in the Lutheran service, and many, *many* more instances all testify to the power of music in the spiritual experience. From the perspective of religion, music, especially sung music, has been vital to the experience.

The relationship is reciprocal – religion has been vital to the choral experience. In our western art music tradition, the Christian church has been the primary agent for commissioning, performing, and archiving written vocal music for over a thousand years. One way I think of its hegemonic rule over the choral repertoire is to remember my doctoral coursework and examinations. From about 1000 to 1800 CE, the history of European choral music could be – and was – taught as a history of the mass, the motet, the cantata, and the oratorio. Indeed, the first question on my doctoral examination was to trace the history of choral settings of the Catholic mass up to 1749, and I needed half a day to do so.

Beyond our schooling, the economic market for musicians testifies to sacred music's dominance. In a recent national survey, 44% of the American Choral Directors Association membership identify as working in a 'music in worship' role.[93] And what sort of jobs do singers typically have during and after college? They become church section leaders, cantors, choristers for Jewish High Holy Days services, etc. In short, when we think about choral music, we acknowledge the enormous role that religions and sacred institutions have played and continue to play in our repertoire, ensembles, and professional lives.

We acknowledge the enormous role that religions and sacred institutions have played and continue to play in our repertoire, ensembles, and professional lives.

Therefore, a thoughtful curriculum for choral music *will* include works from sacred traditions. Here, I am thinking back to colleagues who say they "don't bother getting into that argument" and dismiss the sacred canon of repertoire. Please take a minute to write down your personal top-ten choral works you've ever sung on a sheet of paper. Think of choral music that changed your life, that inspired you to become a conductor, that spoke to you—choral music you would take with you to that metaphorical desert island. Now cross off the list any of those ten that would be defined as sacred repertoire. Imagine the choral music scene if no singer ever encounters Palestrina, Brahms, or Gospel. In an effort to avoid a conversation that will assuredly be complicated, we cut out an *enormous* swath of the canvas of the choral repertoire when we teach only secular texts. This is simply not fair to our singers or our art.

LEGAL ISSUES

I worry that we are excising the entire sacred canon because we are afraid of being sued or fired. This is not an unreasonable concern. For those directors who work in public institutions, what is the law regarding religion and instruction? It would be good to know our rights. In the broadest sense, we can look to the First Amendment of the Constitution:

> Congress shall make no law respecting an establishment of religion, or prohibiting the free exercise thereof; or abridging the freedom of speech, or of the press; or the right of the people peaceably to assemble, and to petition the government for a redress of grievances.[94]

In essence, government will be neither for the establishment of a specific religion, nor against the free exercise of a specific religion. Thomas Jefferson described it as a wall between the state and church. Of course, many teachers in public education in the past, working in a model that promoted school as assimilatory and morally-rectifying, often used Christian religious instruction in class, both as an agent of cultural literacy and as an agent of conversion. One specific school district's approach even led to the Supreme Court case of *Abingdon Township of Pennsylvania v Schempp* (1963), which guides those of us who teach in public institutions.

The Schempp family sued the town of Abingdon over the school's compulsory morning prayer, which included reading Bible passages and reciting the Lord's Prayer. Let us work through passages of the majority opinion, written by Justice Thomas Clark, which sided with the Schempps against the school's mandatory prayers. First, Justice Clark devised this test for any law related to religion in the public sphere: "what are the purpose and primary effect of the enactment?" If the purpose of a law is to advance or inhibit religion, then it 'exceeds the scope' of the Constitution. In other words, "there must be a secular legislative purpose and a primary effect that neither advances nor inhibits religion." The problem with Abingdon's school district laws were that they "require religious exercises, and such exercises are being conducted in direct violation of the rights" of the plaintiffs. It is unconstitutional to force public school students to pray.

Couldn't the Schempp kids just sit quietly while the rest of the class prayed? Justice Clark goes on to clarify, "nor are these required exercises mitigated by the fact that individual students may absent themselves upon parental request." In other words, if a religious exercise is required, allowing a parent to request the student not participate is still discriminatory, and ergo illegal. This may come as a surprise to those choral directors who program Christmas concerts and tell their Jehovah's Witness singers, for example, to simply go offstage, or mouth the words. What we run into here is the distinction between "but *most* of us are fine with this" and "what is legal." Creating an 'opting out' plan is not enough.

Justice Clark clarifies the issue from the perspective of favoritism and deterrence. He notes that true religious liberty requires "that government neither engage in nor compel religious practices, that it effect no favoritism among sects or between religion and nonreligion, and that it work deterrence of no religious belief." While a Christmas concert, for example, is not a religious practice (like a Mass), in this case it certainly effects a favoritism for Christianity. Clark argues for the distinction between "the teaching *about* religion, as distinguished from the teaching *of* religion, in the public schools."

The Supreme Court ruling was thus abundantly clear that the answer was not a complete avoidance of religious texts and issues, just an avoidance of endorsing a religion.

The Supreme Court ruling was thus abundantly clear that the answer was not a complete avoidance of religious texts and issues, just an avoidance of endorsing a religion. The majority ruling argues "that the State may not establish a 'religion of secularism' in the sense of affirmatively opposing or showing hostility to religion, thus 'preferring those who believe in no religion over those who do believe.'" Clark writes, "It might well be said that one's education is not complete without a study of comparative religion or the history of religion and its relationship to the advancement of civilization."[95]

Stephen Webb notes that, although many educators since the ruling have become "nervous about introducing any religious material into the classroom, the Court did not completely ban religion from public education. Instead, it enshrined the distinction between teaching *about* religion (which is acceptable) and the teaching *of* religion (which is not)."[96]

In simpler terms, we might transcribe this ruling as follows:

- What is the *purpose* of your religious activity in question? If it is to promote or attack a religion, it is not legal.
- Are you *requiring* a religious activity? Exemption from the activity for those who do not want to does not make it better. Requiring the religious activity is illegal.
- Are you showing *favoritism* to one religion, or an explicit *discrimination* against another? That is not legal.
- You can teach *about* religions. You can explain religious concepts and terms and beliefs. You cannot teach religion, as in "this is what you should believe." Having all the public school students recite the Lord's Prayer was a clear example of 'the teaching of religion.' Those students were not analyzing and discussing text – they were praying.
- You cannot teach *against* religions. Neutrality is different than an explicitly hostile-to-religion stance in your teaching.
- You do not need to *exclude* religious texts from your curriculum.

This can all start to feel too abstract or complex. Indeed, President Clinton issued a directive in 1995 to help clarify that this was *not* a prohibition on teaching religious content:

> Because many schools had gone further than the Court had required in limiting religious expression, President Clinton felt it was necessary to remind teachers that students may discuss and advocate religious belief in the classroom and in written work. The directive rightly suggests that teachers should encourage this freedom in responsible ways.[..] Most explicitly, the directive forbids teachers from advocating any religious doctrine or idea.[97]

As Webb concludes in his study, "If schools do not let students raise the most fundamental questions about the ultimate meaning of human existence, then they deprive many students of their very motivation to learn."[98] So let us move forward with a guiding question for choral conductors that will help us handle these important and difficult conversations.

To be clear, cases have been filed and lost in the argument against singing sacred music in public education, reinforcing the distinction between teaching religion (unconstitutional) and teaching that involves religious concepts (constitutional). In Bauchman vs West High School (1995), for example, the Bauchman family sued Salt Lake City West High School, arguing that the prevalence of Christian repertoire amounted to a curriculum of sung prayers, and this was dismissed, both at the District and Circuit Court of Appeals. Florey vs Sioux Falls (1980) also upheld that the singing of Christmas carols was not explicitly to teach a religion or to exclude others.

Perhaps one of the nuances that is lost in our concept of the Christmas concert is the distinction between performing sacred choral repertoire and creating an atmosphere (candles, wreaths, carols, et al) akin to an Advent worship service. Joshua Jacobson notes in his letter to the editor in the February 2016 *Choral Journal* that he loves teaching and performing sacred works, but pushes back on the group singing of carols in the public education setting, noting:

> Singing carols feels like a community event—people sharing a common experience through singing together. What Benedict Anderson called "unisonality." Like singing the national anthem at the ballpark or singing a hymn in church. Your primary motivation is probably not musical excellence but rather the joy of belonging to a social-religious community. But what if you're not a part of that community? And what if the lyrics of the song include words that directly contradict your own faith or your own political beliefs?[99]

In short, the concern has never been about a war on Christmas, but rather on the pedagogical goals of the curriculum.

WHAT IS YOUR CURRICULAR GOAL?

This one question usually helps us to see whether we are in the right or not. When we program concerts, we consider a *lot* of factors, including the flow and pace of the event, the time of year, what sounds great, what we know, and, of course, what our singers need in order to grow and sing well. I will be the first to admit that my programming has often been heavily influenced by what I already know and by what will sound great. Those are important considerations and will often lead to good performances, but this is not enough for great pedagogy.

Great pedagogy starts with discerning what our singers already know, then asking what they need to learn in order to progress in their education, and then finding repertoire that serves those purposes. Put simply, when our concert is programmed by "this sounds cool," and our rehearsals are spent teaching them how to sing something that sounds cool, the summative event of the singers' rehearsal process (the concert) is the tail that wags the dog of the broader purpose of a choir in a school setting (music education).

I share this because many of us know how to program a great Christmas concert that will sound wonderful. Many of us know the Christmas repertoire through and through. And we have outstanding models from faith-oriented institutions, and the models of Christmas concerts at St. Olaf, Concordia, Luther, or Millikin, for example, are deservedly celebrated in my region. While they as private sectarian colleges may present religious programs, a public high school teacher cannot use that same format. In short, if the unifying curricular goal of the concert program is, essentially, to celebrate the birth of Jesus Christ, you are teaching *of* religion, not *about* religion.

If the unifying curricular goal of the concert program is, essentially, to celebrate the birth of Jesus Christ, you are teaching of *religion, not* about *religion.*

If a public school teacher did want to do a Christmas concert, I suppose the educator could set out to teach a comparative religions choral curriculum for a school-year – teaching *about* religions through the perspective of singing. In that model, the teacher would program, for example:

- a concert in October that thoughtfully examines choral repertoire drawn from High Holy Days of Rosh Hashanah and Yom Kippur (singing a variety of excellent compositions, doing thoughtful research on history and context, preparing to be proficient at teaching/listening/coaching Hebrew, guiding conversations with students about deeds and atonement) – a meaningful engagement with the Jewish tradition
- a concert in December that thoughtfully examines Advent and Christmas (singing a variety of excellent compositions, doing thoughtful research on history and context, preparing to be proficient at teaching/listening/coaching Latin, guiding conversations with students about expectation and fulfillment of promise) – a meaningful engagement with the Christian tradition

- a concert in February that thoughtfully examines Ramadan (singing a variety of excellent compositions, doing thoughtful research on history and context, preparing to be proficient at teaching/listening/coaching Arabic, guiding conversations with students about positive benefits of submission and purification) – a meaningful engagement with the Muslim tradition
- a concert in May that thoughtfully examines Beltane (singing a variety of excellent compositions, doing thoughtful research on history and context, preparing to be proficient at teaching/listening/coaching Gaelic, guiding conversations with students about fertility and social dance and lunar calendars) – a meaningful engagement with the Wiccan tradition

If we can imagine that someone would be uncomfortable singing a concert of Muslim or Wiccan prayers for an entire rehearsal process and concert, we can begin to see how students who do not identify as Christian might feel singing a Christmas concert. While the number of students who do not identify as Christian may be a smaller percentage than the number who do identify as Muslim, both sets of students are *legally protected* from being either taught religion or discriminated against because of religion. To borrow from Jesus in Matthew 25:40, "Truly I tell you, just as you did to the least of these, you did to me." Unless you have a strong curricular goal of comparative religions and a clear process for teaching all the repertoire with equal respect (energy, quality, attention), you cannot program a sacred concert in a public school setting.

You can, however, present plenty of sacred repertoire in your curriculum and concerts if you have clear *curricular* goals that are not centered on the teaching of religion. One example would be to have your choirs dive into a place and time, such as Vienna 1750-1850. Here we would encounter all the glories of Mozart, both Haydns, Beethoven, and Schubert, and be able to speak to their work in relation to or opposition to the Hapsburg empire. We would include choruses by Cristiano Lidarti and Mahler, who were Jewish. And we could of course include works that were not sacred, like part-songs. We could imagine a concert that saw the world 500 years ago, and find as much music from 1517 as we could. We would include motets of Josquin, Tallis, Isaac, etc, as well as dance music and canzonas. We could imagine a concert that centered on a specific emotional theme, like "Enduring Tribulation," that thoughtfully examines how music has given voice to this spiritual idea. We might include, for example, Bach, Bloch, spirituals, settings of social justice advocates, and so much more. As scholars of religious pedagogy Phillip Clayton and Mark Railey note, "when the instructor keeps in mind the question of purpose, it is much easier to decide when to advocate a particular position strongly and when to list multiple options and allow students to reach their own decisions."[100] The guiding principle of the concert would have to be something that is clearly curricular and identifiable, from which some songs may be drawn from sacred traditions.

In December of 2016, the National Association for Music Education released a policy statement that confirms these suggested approaches. They begin with the affirmation "that the study and performance of religious music within an educational context is a vital and appropriate part of a comprehensive music education" and that "the omission of sacred music from the school curriculum would result in an incomplete educational experience."[101] Citing the 1971 Supreme Court case Lemon v. Kurtzman, the NAfME statement cites these guiding questions from Chief Justice Burger:

1. What is the purpose of the activity? Is the purpose secular in nature, that is, studying music of a particular composer's style or historical period?
2. What is the primary *effect* of the activity? Is it the celebration of religion? Does the activity either enhance or inhibit religion? Does it invite confusion of thought or family objections?
3. Does the activity involve excessive entanglement with a religion or religious group, or between the schools and religious organizations?[102]

Finally, the position statement closes with these guiding questions for educators planning their upcoming programs:

1. Is the music selected on the basis of its musical and educational value rather than its religious context?
2. Does the teaching of music with sacred text focus on musical and artistic considerations?
3. Are the traditions of different people shared and respected?
4. Is the role of sacred music one of neutrality, neither promoting nor inhibiting religious views?
5. Are all local and school policies regarding religious holidays and the use of sacred music observed?
6. Is the use of sacred music and religious symbols or scenery avoided? Is performance in devotional settings avoided?
7. Is there sensitivity to the various religious beliefs represented by the students and parents?[103]

In short, those who teach in public schools can and should teach music from sacred traditions, but only inasmuch as it has curricular value as part of a comprehensive musical education.

Here are relevant excerpts from the ACDA position statement guidelines from 1993 ("ACDA Policy Statement" *Choral Journal*, Dec. 1993, p.53.):

III. GUIDELINES

A. The school's approach to religion is academic, not devotional.
B. The school may strive for student awareness of religions but should not press for student acceptance of any one religion.
C. The school may sponsor study about religion but may not sponsor the practice of religion.
D. The school may expose students to a diversity of religious views but may not impose any particular view.

E. The school may educate about all religions but may not promote or denigrate any religion.

F. The school may inform the student about various beliefs but should not seek to conform him or her to any particular belief.

V. WHAT SCHOOLS MAY DO

A. Schools may use the Bible or other religious books as source books in teaching about religions.

B. Schools should recognize the multiplicity of explanations related to human origins in their appropriate curricular place.

C. A student has the right to pray at any appropriate time.

D. Schools may offer objective instruction about religion as literature and history, and about religion's role in the story of civilization.

E. Students are free to recite such documents as the Declaration of Independence which contain references to God.

F. Students may sing the national anthem and other patriotic songs which contain assertions of faith in God.

G. Rhetorical or personal references to religious faith in connection with patriotic or ceremonial occasions are permissible.

H. Students may be excused from classes for sectarian instruction off school premises.

I. Schools may excuse a student from engaging in an activity which offends that student's religious belief or conscience.

J. Classroom instruction, where its content is in the area of religious holy days or celebration, should be carefully tied to educational objectives. These educational objectives should be specified in writing and should be consistent with the overall curriculum of the school.

K. The school calendar, vacations, and holidays may be scheduled to permit observances of religious holy days when school is on a holy day, upon the request of students' parents.

VI. WHAT THE SCHOOLS MAY NOT DO

A. Schools may not incorporate religious worship or indoctrination into their sponsored programs.

B. School programs may not provide for compulsory reading from the Bible as part of a non-instructional activity.

C. Schools may not promote or indoctrinate any religion, including theism, atheism, agnosticism, humanism, secularism, sectarianism, yoga, or transcendental meditation.

D. School officials may not compose, authorize, or sanction prayers.

E. Sectarian instruction may not be offered to students in public schools during school hours.

F. Sectarian instruction may not be offered in any school-sponsored activity.

G. Official public school musical groups may not participate in religious services under the auspices of the public school.

H. Non-student members of religious groups are not permitted to participate in performances.

At the risk of sounding repetitive, curricular goals must take precedence over programming goals.

Finally, we need to remember that not all group singing is universally appropriate for the concert setting. Nick Page observes: "Singing is universal, but our reasons for singing are not. Within the Western music tradition, we sing primarily for performance and for worship, two very different reasons. There are many other reasons for singing."[104] Moreover, Page reminds us that our particular mindset about performance assumes that we can sing sacred songs in any context or time. And yet, "None of us would ever perform communion at a public school. We know better."[105] So, too, must we learn that there are sacred songs from many traditions that are not to be performed in school auditoriums for concerts. Context maters.

STRATEGIES FOR TALKING ABOUT RELIGION

First, we *ought* to talk about it. In our quest to be neutral, we need to make sure we are also not depriving sacred works of their dignity and worth as a part of the human experience. It is good and important to talk about religions in the context of sacred choral repertoire. For one thing, if the composer identifies as deeply religious, writes for the religious institution, and writes with explicitly religious aims, we do a great disservice to our teaching and that composer's worldview if we ignore that context. How are we supposed to understand a Bach cantata if we ignore the profound value he placed on Lutheran worship? How could we understand Britten's *War Requiem* if we ignore the profound value he placed on pacifism? Is it ethical to sing a spiritual like *Didn't My Lord Deliver Daniel?* and *not* acknowledge the religious context? Given that Rev. Dr. Martin Luther King, Jr was a Doctor of Theology and a preacher, how can we sing settings of his words and not foster conversations about the religious context from which he wrote them? I would maintain that it is unfair to the composer, the culture in which they lived, and ultimately to our singers if we do not deeply explore the context of sacred works.

Second, there is an important distinction between talking about something and judging something. We want to foster respectful conversations that help our singers understand text and meaning more deeply; we need to be uninterested in value statements about something being better or worse. Sometimes this is obvious – if we laugh at or otherwise actively dismiss a religious claim from a song we are singing, we are judging it. More often, this is less obvious in that we teach deeply what we know, and we teach what we do not know only at a surface level. If you have a rich lesson plan for a motet with the text O *Magnum Mysterium*, but you have neither the Hebrew familiarity nor any conceptual understanding for *Hanerot Halalu*, you are favoring one religion over the other with the most important thing you can provide – your teaching. And, on that note, if we are trying to teach about Judaism by singing a Chanukah song, we are not demonstrating an understanding of the major and significant spiritual days in Judaism – we're just celebrating the event that comes closest on the calendar to the Christian event we wanted to celebrate. It should be our goal that we bring the same level of teaching proficiency to all the music we sing. Otherwise, we continually degrade the music of people unlike ourselves by giving their music a surface treatment while we give our own music our best work.

Third, we should start every rehearsal process by acknowledging that many of our singers do not know anything about the context of what we are singing, and that some might know much more than us. If we assume they do, then we presuppose that the dominant culture is the only culture, and it is not. Even when we sing something from the Christian tradition, many singers do not understand the references or their religious importance. According to the Pew Research Foundation's Religious Landscape Survey, only 55% of 18-29 year olds identify as Christian,[106] and of those 55%, only 17% say they read scripture more than once or twice a month.[107] If we value the texts we sing as being important, and we should value all of them, we owe it to our singers to guide them toward a richer understanding of these texts.

Fourth, we should plan for and encourage many questions. If we give space in our rehearsal for singers to openly express their confusion or clarification or interest, they will take it. Anticipate as many questions as possible, and respect them. Clayton and Railey suggest:

> Given that knowledge applied is better assimilated than knowledge memorized, inviting the students to participate in the construction of a portion of the class curriculum—built perhaps around questions that the students themselves have about relating science and religion—often proves helpful in motivating students to learn.[108]

This constructivist approach allows for singers to self-select where they want to explore. If we select repertoire and texts that are rich for study, we will be able to provide them with excellent learning opportunities. As Thomas Lloyd notes, teaching sacred texts in secular contexts is like the work of an actor in the theater. "An actor tries to understand his or her character on· its own terms, trying to find emotional connections between the character and one's own experience. Yet the challenge and reward of acting is taking on some of the characteristics of someone who is different than you, knowing that once you leave the stage you resume being yourself, though perhaps with a richer understanding of what it means to be human."[109]

RESPECTFUL PERFORMANCE VS EMBODIMENT

When we sing the words of another tradition than our own, how do we place ourselves in this experience? Once I worked with a singer who identified as evangelical Christian and refused to sing a setting of a prayer by the esteemed Buddhist monk and author, Thich Nhat Hanh. Her argument was respectful and clear: the Lord of Israel proclaims in Exodus 20:3: "You shall have no other gods before me," and this song included the text *Homage to Lord Buddha*. I had recently read a lot of Hanh's writings in preparation for this song, so my first strategy was to clarify that, to Hanh, the Buddha is not a Lord in the way we might speak of the Lord God of Israel. Rather, to Hanh, Gautauma Buddha was awakened through meditation to the truth of why people suffer, and that anyone who understands the four principles is likewise a Buddha (an awakened one). My Christian student's response was, "Yes, but it still says '*Homage* to *Lord* Buddha,' and I am not comfortable with that." Then I tried to look at how we use Lord in other contexts, like "Lord Byron," as in 'a person worthy of great respect.' When that did not work, I turned the discussion around and asked her what the singer on her right, who was Jewish, ought to do when we sing *Messiah* later that year, and what the singer on her left, who was an atheist, ought to do for either selection. Her response was that it was up to each singer's conscience to make those decisions.

I share this conversation because a) we were both respectful throughout, which many readers might not encounter in their own experiences with younger students or families, and b) to acknowledge that religious arguments are *rarely* easy. Had she wanted clarification or further context, that conversation would have helped. But she was resolute that there was a line to be drawn between being open-minded and dishonoring God, and this was the latter to her. She did end up singing the song, which leads me to a final observation that sometimes people need time and freedom to think through these big issues.

What my singer was concerned about is what some scholars call the problem of embodiment. When we sing, we put someone's experiences and beliefs into our bodies, and we literally give it voice. But thoughtful study and performance of artwork is rarely the pure embodiment of that worldview. Rather, it is hopefully a respectful engagement with a cultural and artistic experience, which may or may not be outside of your own. We may see purposeful embodiment in a church choir singing their faith or an activist organization singing freedom songs, as these groups resolutely connect 'what I'm saying' to 'who I am with.' But much of the music we sing as curriculum lies outside of our own experience and has to be thoughtfully laid out.

Thoughtful study and performance of artwork does not need to equate with negation of our own experience. As a tenor whose voice best suited the music of Benjamin Britten, I sang works that he, as a gay composer, wrote for his spouse, Peter Pears, using texts of gay poets like Michelangelo, and I did so thoughtfully and respectfully without also becoming gay or negating my heterosexual identity. I have performed in Jewish synagogues for High Holy Days with thoughtful respect and not negated my own religious identity. I have performed Captain Hook without becoming a pirate.

By contrast, thoughtless performance of artwork outside our own experience is profoundly dangerous. An intellectually lazy performance of music from other cultures reduces that music or tradition to *exotic, other,* and, no doubt, *inferior* to our own music. Thoughtless performance centers on parody, and I hope no one ever parodies the cultures I value as my own. It is therefore incumbent upon me to teach with the respect due to any culture I perform.

It matters what our curricular goals are for performing music. If I program the text of Hanh so that I can teach and promote Buddhism, I am marginalizing that singer's Christian identity and forcing her to embody something she does not believe. If I am programming the text of Hanh as one of many voices that speak to a concert theme of "Music in Times of Conflict", then this poem, written during the Vietnam War and calling for peace between north and south, is curricular. *How* Hanh calls for peace is through the lens of the Buddhist religion, which many Vietnamese identify as; *what* he is calling for is the center of the pedagogical concern for this curriculum on war and peace. From this lens, the evangelical Christian student was able to find commonality with Jesus' proclamation, "Blessed are the peacemakers: for they shall be called the children of God" (Matthew 5:9), and then she was comfortable performing the song.

THE FRUITS OF YOUR LABORS

Finally, I would say that it matters what sort of culture we build with our choirs. If we aim for true embodiment of text and voice in 97% of our music, and then ask our singers to flip a cognitive switch to sing one song per year outside of that expected mode, we set ourselves up for difficulty. If, however, we acknowledge that every song we program will spark competing viewpoints, different identities intersecting in different ways, then we understand that every song we sing is in some way representative of our pluralistic democracy. If we build in the space and time for ourselves to understand what we are teaching with all our music, we can be better guides through discussion and rehearsal. If we build in the space and time for our singers to ask questions, to probe and ponder these most important questions of human existence, then we teach wiser, more considerate singers. This kind of culture is a long-term project, and we can tear down several years of growth with one biting or dismissive comment. **Talking about religion with choirs is very difficult work - and it is supposed to be.**

CHAPTER 7
Choir and World Music

I came of age musically during the rise of multiculturalism. In the singing of music indigenous to 'other' people, I was supposed to develop a fuller appreciation for the diversity of our world, celebrate the many different threads of our international musical fabric, and co-create - with our voices - global harmony through choral community.

When I became a conductor, I promised myself I would give my singers a similar experience. I knew that I had this responsibility and opportunity to make the world better by teaching my singers that they live in an unimaginably rich global community of musical traditions. Within the first two years of my present teaching position, choirs I taught had sung in over twenty languages. I was working toward the mission of making a more respectful, empathetic, and loving world. I share this to help the reader understand how much I have struggled to reconcile these goals of teaching music around the world with conversations about history, power, marginalization, and culture.

WHAT DO WE MEAN BY *CULTURE*?

If we sing the music of many cultures – that is what multicultural implies, right? – then, what do we mean when we use that word *culture* in the first place? It benefits our conversation to take a minute to explore some of its primary definitions. The Oxford English Dictionary offers, among other meanings, "the distinctive ideas, customs, social behavior, products, or way of life of a particular nation, society, people, or period," as in "exploring the unique culture and history of Hawaii." In the singing of one another's music, we aim to better understand each other's distinctive ideas, customs, and way of life.

When we fail to comprehend the difference between culture and ethnicity, we end up offensively assuming differences or similarities.

I want to suggest that there are two other uses of the word *culture* that we frequently meld with the meaning above. The first is to overlap the idea of *culture* with the idea of *ethnicity*. Indeed, by the OED's standards, the loop is nearly circular, for it defines ethnicity as: "status in respect of membership of a group regarded as ultimately of common descent or having a common national or *cultural* tradition" (my emphasis). I mean by this that when we sing an Irish folk-tune set for chorus, for example, we imagine a culture in the sense of the "distinctive ideas, customs, social behavior" of

Irish people, *and* we assume a specific Irish ethnicity – probably White, possibly even red-haired with freckles.

When we fail to comprehend the difference between culture and ethnicity, we end up offensively assuming differences or similarities. We can see the underlying equation of ethnic heritage and culture by someone asking an Asian-American person where they are from, and, hearing "Akron, Ohio," in response, then asks, "right, but where are you *from*?" Such an offensive question speaks to the cognitive dissonance between being American in culture (wears Old Navy clothes, speaks with Midwestern American dialect, eats hot dogs, etc.) and not-American in ethnicity (i.e. not White; thus the quick assumption of a recent immigrant).

Another way we use the word culture is in relationship to power. Culture informs who determines power, and how power is structured. We turn to the sixth definition in OED,[110] namely "refinement of mind, taste, and manners." The implication here is that culture is a sort of intellectual/artistic capital, held in abundance by those with power. If you go to the opera, quote Shakespeare, invest in stocks, speak French, and know which fork is for salad and which is for dessert, you possess cultural power in the sense that you are fluent in the expected manners and knowledge of wealthy Americans. As sociologist/anthropologist Pierre Bourdieu observed, those of us who learn these skills develop a kind of 'cultural capital': an embodied capital that "cannot be transferred instantaneously like a gift or bequest," though can be acquired "in the absence of any deliberate inculcation," leaves its mark in subtleties like how one pronounces words, and "thus manages to combine the prestige of innate property with the merits of acquisition."[111] More specifically, this 'cultural capital' is a sign of a person's power within the dominant, Euro-American, wealthy culture. Speaking French may be, in fact, an irrelevant cultural marker to a majority of populations across the American landscape. But those in actual political and financial power are those that define 'cultural power' in the dominant paradigm.

When we use the word *culture*, we tend to conflate many meanings like this:

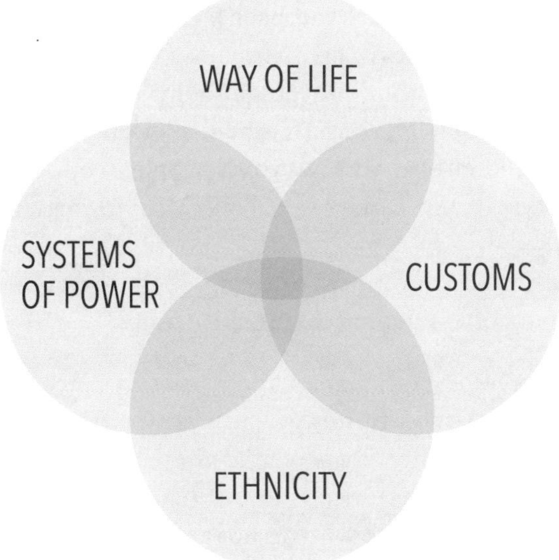

In our world as conductors, we can use the word culture in many overlapping meanings. From the biology-laboratory sense, we 'culture' certain kinds of music the way lab scientists culture bacteria – we grow it, nurture it, study it, and teach about it. In the ethnicity sense of culture, we can name music by its ethnic roots, as in 'a Kenyan folk-song.' But we do not always do this. If the choral work comes from a White composer, we simply call it music. But if the work comes from a composer who we identify as outside that Euro-American White ethnic identity, we often call it 'music from a global perspective' or 'global music', and I feel compelled to point out that all music is global in origin unless it is created in outer space. From the perspective of culture as testimony to power, we learn the repertoire endorsed by the dominant cultural mode of discourse (Josquin-Palestrina-Bach-Mozart-Beethoven-Verdi, et al.) and we define it as cultured music in the 'refinement of mind, taste, and manners' sense. Culture, ethnicity, power, and music are accordingly inter-related.

MUSIC AND BORROWING

"Lesser artists borrow; great artists steal." – Igor Stravinsky

"Books serve to show a man that those original thoughts of his aren't very new after all." – Abraham Lincoln

"The great thinker is one who can hear what is greatest in the work of other "greats" and who can transform it in an original manner." – Martin Heidegger

Everybody borrows, of course. Art, it is often said, does not exist in a vacuum. Most of us who took music history courses likely explored the fertile interaction between the English and the Franco-Flemish, Josquin and the Italians, the Italians and the Germans, and on and on. Indeed, all music comes from people who have heard and studied other music. Young Wolfgang Mozart was heavily guided by his father Leopold, and then influenced by the Viennese composers of his day (e.g. Michael and Josef Haydn), then by composers of the past (e.g. Handel and Bach). Everybody borrows.

Some music, however, explicitly and consciously borrows the musical language of others. When Mozart labels the third movement of his piano sonata K.331 *Turkish*, he no longer borrows from people like him (German-speaking, Catholic members of the Holy Roman Empire) and instead borrows from people in opposition to that identity (the Janissary band style of the Turkish-speaking, Muslim members of the Ottoman Empire).

We have alluded to the concept of 'other-ing' before; now we need to define it properly. Alison Mountz offers this succinct explanation:

> The term 'other' serves as both a noun and a verb. By placing one's self at the centre, the 'other' always constitutes the outside, the person who is different. As a noun, therefore, the 'other' is a person or group of people who are different from oneself. As a verb, 'other' means to distinguish, label, categorize, name, identify, place and exclude those who do not fit a societal norm. In geographic

> terms, 'to other' means to locate a person or group of persons outside of the centre, on the margins. 'Othering' is the process that makes the 'other.'[112]

One good way into this understanding of othering another culture is through the writing of Edward Said, whose book *Orientalism* in 1978 brought keen attention as to how we see ourselves versus people who are not like us. He writes:

> I mean to ask whether there is any way of avoiding the hostility expressed by the division say, of men into "us" (Westerners) and "they" (Orientals). For such divisions are generalities whose use historically and actually has been to press the importance of the distinction between some men and some other men, usually towards not especially admirable ends.[113]

Said develops this by critiquing the very idea of Orientalism as a form of study as, indeed, a form of oppression:

> Orientalism is never far from what Denys Hay has called the idea of Europe, a collective notion identifying "us" Europeans as against all "those" non-Europeans, and indeed it can be argued that the major component in European culture is precisely what made that culture hegemonic both in and outside Europe: the idea of European identity as a superior one in comparison with all the non-European peoples and cultures.[114]

What we are addressing here is the process of first, looking at those we consider 'not ourselves,' then, turning them into an exotic 'other,' and, finally, contextualizing them as fundamentally different from (and less than) us.

What do we mean when we name 'others' as exotic and/or different? This is probably easier to recognize by sight than by words. Most advertisements we see serve to reinforce the norms of our society. We are shown an idealized 'us' in the ad, an 'us' who use the product to help us solidify that membership. When I see that strong, dependable, humble man driving a Chevrolet pick-up truck, I want to be like him (I share those moral values), so I think maybe I need a truck. Some advertisements, however, focus on identifying the 'other' as wild and different, and then offer you (the unmarked viewer) the chance to be exotic through their product. In this 2004 advertisement for Magnum ice cream, two White European models are naked, body-painted much darker to be 'other,' engaged in romantic touch –and, just to clarify their 'otherness,' they share a hot pepper (see "ethnic foods"). Thus the ice cream unleashes their primal, sexual, non-European selves[115]:

In this 2016 advertisement[116] (same company), an Asian woman and a tiger are both symbolic of unleashing one's inner animal. By eating this ice cream, we can become wild again, like a tiger – or an Asian woman:

Note that this particular conflation of these two images shows up in racist language, for example referring to Asian mothers as "tiger Moms".

By contrast, if someone is marked as 'other,' looking in at the 'unmarked' Euro-American White category, an advertisement might serve to show them how they can become less 'other.' Consider this 2011 advertisement[117] for shaving gel. We see a Black man who has figuratively killed his primal, uncivilized self, so indicated by his afro, beard, and violent disposition. Now he embraces the trim, clean-shaven look and business-casual attire associated with hegemonic White power. The history of White perspectives on Black hair would fill another book, but I would note briefly that this image channels the violence, oppression, cultural erasure, and capital-R Racism of that history, proving the adage that a picture can say a thousand words.

These ads – and thousands upon thousands of representations in literature, television, film, and beyond – reinforce the discourse that White/European is normal, intelligent, capable, and civilized, and that non-White/non-European is primal/other.

When we look at our choral repertoire choices, then, it is essential that we are as aware as possible of the influence of viewing other cultures as 'exotic' or 'other.' Does a composer borrow from an 'other-ed' musical tradition through this lens of 'wild, primal, uncivilized,' or with clear respect and consideration for these people and their music? I ask us to question what we are endorsing when we perform music that borrows 'other-ed' musical language for its 'wild' or 'exotic' influence.

If a musical style sounds "weird" or "exotic" to our ears, we are presented with an opportunity to be curious learners. Music educator and scholar Juliet Hess thoughtfully described her first aural encounter with Carnatic music as an epiphanic moment. Lacking any musical background and training in this music, Hess writes that she, "could not make sense of the music, but it struck me quite clearly that there had to be an inner logic to the music I could not hear." Hess had been studying Ghanaian polyrhythms, so she "realized that if I were to learn about the music on its own terms, it would become intelligible to me over time".[118] Too often we respond the other way, with prejudice instead of curiosity. When students encounter unfamiliar musical styles which without the tools to comprehend what they are listening to, it may "serve to affirm its 'outsider' status" as 'exotic' and 'other.'[119]

One of the great challenges of helping students navigate these encounters with unfamiliar musical styles is that we teachers usually have pockets of expertise we lean heavily into, and little experience with most musical styles. We embrace the opportunity to teach our expertise to students, even if they have no familiarity with the music we know and love. For example, students typically have no culturally entrained familiarity with German cantatas from the 1730s or Latin motets from the 1580s, but choral directors are often highly experienced with this repertoire and enthusiastically welcome the opportunity to teach these great, albeit wildly unfamiliar choral styles to our singers. As Molly Stone et al observe, "teacher-training programs do not give student sufficient engagement in musical traditions outside European written music, so teachers continue to enter the profession untrained in any other ways of making music.[120] And we are often apprehensive, or overwhelmed, or uninterested in teaching what we do not know. This often leads to mental shortcuts which end up doing more 'exotic other' harm. As Sharon Davis Gratto succinctly puts it: "Contrary to common belief and practice, not all African choral music should be accompanied by drums."[121]

How can we best teach musical styles with which we are not yet expert? Stone et al argue that our job is:

> "to learn enough to make informed choices about which elements of authenticity to strive for at each new stage of our relationship with the genre. As we continually interrogate our own decisions, we can ask: "What aspects of authenticity are most important at this stage of my learning? What can't I achieve right now, and what would it take for me to be able to achieve it in the future? What are possible negative consequences for omitting the things I can't achieve, and do the benefits outweigh those consequences?"[122] We need the courage to enter into these spaces where we are not experts, knowing that we are not experts.

In other words, while we want to and should teach a range of musical styles, we cannot transform overnight into teachers who have expertise with multiple cultural/ musical traditions. Borrowing from James A. Banks' work, ethnomusicologist Patricia Sheehan Campbell identifies Four Levels of Curriculum Reform:

1. Contributions: Focuses on heroes, holidays, and discrete cultural elements.
2. Additive: Content, concepts, themes, and perspectives are added to curriculum without changing its structure.
3. Transformation: Enabling students to view concepts, issues, events, and themes from the perspectives of diverse ethnic and cultural groups.
4. Social action: Students make decisions on important social issues and take actions to solve them.[123]

In the first stage, teachers seek out music by women for March, music by Black composers for February, Irish folk music for St. Patrick's Day, and so forth. This is a working definition of tokenism. In the additive level, teachers still rehearse all music through the same pedagogical lens (I'm the teacher, you're the learner; let's start with Solfege, then sing-counting,...), but include works by a range of cultures within that framework. At the transformative level, students encounter music through a culturally-relevant lens. A folksong that is aurally transmitted and corresponds to movement is taught aurally with movement, for example. In the fourth level, the work of singing and the work of being in community merge and transcend discrete standards-based learning goals.

Part of our challenge is to expand how we conceive of curricular material. As Sheehan Campbell notes, "The multicultural flurry in music education was for many years a frenzied search for material, preferably melodies, rhythms, and multiple parts that were fully notated via standard western staff notation." This fixed and immutable representation of sound as defined through twelve half-steps and notated meter is profoundly limiting, and "little to no attention was given to personal interpretation—much less improvisation"[124] I will share here that teaching a song aurally is an enlightening process. In my experience in a college/conservatory setting, it flipped the roles of who had culturally-relevant power. Music majors who were trained in sight-reading found themselves flustered and hesitant to trust their ears, while students majoring in humanities and sciences with little to no choral background emerged as leaders.

CHORAL MUSIC AND CULTURAL APPROPRIATION

When does borrowing from another musical idea or style become more than borrowing? When do we go from being inspired by a new influence to appropriating that music for a new purpose? Mozart's *Rondo a la Turca* sounds like Mozart, but most South African freedom song arrangements are explicitly designed to sound and feel just like freedom-songs from South Africa. Is all appropriation bad? How do we as respectful conductors distinguish between benign appropriation and harmful appropriation?

James Young and Conrad Brunk investigate these questions thoroughly in their recent collection of essays, *The Ethics of Cultural Appropriation*. They note in the introduction that cultural appropriation can be wrong...

> …precisely because it fails to indicate due respect for a culture, its beliefs, its values or its members. Certainly, considerations of respect are often crucial. Perhaps, however, the concepts of respect and offense are closely related. To be offensive is to show a lack of respect. Conversely, the showing of proper respect for a culture involves, minimally, avoiding actions that are gratuitously offensive.[125]

That is, if composers are borrowing a musical language just because they like it, they might not be taking into consideration all of the other factors surrounding that music and its role(s). Let us suppose that aliens from another planet visited a Chicago police funeral and enjoyed the sound of bagpipes playing Amazing Grace during the funeral procession. Lacking the cultural knowledge of what was happening—a ritual of grief, with a theologically cathartic hymn – they might argue that a song is just notes and rhythms, and use the tune with new lyrics to teach their children potty-training. We would in this case say that they were not taking into consideration the factors surrounding that music, and would describe this as harmful appropriation. Let us hope, though, that most composers are not horrible people seeking actively to exploit other cultures. How can we tell if a composer who borrows from other musical languages is doing so respectfully?

James Young outlines many of the ways in which cultural appropriation could be harmful in his book *Cultural Appropriation and the Arts*. Initially, he considers *subject* appropriation, in which outsiders misrepresent a culture with the very content itself. "Outsiders could create or perpetuate harmful stereotypes that hurt members of a culture," as often seen in stereotyped Native American characters in mid-20th century Westerns. These distorted images of a culture would then lead to "discrimination in employment or education," which leads to "economic problems," for example employers not hiring Native Americans based on their engagement with these Westerns.[126]

Next, Young considers *content* appropriation, in which "outsiders clumsily appropriate the styles of insiders". The distinction here is that the borrower has not necessarily cast the borrowed group as an inferior subject, but rather does an inferior job of appropriating its content. The obvious risk here is that "the aesthetic rubbish that the outsiders produce will give a wide audience a false picture of the insiders' culture." For example, I might visit another culture for three days, hear a tune I like, and arrange it for choir, but do so poorly: I get the notes and rhythms wrong, I use the wrong instruments, I mess up the text, and I set it in the wrong performance context. But what if my arrangements are the only exposure fellow Americans have to this music? When a majority culture appropriates and (mis)performs the music of the minority culture poorly, it redefines the music, and "the distinctness of the minority culture may, consequently, be eroded".[127] If we think the entire musical output of Peru is confined to New Age pan-flute recordings, then we see an indigenous musical culture being redefined, appropriated, and eroded.

Young finishes his text with the following guidance for those who wish to borrow from another culture explicitly:

> Artists ought be as respectful as possible when appropriating content. This imperative is particularly strong when artists borrow from a disadvantaged minority culture. The members of such a culture will quite reasonably be particularly sensitive to further indignities and artists ought to strive to avoid giving offence where possible. Presumably artists who appropriate content from a culture do so because they find something of value in that culture. This ought to be apparent from all that they say and write about the culture from which they borrow.[128]

And so we arrive, as we so often have before, at the idea that respect is paramount.

In connecting appropriation with choral pedagogy, Ryan Cho offers this working definition of cultural appropriation: when "people from a more powerful culture adopt the art, symbols, or elements of a less powerful culture without understanding or respecting the context or history of that material." In the imagine case of the intergalactic travelers to Chicago, "Amazing Grace" was not meant to be arranged for toilet-training. Cho notes that "one negative result of this can be that elements of an appropriated culture are (intentionally or unintentionally) distorted and/or used as a gimmick or a costume when normally they would be treated with some respect or reverence. As opposed to cultural exchange, where there is a sense of reciprocity or mutual respect, cultural appropriation reproduces or exacerbates an exploitative power dynamic that already exists between groups of people in society."[129] In the case of mid-20th century Westerns, for example, Native American cultures are reduced to caricatures.

How do we know when a composer or conductor is borrowing music respectfully? We can ask ourselves if the composition or performance intends to honor a traditional performance style through extended research and mutual discussion, or offer a parodied caricature of 'the way these people do it.' We must always be aware of the implicit danger in our assumption about 'others'—that we are the central observer, looking into these specialized cases of human experience. As Coleman and Coombe write,

> High Culture (Euro-American, White, etc) has historically been used as 'the spiritual badge of a privileged group' and the collective works that constitute canons are offered as evidence of the timeless unity of the human spirit;... The point about Culture is it is cultureless; its values are not those of any particular form of life, simply human life as such. The universalist self-understanding of Culture puts it in a relationship of superiority to 'mere cultures' as blatantly historical forms of life that value collective particularity.[130]

One good way to see Culture in our lives is to consider that we assume western art music progresses as both ahistorical and continuously mutable (it has ever been the case that we make great music, though it changes), but we also assume that folk traditions like Bulgarian women's choir repertoire are fixed, historical, and particular to Bulgarians (that is how they sang a hundred years ago and how it shall ever be sung). In this case, we, as Culture, determine that Bulgarian women's choir is a mere 'culture,' one that we can identify, classify, store in a museum, and take out and admire the way we admire a Rembrandt painting – as an aesthetic artifact. As teachers who respect all singers, we can go beyond this mode of thinking.

We may like a certain thread of music from a community, but when we teach as if that is the only thread that exists in that community, we fail to show the kind of respect for others that we would want.

We can also ask ourselves whether those who appropriate others' music are seeing and honoring the bigger picture of the entire cultural musical landscape, or just the corner of it that they like. If everyone keeps borrowing one small part of a culture, do we around the world get a respectful sense of this culture? This is Young's concern with Subject Appropriation above. Coleman and Coombe, too, note that our appropriation of 'folk culture' is often alarmingly narrow:

> One irony of the artistic appropriation of Indigenous music is that, although the musicians who appropriate the music declare their 'fundamental respect, even deep affection for the original music and its makers,' their music focuses on a small sample of the repertoire of the originating culture, in turn misrepresenting its musical achievements.[131]

One example for us as choral directors would be if we teach as if Irish music consists exclusively of songs for fiddle, tin-whistle, and Bodhran to be sung at pubs, neglecting its symphonies, operas, rap, pop, and other genres of music. The Korean peninsula has more music to sing than "Ahrirang." We may like a certain thread of music from a community, but when we teach as if that is the *only* thread that exists in that community, we fail to show the kind of respect for others that we would want as a residents of a complex and multi-faceted society.

Additionally, we can ask how the borrowers are treating those whose music is borrowed. You and I have been taught to perceive music through specific authorship. We understand that Eric Whitacre has rights and claims over *Water Night* as *his* composition, and that I cannot write a composition that borrows 75% of its content from him without acknowledging his original authorship and paying him. Yet some musical-cultural traditions do not have the same emphasis on personal authorship as central to a song's identity. When a western composer borrows a melody from such a culture, who do they acknowledge, and how do they acknowledge their borrowing? Do they feel like they have to acknowledge anyone, or will a broad nod to 'the folk tradition' suffice? That is, "Progressive evolution in music came to be associated with writing, relegating the sonic endeavors of others with oral histories to the lesser domain of folklore, conceived as primitive, static, and incapable of development."[132] Who do arrangers share the financial profits with? Our system makes it easy to 'steal' from a vibrant musical culture, re-package it as a new composition, and make a profit.

On the other hand, we cannot assign copyright to everything. As James Young and Susan Haley note,

> [C]ultures do not own subject matters... Usually, subject matters are part of the public domain. Anyone may write about or otherwise represent what falls within his experience or within the ambit of his imagination. An exception to this rule can occur when members of a culture wish that something about their culture remain private.[133]

So, for example, honoring dead ancestors is a subject matter, and 'of the public domain.' Painting one's face to look like a skull on November 2, however, starts to feel like appropriation of the specific cultural practice of the Day of the Dead.

We can consider who is borrowing from whom and whether there are any issues of power and oppression that need to be acknowledged.

Further, we can consider who is borrowing from whom and whether there are any issues of power and oppression that need to be acknowledged. As Brunk and Young note when considering religious appropriation, "On the face of it, people would seem to have the right to adopt whatever beliefs make sense to them, regardless of their origin or who else holds them, and regardless of the unique cultural or other significance these beliefs may hold for others," but "the relationship between a colonized and nearly extinguished culture and a dominant, colonizing or settler culture is hardly between 'free and equal' parties."[134] Or, as Lauren Michele Jackson puts it, "when the powerful appropriate from the oppressed, society's imbalances are exacerbated and inequalities prolonged."[135]

Finally, we can ask ourselves whether the music being borrowed belongs to a broader and culturally relevant practice. As Brunk and Young point out, we are rarely discussing abstract philosophical beliefs in our discussion of appropriation. Rather, the concern is more likely over how we borrow another culture's stories, practices, and performances. Young and Haley argue:

> Just as plagiarism is a form of theft in Western culture, so the appropriation of religious stories and practices is theft. Respecting this right does not inhibit anyone from adopting the underlying belief about the world or the moral teaching... Those who wish to adopt the belief may do so without appropriating the particular cultural expressions of those beliefs—and if they respect the culture, they will respect its norms of exclusive use.[136]

For example, let us imagine if a Muslim vocal ensemble presented a 'historical performance practice revival' concert of an 18th-century Mass setting, complete with a performed reenactment of Communion. Catholic readers would immediately recognize that a performance of the Holy Eucharist would fit under their "exclusive use" terms, as in "something only we get to do"; this is not something that can be appropriated and performed by others. Do we examine the context and practice of the labor songs, wedding songs, and prayers we sing from 'other' cultures with the same care that we would ask for?

While the motives of multicultural world music may be well-intentioned, I question whether our process has been as benign as we imagined it. As a White person singing choral music, I have the privilege of not being conscious about my race or ethnic identities. Since the overwhelming majority of repertoire I sing is written by people who look like me, I rarely think about identity – I just sing. Likewise, when I go to buy hair-care products, I find them in the aisle marked 'hair-care,' and when I buy food I find it in every aisle. I am an 'unmarked category.' But a Black person finds their hair-care products in the section marked "ethnic" or 'multicultural' hair-care, and a Mexican person finds their food in the "ethnic foods" section – they are marked as 'other.' Our choral music, as with our grocery stores, may too easily treat White/European as an 'unmarked,' a default, and treat our singers from any other background as multicultural. We have to acknowledge the problems in this and begin to do better.

We can celebrate the music of the world. I still hold fast to that dream of a multicultural choral world. I question how we have defined and implemented it thus far. Without a doubt, it is very easy to find cultural parodies, and much, much harder to find great music from under-represented identities.

CULTURALLY RESPONSIVE TEACHING

So far, we have looked at the ways we can approach multicultural music education from a teacher-oriented perspective. We can check our tendency toward programming repertoire for tokenistic or exoticizing purposes. We can do the work to know more about what we're teaching. We can, in short, take seriously the music we are teaching. In the traditional school ensemble, the director is the locus of expertise, guiding students who do not yet know how to perform this music well; therefore, a thoughtful director needs to demonstrate expertise in any music they teach. In the traditional school ensemble, the director selects repertoire and then works to generate student engagement with that repertoire. I want to suggest that there is another way to approach multicultural music education that starts with the idea that it is okay to admit that we are not experts in all musical traditions. There is another approach that starts with knowing who our students are and what musical knowledge and skill they already bring to the ensemble space.

"Culturally relevant pedagogy", "culturally responsive pedagogy", and "culturally sustaining pedagogy" are all terms that have emerged in education studies to describe a learning environment in which students' assets drive the learning process. Leading scholar Gloria Ladsen-Billings describes how she first began her work, observing that "when I originally began searching for research on successfully educating African American students, I found nothing."[137] Instead, she found an abundance of deficit-centered scholarship that focused on the learning gap, the achievement gap, and other ways of attributing blame or deficit to Black children in schools. Gladsen-Billings continues: "instead of asking what was wrong with African American learners, I dared to ask what was right with these students and what happened in the classrooms of teachers who seemed to experience pedagogical success with them."[138] Her work led to an abundance of research in what was then called 'culturally relevant pedagogy', and is designed to be a paradigm shift in how we train teachers and think about schooling. Paradigm shifts are hard, and we often look for shortcuts. Gladsen-Billings observes that school districts and departments often produce "a distortion and corruption of the central ideas I attempted to promulgate. The idea that adding some books about people of color, having a classroom Kwanzaa celebration, or posting "diverse" images makes one "culturally relevant" seem to be what the pedagogy has been reduced to."[139] What, then, is the paradigm shift of culturally responsive pedagogy?

Scholar Geneva Gay offers a precise definition here:

> Culturally responsive teaching is defined as using the cultural characteristics, experiences, and perspectives of ethnically diverse students as conduits for teaching them more effectively. It is based on the assumption that when academic knowledge and skills are situated within the lived experiences and frames of reference of students, they are more personally meaningful, have higher interest appeal, and are learned more easily and thoroughly.

Further, Gay explains that culturally responsive teaching has five characteristics:

1. Developing a knowledge base about cultural diversity;
2. Including ethnic and culturally diverse content in the curriculum;
3. Demonstrating caring and building learning communities;
4. Communicating with ethnically diverse students;
5. Responding to ethnic diversity in the delivery of instruction.[140]

Let's unpack this for a moment. If we engage in culturally responsive teaching, we use our students' cultural perspectives and experiences as conduits for learning. By situating the lesson within their lived experiences, we increase relevance, student engagement, and learning. Whether our students listen to Billy Eilish or Nas X or Mariarchi Vargas de Tecatitlán or BTS or Schütz, we can teach musical concepts such as form, meter, articulation, dynamics, breath support, harmony, tone, and timbre, and not as a "fun reward" song on a 'pops' concert, but as thoughtful, intentional instruction in group singing.

Put differently, teachers often program 'multicultural music' as a box to check. The internal script might go something like: "now that I've added this song to my mostly Euro-American set, or added this concert to my mostly Euro-American year, I have fulfilled my 'diversity requirement.'" But as Joshua Palkki observes in his study of two Latina students in a select high school choir, "teachers employing culturally relevant pedagogy in music education seek to get beyond colonizing, tokenizing practices and look into the community—both within and surrounding the school music program—to draw upon resources and musical traditions that speak more directly to the specific student population of that school."[141] Jennifer Walker makes a similar argument: "Culturally responsive teaching goes beyond teaching ethnically based music literature or content to students. Rather culturally responsive teaching is a comprehensive approach to demonstrating understanding of who students are (and who we are, as teachers), how, and why they operate in the world, and then making decisions about what will be learned based on this information. For music teachers, this approach is much more student driven and culturally relevant to students than the more curricular-driven idea of multicultural music education."[142] Culturally responsive pedagogy pushes us to think beyond just programming alterations.

In other words, to fully embrace culturally responsive teaching, teachers need to de-center the idea of "repertoire first, engagement second", and learn to start by getting to know our students and then build out our work from there. Julia Shaw states:

Many music teachers approach curriculum design from a 'repertoire at the center' perspective. This perspective may limit teachers' attempts at practicing CRP [Culturally Responsive Pedagogy] to an approach that more closely resembles an "additive approach" to multicultural education, in which ethnic content and perspectives function as appendages to the curriculum...In contrast to repertoire-centered or sequence-centered approaches to teaching, culturally responsive pedagogy places students at the center of the curriculum. An additive approach to incorporating diverse content into the curriculum can fall short of cultural responsiveness when no attempt is made to align learning experiences with the cultural perspectives of particular students.[143]

And in this regard, culturally relevant pedagogy, like Universal Design for Learning, is not a script to follow, but rather a way of being and doing. As Geneva Gay states, "Culturally responsive teaching, in idea and action, emphasizes localism and contextual specificity."[144] There is not a technique or guideline for teaching all White students or all students in Texas – that would be culturally prescriptive pedagogy, reducing the specific constellation of cultural influences that each student brings to an essentialized nugget. We have to know these particular students in this particular classroom.

A major roadblock to culturally responsive pedagogy is that many of us are afraid to tackle issues of difference in cultures. As Gay observes, "in the United States teachers are predominantly middle class, female, monolingual, and of European ancestry, while students are increasingly poor and linguistically, ethnically, racially, and culturally diverse."[145] And since White teachers, being White in America, tend to be very apprehensive to "take on taboo subjects like race or feel unqualified in cultures beyond their own, teachers may concentrate on only "safe" cultural diversity such as cross-group similarities and intergroup ethnic customs, cuisines, costumes, and celebrations".[146] We are not going to teach with culturally responsive pedagogy if we are afraid of talking about culture or of not being the expert.

In short, the charge to do more in multicultural music education tends to paint many teachers into a corner. The thinking often flows like this: as the teacher, I have to be the expert; as a teacher in this district, I have to achieve the following musical standards and assessments; as a teacher who wants to do well, I am learning that I have to teach multicultural music outside my expertise; as someone who understands history, I acknowledge that those songs will come from cultures that have been oppressed or marginalized by White people historically; as a White person, I do not 'want to go there' in class discussions, nor do many of my White students or their families; as someone learning about 'othering', I know that not 'going there' means that I will end up passively 'tokenizing'; maybe I'll just teach what I know. This line of thinking starts with the faulty premise that we need to be the expert. What we really need is permission and help. We need permission to *not* be the musical expert in all things, permission to try and fail and try and fail without being cancelled or called out. And we need help from musical experts.

When we teach music that we know in our bones, we share our contextual and scholarly passion with our singers and we bring a pickiness to the style that helps our ensemble achieve at the highest level. If we do not know a particular musical style at all, our singers are not likely to be pushed to that high level of understanding and performance. I have strong opinions on how to perform Bach's BWV 80, but no concept of or frame of reference for Balinese Gamelan. I would know in a heartbeat if my students were performing the Bach inaccurately or poorly, but I have no similar pickiness about Susanto's gamelan-inspired choral work, "Janger". We need to work with culture-bearers. Ethnomusicologist Patricia Sheehan Campbell states: "musically speaking, culture bearers are often locally living artist-musicians who come into schools from their nearby communities to make their contributions as full-fledged performers; as demonstrators of musical genres, instruments, vocal styles, and dances; and as storytellers who give credence to the music by way of what they say about how the music functions or what it personally means to them and others within their communities."[147] Within your choral community, there are students, family members, neighbors, arts organizations, and communities in which musical traditions are celebrated, taught, and performed. Tiffany Walker suggests that we need the courage to step away from seeing ourselves as "teacher-as-master" and enter into the space of "facilitator" between the ensemble and the culture-bearer. She writes: "you can start by choosing a culture that relates to your students, and find experts within that culture to obtain more information. These experts are also called culture bearers or informants. They can range from known researchers in a specific culture to the very students in your choir or their families."[148] Just as we seek out a French teacher down the hall to help with pronunciation of "Dirait-on", we can and should seek out musical experts in our community for help with music in which we are not fluent.

In a recent interview with leading conductors in this work, Stone et al offer guidance on how to engage with culture-bearers effectively. First you can prepare in advance of the culture-bearer's work by learning the obvious background information with the class on your own, so as to demonstrate your respect for their time and expertise. "Where is Laos?" is something the teacher and students can Google. "What does this text mean?" is usually something that the teacher and students can Google. "What does this text mean to you?", by comparison, would be a question creates space for rich discussion. Next, when the culture-bearer comes, the teacher needs to get out of the way and not step in every two seconds to reassert their authority. Additionally, be sure to pay culture-bearers for their time and expertise. No one pays their mortgage with exposure or heartfelt thanks for the opportunity to share their expertise. Also remember, if you are reaching out to a spectacular conductor who also happens to be a culture-bearer in a specific repertoire, reach out to them for more than that one song. Otherwise, you're missing out on their demonstrable expertise in your 'standard' repertoire, and you are communicating, "I think of you primarily as the Black/Hispanic/etc conductor". Finally, as the choral classroom learns and improves through their work with the culture-bearer, remember that the audience in the concert also will need some help. Stone et al write: "because audiences typically don't get to take part in workshops, sharing the clinician's teachings in creative ways during the performance can have a powerful impact."[149]

It is important to remember that the culture-bearer speaks for themself, not for an entire culture. To put it simply, I have cultural knowledge of how to perform the hymn "Amazing Grace" and might serve as a culture-bearer to the intergalactic aliens mentioned above. For example, I would teach them to hold the seventh measure an extra three beats as an unwritten performance practice, and I would clarify that the context is one of profound spirituality, not potty-training. But I would not speak for all Americans or all Christians. We should not treat one colleague's guidance on one arrangement to speak for all music from that culture past and present. Culturally responsive teaching is a local practice, not a universalized practice.

We have addressed ways that the teacher can enact culturally responsive teaching, but the heart of the paradigm shift is the call to engage more intentionally with our students. Culturally responsive teaching starts from the idea that our students know about and care about music, and that our role is to work from what students already know toward what they will learn. Sheehan Cambell observes that an effective culturally-responsive teacher "is not the hub of classroom activity, or the star around which students orbit. Musical and multicultural understanding develops when there is ample humility on the part of the teacher, an openness to student ideas and interests, passion and compassion (for the music and the learners), and a willingness to learn from reputable sources—including students who frequently bring an astonishing extent of experience, intuition, and discernment to the learning process."[150] As Vanessa Bond writes, "Choral educators can help students connect their home and school experiences by engaging with the music that students listen to outside of the classroom."[151] Of course, not every student listens to the same music, so what we foster in the choral classroom will necessarily involve some new encounters, just as our Palestrina motet is a new musical encounter for almost every student. Bond writes, "a responsive director will also recognize that students must challenge themselves to learn in ways that might not be comfortable initially and should encourage students to use their support network of classmates to work toward fluency in many ways of musical knowing."[152] These challenges might include: how we learn (aurally versus visually), how we embody (moving versus standing still), how we speak (unknown versus known languages/phonemes), how we sing (range of techniques/timbres), how we decide (authority versus consensus), how we rehearse (drill versus discussion), and much more. But as we teach students to navigate the unfamiliar with patience and curiosity, we set them up for much more success in life. As Hess notes: "As we consider making many different possible encounters possible in our music classes, we may actually be setting the conditions for profound realizations later in life. If we encounter diverse musics on their own terms as young people, even when these experiences mean little at the time, they may create the conditions for important learning at a later time."[153]

I return to Gladsen-Billings' cause for investigating the possibilities of culturally responsive pedagogy: the deficit-mindset of teaching minoritized students. Her initial work focused on what successful teachers of African-American students held in common, and she observed: "The common feature they shared was a classroom practice grounded in what they believed about the educability of the students."[154] She notes that they reflected this belief by fostering "a community of learners rather than competitive, individual achievement. By demanding a higher level of academic success for the entire class, individual success did not suffer."[155] Gay reiterates that teachers need to avoid a mindset of 'how to fix the poor/powerless', arguing: "there is, indeed, power, potential, creativity, imagination, ingenuity, resourcefulness, accomplishment, and resilience among marginalized populations."[156] Gay finds that successful culturally-responsive teachers "genuinely believe in the intellectual potential of these students and accept, unequivocally, their responsibility to facilitate its realization without ignoring, demeaning, or neglecting their ethnic and cultural identities. They build toward academic success from a basis of cultural validation and strength."[157] Simply put, we have to interrogate our biases as teachers if we hope to help our students thrive in choir. Do we engage in "those kids" language? Do we forecast which students will be in jail? Do we think of some musics as awful, weird, or of no use to an ensemble setting? Can we see in all students a level of expertise and passion, and meet them there, while holding high expectations?

PEDAGOGICAL APPLICATIONS FOR CHORAL DIRECTORS

Step 1: Acknowledge the playing field's tilt.

Most of us received our education and training in the Euro-American White art music tradition, complete with thousands of hours of readings, performances, and engaged experiences. We may have dabbled in music outside that culture in shallow and unstructured ways. Even this inequity is okay in the sense that we cannot become experts in everything. But we must recognize that when we program concerts and teach music, we teach from a position of expertise in the Euro-American White art music tradition, and as novices outside of it. Our playing field is strongly tilted, and we need to acknowledge that reality.

Step 2: Decide why or why not to include music outside your expertise.

As Simon Sinek so famously puts it, start with *why*. Consider if singing the music of other cultures is something you value as a pedagogue. I make a case for it here, but each of us needs to decide for ourselves. Do not play "representation Bingo" with your curriculum. It is all too easy to program with a checklist mindset: I have a Black composer, a female composer, a 'World Music' composer, and an LGBTQ+ composer – bingo! As Ryan Cho wisely cautions, "if you are exploring cultural music that isn't yours, remember that the draw should be that you are doing that music well, not just that you are doing that music."[158]

Step 3: If you decide to do music from less-represented cultures, give yourself and your group twice the usual amount of time in your preparation.

When I teach the Mozart *Ave Verum Corpus*, I am already familiar with Latin, D major, 2/2 meter signature, Vienna, Catholicism, *bel canto* singing, ABA form, word-painting, and dozens of personal performance experiences. When I taught Clayton Parr's excellent arrangement of the Georgian folk-song *Sach-idao*, by contrast, I had to learn how to pronounce Georgian text, hear a new musical mode, feel a specific kind of accelerando, coach a different vocal production, and learn about Georgian wrestling. It takes more time, because my playing field is strongly tilted toward Mozart. My singers shared in the experience, and it took them more time to learn this repertoire that was not a part of their prior musical training.

Step 4: Get help from experts, or find the people who will connect you with the experts.

I hope most of us already do this, but when we encounter a song whose language is unfamiliar to us, it both helps the teaching process and respects the song to have an expert in the language introduce it and then coach it. Most conductor-editors love to see their editions performed and are very generous with their time. In the case of *Sach-idao*, Dr. Parr sent me audio and written IPA to help me teach the choir, and then Skyped in to a rehearsal to coach the choir's pronunciation. Put differently, have you ever heard a choir from overseas sing American songs dreadfully, and thought to yourself, "Gosh, if I could have had just 30 minutes with that group, it might have actually sounded like *Amazing Grace*?" We want our songs to be performed with good pronunciation, with a clear understanding of the song's context and meaning. Let us treat others in the way we would wish to be treated.

Step 5: What is the curricular goal with your repertoire selection?

Too often I have found myself fighting uphill with a song and realized, too late, that I had selected this song simply because it was 'different' or 'rhythmic' or 'sounded cool.' There is very little deep teaching to discover under those criteria. I've already picked it, so we achieved 'different.' We learned the rhythms, so there's the second goal. It just never arrived at 'sounding cool' because we had no depth of understanding on the song, no sense for its context or motivation.

Let us suppose that a choir in China programs a rich concert of varied choral repertoire from its art canon, and then adds *Jingle Bells* toward the end of the program as a lively, multicultural song that, according to the internet, is wildly popular in America. It is all those things – lively, wildly popular, and multicultural from a Chinese choir's perspective. It is also true, however, that it is a Winter song (season-specific), and most popular with young children. It is perhaps not exactly the best musical example to come out of the American tradition.

The clearer we are with how a song fits within our curriculum, the better things will go. When we have a clear vision for each song as part of the learning process, we show greater respect our singers. When we do the research necessary to build curriculum content around a song, we honor the culture from which the song comes.

Step 6: Look at relationships with clear eyes.

Every song has relationships between composer, music, text, culture, performer, and audience. Some are very clear-cut: Bach's cantatas were Lutheran texts and chorale tunes set by a Lutheran composer to be performed by a Lutheran choir for a Lutheran church. Some relationships are fraught with problems right away: Steven Foster published *Camptown Races* for White people to sing while dressed up to 'look Black' so White audiences could laugh at enslavement. Sometimes the original collaboration between arranger and culture-bearers was respectful and intentional, but then the performance practice and cultural relevance are lost in the mass-market dissemination of the arrangement.

Step 7: If there is a power differential in any of these relationships, name it.

If you and your choir are primarily White and the music comes from a non-White tradition, recognize that. If you and most of your choir come from a culture that has historically oppressed the culture from which the music you are singing comes, recognize that. It *does not* mean you cannot perform the music. It does mean that you need to be aware that you have an important pedagogical responsibility to navigate this very carefully. If a White choir in South Africa sings Black freedom songs, you would expect that there would be some thought and care into how and why that is done. For example, I recognize that I am part of an America that systematically killed and oppressed millions of Native Americans. I want to go into my programming of a Cherokee song with a keen eye to how it fits in my curriculum and how I will navigate those conversations.

Step 8: Zoom out and ask yourself how you are representing other cultures.

Jingle Bells is a catchy song and probably works in several concert contexts, but it is only one kind of song that we sing in America. Mariachi is great and works in many concert contexts, but it is only one kind of song from Mexico. As we look over our programming from year to year, let us be sure that if we are seeing fun songs from specific cultures, we are also artistically rich and compelling music from those cultures, rich texts in those languages, and art music of the past and present from those cultures.

Step 9: Leave a LOT of time for finding great repertoire!

Once we realize what we are looking for – curriculum, not parody – we see more clearly how easy it is to find the latter and how hard it is to find the former. Leave a lot of time for this part of the process. Again, the clearer the curricular goals, the clearer your search will go. The best resources are colleagues you respect and your ACDA R&R coordinators. Look for what Dr. Derrick Fox calls "ethical arrangements". These are scores where the arranger demonstrates that they are a culture-bearer or work intentionally with a culture-bearer. They include rich resources for text, translation, and pronunciation. They situate the song in its cultural context. They provide aural examples to help singers with a tonal concept of the song.

Step 10: Guide your singers to respectful behavior.

When we do the kind of preparatory work that honors different musical cultures, we create an environment where all people are respected. Our singers might not know how to embody that respect in appropriate behaviors, and we must be there to guide and teach them effectively. When we rehearse a song from a culture that most singers are not familiar with, we might see singers enact stereotypes about that culture. It is normal, but not okay, for students to mock a specific vocal production style, or perform a caricatured version of a culturally specific dance, or make up nonsense words that resemble distinct phonemes in the song's language. We must identify and name such behavior as inappropriate. Our silence in the presence of such offensive behavior serves to condone this kind of discrimination. We can introduce the work with clear guidelines and expectations for respect. But we will likely see such behaviors, and when we do, we must act immediately to clarify that the choral rehearsal room is a respectful space.

Step 11: Be patient and persistent.

You will mess up. In two different instances *after* the first publication of this book, I followed all of these steps to the letter in projects with my choirs. I read dissertations on the work; I found word-by-word and IPA translations of the work; I found excellent audio recordings of the work; I found experts in the languages and musical styles to work with the choir; I left more time to do the work well; and, in both cases, I had mediated discussions with deeply hurt students. Each instance was nuanced, but I learned two lessons: 1) I was still centering *my* expertise. In both cases, the student was a culture-bearer and had no voice in the process. I wanted to show the singers how much I cared about doing this well was working with these outside professional culture-bearers, and completely ignored the lived expertise and passion for this music right in front of me. 2) Feelings of marginalization do not go away lightly. In both cases, I had harmed the relationship with past programming and teaching years before. Having lost each student's trust early in their college experience, my new efforts felt performative. So I am learning to practice patience with myself, that messing up is part of the process. But I also practice persistence, because it matters deeply to do better.

CHAPTER 8
Choir and African-American Music

Trigger Warning: this chapter includes offensive, anti-Black images and words.

This is a chapter that talks about anti-Black racism in America and how it affects choral music pedagogy. I want to begin with two assumptions that I think will be true for most, though certainly not all, White readers of this book. First, you probably do not see yourself as fitting the classic definition of a capital R Racist, believing that different races of people have different fundamental capabilities and attributes. You would not prohibit your White children from playing with Black children. You would not lock your car doors when you see a Black person walking by. You might even get tired of "talking about race" or feel a subtle defensive posture emerge at the thought of reading this chapter. And I also want to acknowledge that if you are Black, you have probably had all of these things happen in your life, repeatedly.

Second, I assume that if you are White, like me, have probably benefited your entire life from being White in ways you cannot readily see. Peggy McIntosh provides a powerful checklist of privileges that those of us who identify as White do not think about, but that those who identify as Black must always think about:

> I can turn on the television or open the front page of the paper and see people of my race widely represented; When I am told about our national heritage or about "civilization," I am shown that people of my color made it what it is; I can be sure that my children will be given curricular materials that testify to the existence of their race; I can swear or dress in second-hand clothes, or not answer letters, without having people attribute these choices to the bad morals, the poverty or the illiteracy of my race; I can be pretty sure that if I ask to talk to "the person in charge," I will be facing a person of my race; I can take a job with an affirmative action employer without having co-workers on the job suspect that I got it because of race; I am never asked to speak for all the people of my racial group; I can do well in a challenging situation without being called a credit to my race; If I should need to move, I can be pretty sure of renting or purchasing housing in an area which I can afford and in which I would want to live; I can be pretty sure that my neighbors in such a location will be neutral or pleasant to me; Whether I use checks, credit cards, or cash, I can count on my skin color not to work against the appearance of financial reliability.[102]

So as we begin to unpack some of the issues surrounding music and race in America, we must let down our guard in important ways.[159]

We have to be able to talk and learn about racism without feeling accused. If we start from a defensive posture, we cannot make any progress. So we have to draw a distinction between being Racist, which I hope you are not, and being part of a racist paradigm, which I think everyone is. That is, we can start to understand that the playing field has never been fair, and that America's choral tradition has not been exempt from that oppression. We can learn to see ways in which our American history, and the music that reflects it, have not lived up to our goal of respect for all.

We are all participants in a system whose inequality is so old, so entrenched, that we may not readily see it.

Some part of White Americans' resistance to talking thoughtfully and empathetically about race may stem from a lack of deep familiarity. If a man has a hard time understanding gender issues, he at least has the frame of reference of loving relationships with a mother or sisters or daughters, so he can expand his empathy and understanding by seeing through the eyes of people he loves and understands. But with race conversations in America, many White readers will realize, upon reflection, just how *segregated* our lives are – how little integration and substantive relationships we have had with people of color. Too, we are all participants in a system whose inequality is so old, so entrenched, that we may not readily see it. Finally, if we do begin to see just how troubling America's relationship with race has been, we may feel a kind of horror that we do not know how to process.

The term 'White fragility' has emerged to describe White Americans' reluctance to engage in these conversations out of fear of that feeling. I need to add here that the concept of White fragility is not something we need to praise White scholar Robin DiAngelo exclusively for. James Baldwin said in 1962: "A vast amount of the energy that goes into what we call the Negro problem is produced by the white man's profound desire not to be judged by those who are not white, not to be seen as he is, and at the same time a vast amount of the white anguish is rooted in the white man's equally profound need to be seen as he is, to be released from the tyranny of his mirror."[160] As we reflect back on the image of Dorothy Kounz on her first day of school in Chapter 1, we will not be directors who stay safely at home sending good wishes to her. We commit ourselves to learning and doing, because 'bystander' is not how we want to be remembered when our photo is taken.

And, to be clear, there is not a neutral stance of 'not racist'. Dr. Ibram X. Kendi writes, "one either allows racial inequities to persevere, as a racist, or confronts racial inequities, as an antiracist… The claim of 'not racist' neutrality is a mask for racism."[161] Think of it this way: our boat is taking on water. We can add more water to the boat to sink faster, or we can try to stop the leaks and scoop water out of the boat, but sitting passively lets the boat continue to sink.

We have to jump over the conceptual hurdle of fixed versus growth mindset when we talk about racism. Just as most of us grew up in a fixed-mindset language of talent as a fixed attribute, most of us grew up with "racist" as a fixed-identity label. Steve might be labeled as 'talented', or 'brunette', or 'tenor', or 'racist', as immutable characteristics of a person. But Kendi reminds us that "we can be a racist one minute and an antiracist the next. What we say about race, what we do about race, in each moment, determines what—not who—we are."[162] Our actions, moment to moment, each help or hurt in the pursuit of equity.

I find it helpful, both in my own life and in my teaching, to think of racism the way I think of intonation. I value good intonation, and I think of myself as an in-tune singer. I aspire to be in tune every time I sing in choir, but the reality is that I will sing under or over the pitch at times. When I am flat or sharp, please tell me. I want to be a great contributor to the choir, and if I fail to hear that I am sharp, I want to know. I might feel a little defensive, but that defensiveness needs to be much smaller than my feeling of gratitude for the opportunity to improve. It is easy to imagine other reactions: "I'm not sharp, you're flat" (worry about yourself, not me); "I didn't mean to" (my intention is more important than my impact); "quit making this about pitch" (there are other rehearsal issues to address); or, "I don't hear tuning". Any singer desiring to perform well needs feedback when they are out of tune. We do not always like that feedback, but we should welcome the opportunity if we hope to perform well. In fact, we expect our singers to welcome *our* critiques every rehearsal. At a meta-level, we are communicating to our choir, "I will give you dozens of corrections to make in the next 50 minutes, and remember, it is all for the common good". So, when someone calls me in with a quick chat to say, "this thing you said felt racist to me", I could say "I'm not racist, you're racist", or I could say "I didn't mean to", or I could say "why are you making this about race?", or I could say "I don't see race", but instead, I try to thank that person for the correction. Yes, I know that it is significantly harder on the psyche to receive feedback about racism than to receive feedback about intonation. Remember that we used to be terrified of our music teacher's feedback when we were adolescent musicians, but we learned, through hard experience, that it mattered to our development. All of which is to say, as we work through this chapter, and as we work through each day, let us cultivate a feeling of gratitude for the opportunity to do better.

PREFATORY NOTE

I cannot imagine censoring or shaming a colleague's musical choices, and it is not my intention to do so in this chapter. I recognize that I have taught with racist practices for years. My role here is not to wag fingers or prescribe the one right way to do things. I write here to acknowledge my responsibility to help to build a more respectful choral experience for my singers, and to stop being a passive bystander to historic problems that continue on in our music. Although this chapter takes a long look at historical racism before getting to musical issues, I believe it is absolutely necessary.

AMERICA'S RACE PROBLEM

Let us begin at the beginning, and review some key moments in our shared American history. In 1619, twenty Africans were kidnapped, shipped across the Atlantic, and sold into captivity in the British North American colonies, marking the beginning of European colonists' relationship with Black Africans. In 1641, Massachusetts became the first colony to legalize slavery; in 1662, Virginia passed a hereditary enslaved person law, clarifying that the children of enslaved people were also enslaved; in 1705, Virginia passed a enslaved person code, clarifying that enslaved people were property, not people, therefore acquitting owners who killed enslaved people.

Before we continue, it is worth reading the Virginia Slave Code to more fully wrap your head around the degree to which our nation was formed with European colonists viewing themselves as humans and viewing Africans as disposable property.[163] At the Constitutional Convention in 1787, the drafters of our nation's foundational document could not agree on the value of Black people and therefore compromised that an enslaved man's vote counted as three-fifths a vote (Article I, Section 2, Clause 3 of our Constitution). In 1865 – fully 78 years later - the 13th amendment officially abolished slavery for all of America, leaving a combined legacy of 246 years of kidnapping, rape, torture, and murder of *millions* of human beings – all part of our shared history.

Of course, discrimination against African-Americans did not stop in 1865. In both northern and southern states, policies at the local and state level systemically oppressed and disenfranchised citizens. During the brief Reconstruction era after the Civil War, American legislators had within their sights a comprehensive end to so much violence and oppression, and then failed to deliver. Most of us are familiar with the so-called Jim Crow laws in the South that promoted 'separate but equal' rights to Black citizens, such as segregated drinking fountains, schools, bus seats, and neighborhoods. Between 1882-1962, US federal crime statistics reported *3,921* illegal lynchings of Black people in the South – for perspective, that is almost a thousand more murders than in the 9/11 attacks.

Discrimination in the 20th century could also be found in the north and in systems that appeared fair on the outside, such as real-estate. As Ta-Nehisi Coates writes, Congress developed the Federal Housing Administration in 1934, which adopted a map system that would rate neighborhoods by perceived stability.

> On the maps, green areas, rated "A," indicated "in demand" neighborhoods that, as one appraiser put it, lacked "a single foreigner or Negro." These neighborhoods were considered excellent prospects for insurance. Neighborhoods where Black people lived were rated "D" and were usually considered ineligible for FHA backing. They were colored in red. Neither the percentage of Black people living there nor their social class mattered. Black people were viewed as a contagion. Redlining went beyond FHA-backed loans and spread to the entire mortgage industry, which was already rife with racism, excluding Black people from most legitimate means of obtaining a mortgage.[164]

Indeed, Chicago housing practices were so discriminatory that Rev. Dr. Martin Luther King Jr. took the focus of the Southern Christian Leadership Conference up to Chicago in 1965-66 to emphasize and concentrate on fighting for reforms in this de-facto segregation. As he commented after being hit by a rock in a nonviolent march through a White neighborhood in Chicago, "I have seen many demonstrations in the south, but I have never seen anything so hostile and so hateful as I've seen here today."[165] Re-read Dr. King's statement, consider again what he saw in Selma and Birmingham, and remind yourself that he was describing a major northern city during the lifetime of many Americans alive today.

In response to the Civil Rights movement's well-coordinated protests, Congress passed the Civil Rights Act which struck down segregation laws in 1964. In 1968 Congress followed up with another Civil Rights Act in an attempt to address the housing rights that King was protesting. For most of us, our American History classes may have concluded that racism in America ended at that moment. The evidence, however, does not hold that conclusion. It is useful to see how many representatives in 1968 voted *against* those laws. Senator Strom Thurmond of South Carolina voted against both Civil Rights Acts, yet served in the US Senate until 2003. Let us recognize that a Millennial from South Carolina would have spent the first years of their life represented by a senator who said,

> There's not enough troops in the army to force the Southern people to break down segregation and admit the nigra race into our theaters, into our swimming pools, into our homes, and into our churches.[166]

It would be satisfying to say that Senator Thurmond represented a small, hateful group – 'others' – but, again, the evidence suggests that institutional racism still surrounds us.

While the most egregious results of racism in America today can be seen in the phenomenally biased outcomes in criminal law and in consequence-free murder of Black children, let us stay on topics that provoke a less politically-coached response and look at two examples of purely-numbers data that reflect ongoing anti-Black racism. The Housing and Urban Development office conducted a study on Racial/ Ethnic Minority Housing Discrimination in 2012. Here are two points that leap out of the document.

First, Black home buyers who "contact agents about recently advertised homes for sale learn about 17.0 percent fewer available homes and are shown 17.7 fewer homes than equally qualified Whites."[167] Again, we are talking about 2012 – not 1912 – and about *equally* qualified homebuyers, not wealthy White and poor Black homebuyers. In other words, if I had been shown 30 houses, a Black homebuyer with the same credit rating would be shown 25 houses.

Second, the study demonstrated that "minoritized home-seekers whose ethnicity is more readily identifiable experience more discrimination than those who may be mistaken for Whites." If real-estate agents could tell by name, appearance, or speech that the renter or buyer was Black or Asian, the home-seekers would be "significantly more likely to be denied an appointment than minorities perceived to be White," would be "shown fewer units," and would "face higher discrimination during the in-person visit."[168] The playing field is indeed not level for everyone, including equally qualified home-seekers.

Following up on this research, researchers at Marquette University conducted a study wherein they sent requests to mortgage lending organizations to inquire about loans. The financial information they sent to loan companies was *the same data*, but the names varied to sound racial/ethnic specific. Applications made by a White-sounding name like Jake Krueger received a 72.62% response rate; applications by a Black-sounding name like DaShawn Banks received a 62.62% response rate. The authors write that their study confirms, "that discrimination still exists in the lending industry, and that it exists across a larger sample and geographic scope than previous studies have examined." Further, they conclude that having an African-American sounding name "reduces the probability that a Mortgage Lending Organization responds by the same magnitude as does reporting a credit score that is 71 points lower."[169] Again, we are not discussing response rates for different people – DaShawn and Jake are *fictitious* people with the *exact same* financial data. I suspect that none of the lending organization employees wake up in the morning and make a conscious decision to treat Black applicants differently - that is, to be racist – but the data is troublingly clear that their decisions are.

Our laws are not always working for racial equality, either. As recently as July 2016, a circuit court struck down a North Carolina voting requirement law because of *obvious* discriminatory practices. "Every single one of these restrictions disproportionately burdened Black voters; indeed," as the 4th Circuit writes, "SL 2013-381 seemed to target African-Americans with almost surgical precision. The evidence that the legislature enacted SL 2013-381 for precisely this purpose—to hamper Black voting rights—is almost overwhelming."[170] Sometimes our laws work to *tilt* the playing field.

Yes, we have a difficult time talking about race in America. Part of this is because we continuously want to speak of ourselves as post-racial while at the same time we continue to discriminate. Since this discrimination has endured in different forms for 400 years, it can be difficult to see how it has become so commonplace. Let us look at some of the ways we have normalized racism throughout our history.

SCIENCE'S TROUBLING RELATIONSHIP WITH RACE

Earlier we discussed the classification work of Carl Linnaeus, whose love of taxonomy included the concept of different races of humans, complete with different attributes. Scientists after Linnaeus pursued this, seeking evidence in skulls, as Pieter Camper (1722-1789) showed here in his hierarchy of facial angles:

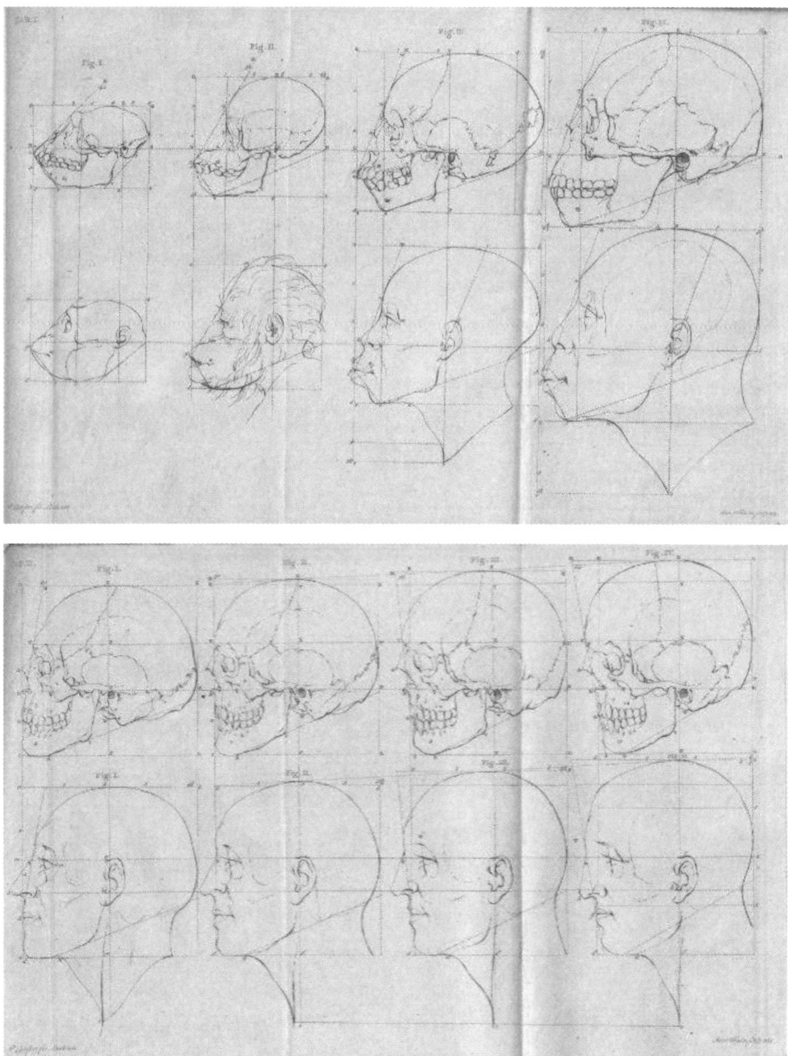

To clarify, the first two are orangutans, followed by an African, an Asian, and then a series of European skulls (showing progress from primitive to civilized). Johann Friedrich Blumenbach (1752-1840) carried this cranial line of research to determine that there were five races – Caucasian, Mongolian, Ethiopian, (Native) American, and Malay (Asian) – which you can see here below with representative skulls[171]:

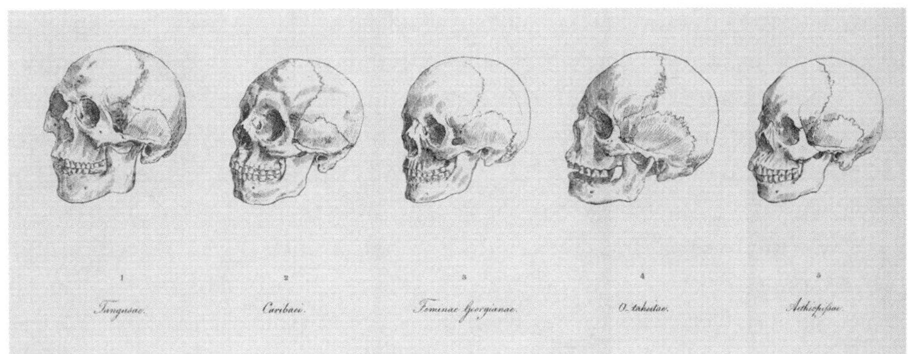

But it was Samuel George Morton (1799-1851) who took this research and attempted to determine racial *intellectual* capacity based on cranial size. Josiah Clark Nott compiled his *Types of Mankind*[172] in 1854 in memory of Morton, in which he continued Morton's theories:

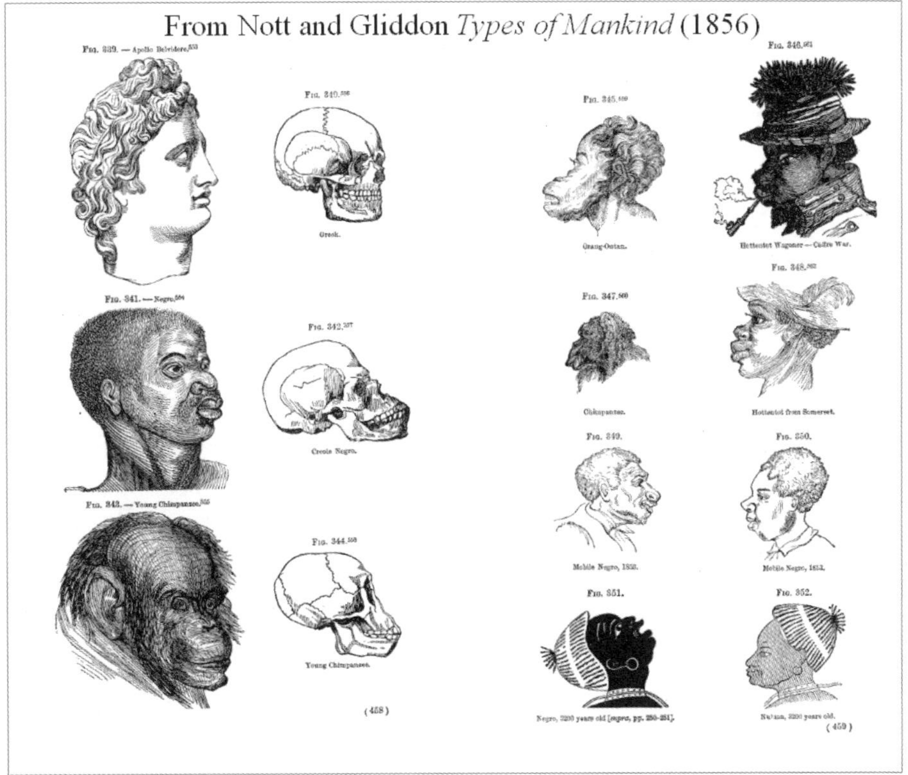

Social Darwinists in the late 1800s seized on the concept of 'survival of the fittest,' and, looking around at the White Americans enslaving Black Americans, argued that chattel slavery was in the best interest of both parties.

Incidentally, this quest to prove distinct races with distinct intellectual capacities through cranium shape connects with how we talk about music. As Loren Kajikawa writes, "just as most colleges were not designed initially to serve nonwhite students, university music schools were never intended to teach anything other than classical music…The adjectives used to distinguish classical music from other forms of music derived from contemporary racial science. The term "highbrow" (in opposition to "lowbrow"), for example, comes from the phrenologist's lexicon and describes the superior cranial shape of northern Europeans. In this way, classical music and whiteness were co-productive, meaning that they defined and reinforced one another through a shared opposition to undesirable racial, ethnic, and class groups."[173] Well, that is awful.

When we take as 'science' that there are different races with different cranial capacities, we invite racial intelligence discrimination into the conversation. But we would need some sort of scientific proof that one race performed higher than another in order to confirm it. Carl Brigham designed the SAT test (that many of us took to enter college) for such purposes. Brigham was personally focused on proving such differences in races, and used the results of his testing of different populations to conclude that American education was declining and "will proceed with an accelerating rate as the racial mixture becomes more and more extensive."[174] Brigham wanted to prove that Jewish immigrants were inferior to White Anglo-Saxon Christians, so he gave his exam to Jewish men who had just emigrated from Russia. A test that used such linguistic comparisons as *runner : marathon* as *oarsman : regatta* was arguably not a great test of "innate race-based intelligence" to give to people who barely spoke English, but it was enough for him to conclude that the data "would rather tend to disprove the popular belief that the Jew is highly intelligent." He found that immigrants from Russia "had an average intelligence below those from all other countries except Poland and Italy." But how could he reconcile data with people's real-world experience of intelligent Jews? His answer was data variability: "if we assume that the Jewish immigrants have a low average intelligence, but a higher variability than other nativity groups, this would reconcile our figures with popular belief."[175] I should clarify that I am not quoting from a blog, but rather Bingham's book, published by Princeton University Press, where he served as a professor of psychology. This was hard science in 1922.

And it is this mode of seeking empirical evidence in the genes of different classes of humans that led to the publication of *The Bell Curve* in 1994, in which Murray and Herrnstein take such tests as incontrovertible truth of racial distinctions in intelligence. They claim:

> The difference in test scores between African-Americans and European-Americans as measured in dozens of reputable studies has converged on approximately a one standard deviation difference for several decades. Translated into centiles, this means that the average White person tests higher than about 84 percent of the population of Blacks and that the average Black person tests higher than about 16 percent of the population of Whites.[176]

I remember that book.

Whatever stories we want to tell ourselves about America, we have to acknowledge that our story is inseparable from racism, and that the arts and sciences were complicit allies. If we are to teach our choirs with respect, we need to consciously, actively, and frequently acknowledge this inherited racism. White people arrived at this point by thinking that different-looking humans were categorically different; then, we established a variety of different kinds of tests designed to both prove our differences and our White superiority; and finally, we confirmed it through our biased testing and have set policies based on those manufactured differences for centuries. I would *love* to teach in a world that was free of racism, but I don't. I have a responsibility as a teacher to see and name the racial/racist structures that have been in place for so long – and continue to be.

I would love to teach in a world that was free of racism, but I don't. I have a responsibility as a teacher to see and name the racial/racist structures that have been in place for so long – and continue to be.

MUSIC'S RELATIONSHIP WITH RACISM - MINSTRELSY

Off the top of your head, which BBC show do you think ran continuously from 1958-1978, won multiple awards, had a weekly audience of 16 million viewers, broke sales records, and spun off a theatrical production that won it a place in the *Guinness Book of Records* as the "Stage Show Seen by the Largest Number of People?"[177] It seems incredible to believe, but *The Black and White Minstrel Show*[178] was that successful, that recently.

Credit: Evening Standard / Stringer

What you are looking at are White British men who have painted themselves to look Black so they can perform as Black men. This is known as Blackface, and it is central to a long and significant part of the American musical canon known as minstrelsy.

Minstrelsy rose to prominence in America in the 1840s-50s as a form of entertainment for White working-class audiences. In a typical minstrel show, White men would use burnt cork to darken their faces, and then do comic routines that mocked Black people. As Matthew Shaftel notes, the public pressure on the troupes was to be as funny and harsh as possible. Blackface troupes risked going under unless they... "emphasized delineations of Negro eccentricities" or focused their acts on that which "the legitimate object of their costumes and colored faces, namely the personation of the witty negro."[179]

Minstrelsy served two important functions: it introduced northern White people to southern Black people and to slavery in particular, and it promoted the agenda that Black people under slavery were doing just fine, singing and dancing and having a great time. In order to meet these goals effectively and entertainingly, a typical minstrel troupe would include several stock characters. There was Jim Crow, the lazy slave, and his northern counterpart, Zip Coon, the freedman who thought himself fancier than he really was.

Jim Crow

Zip Coon

Mr. Tambo and Mr. Bones would play music at the ends of the semi-circle, and an Interlocutor emceed the performance.

The premiere minstrel troupe of the 1840s was Christy's Minstrels, and the composer of their most renowned musical hits was Stephen Foster. I encourage every choral director to take a minute to let that sink in. Though Stephen Foster eventually left minstrelsy in the late 1850s, he made his fame and fortune writing music for Christy's Minstrels. Here are some of the lyrics for the songs that Foster and Christy's Minstrels made nationally famous:

Uncle Ned[180]
Dere was an old nigga dey calld him Uncle Ned
He's dead long ago, long ago!
He had no wool on de top ob his head,
De place whar de wool ought to grow.

Refrain: Den lay down de shubble and de hoe-o-o
And Hang up de fiddle and de bow.
No more hard work for poor old Ned,
He's gone whar de good niggas go.

His fingers were long like de cane in de brake,
He had no eyes for to see,
He had no teeffe to eat de oae cake,
Se he had to luf dat oae cake be.

When Old Ned die Massa take it mighty bad,
De tears run down like de rain;
Old Missus turn pale, and she ges berry sad
Cayse she nebber see Old Ned again.

There are the obvious ways in which this song is *profoundly* offensive: n-words, caricatured dialect, describing his hair as wool, etc. And then there is the offense of political agenda in this song, in which northern audiences learn just how much enslaved people and their abusers loved each other – the *Massa* and the *Missus* weep for Ned's passing, for example.

Here is a song I have sung dozens of times, including while in a college touring choir:

Camptown Races[181]
De Camptown ladies sing dis song—Doo-dah! doo-dah!
De Camp-town race-track five miles long—Oh! doo-dah day!
I come down dah wid my hat caved in—Doo-dah! doo-dah!
I go back home wid a pocket full of tin—Oh! doo-dah day!

Gwine to run all night!
Gwine to run all day!
I'll bet my money on de bob-tail nag—
Somebody bet on de bay.

As it turns out, there is a context to *doo-dah*. The lyrics of the song *Zip Coon* (see the character above) include the chorus: O *zip a duden duden duden zip a duden day!* As Theodore Johnson III notes, "if this sounds similar to the Academy Award-winning *Zip-A-Dee-Doo-Dah*, it's because that song was derived from this chorus."[182] (Look into the Disney movie *Song of the South*, from which "Zip-a-dee-doo-dah" appears, for an example of a revisionist antebellum South.) So in this case we get two disturbing revelations at once – that *Camptown Races* is a minstrel song, and that a Disney song many of us sang as a kid is also based on a minstrel song.

Here is another Stephen Foster song I have sung more times than I can count:

Oh! Susanna[183]
I come from Alabama with my banjo on my knee;
I'se gwine to Lou'siana my true lub for to see.
It rain'd all night de day I left, De wedder it was dry,
The sun so hot I froze to def, Susann, dont you cry.

Refrain: Oh! Susanna, do not cry for me;
I come from Alabama, Wid my banjo on my knee.

I jump'd aboard the telegraph, and trabbled down de ribber,
De lectricik fluid magnified, and killed five hundred Nigga.
De bulgine bust and de hoss run off, I really thought I'd die'
I shut my eyes to hold my bref, Susanna, dont you cry.

Shaftel observes that this song defines "the enslaved person(s) as simple and dim-witted," which is "why it quickly became a mainstay of the Blackface minstrel show" after it was introduced in 1848. He observes that the "nonsense of the lyrics" - like an all-night rain in dry weather or a sun so hot that one could freeze - "characterizes the protagonist as naïve and unsophisticated." This charming idiocy is played up when he confuses the horsepower of an engine (*bulgine*) with an actual horse. Shaftel writes that, "the minstrel audience would have immediately understood the plays on words, taking delight in the singer's confusion of new technologies."[184] In other words, the 'nonsense' of the *Oh, Susanna* is not to capture silliness, as I was always taught, but to capture the idiocy of a southern Black man.

I wish I could say that is the end of it, but here's another:

Old Folks at Home (Swanee River)[185]
Way down upon de Swanee ribber, Far, far away,
Dere's wha my heart is turning ebber, Dere's wha de old folks stay.
All up an down de whole creation, Sadly I roam,
Still longing for de old plantation, and for de old folks at home.

Refrain: All de world am sad and dreary, Ebrywhere I roam,
Oh! Darkies how my heart grows weary, Far from de old folks at home.

All round de little farm I wandered, When I was young,
Den many happy days I squandered, Many de songs I sung.
When I was playing wid my brudder happy was I.
Oh! Take me to my kind old mudder, Dere let me live and die.
One little hut among de bushes, One dat I love,
Still sadly to my mem'ry rushes, No matter where I rove.
When will I see de bees a humming all 'round de comb?
When will I hear de banjo tumming down in my good old home?

Here again we see the political act of romanticizing the enslaved person's life: the charming *little hut among the bushes*, or the *many happy days I squandered* on the plantation. Shaftel notes that while "working on the manuscript, Foster hit an important turning point when he changed the word "Blacks" to "folks" in the line *Dere's where de old folks stay*.[186] I do not know if that change mitigates the incredibly offensive nature of the entire minstrel endeavor, but it should be an indicator to choir directors that when we sing songs with lyrics like *some folks*, we might be in minstrel territory.

Finally, here is a Foster song that I distinctly remember teaching to a high school choir years ago, not knowing this context:

The Glendy Burk[187]
De Glendy Burk is a mighty fast boat,
Wid a mighty fast captain too;
He sits up dah on de hurricane roof
And he keeps his eye on de crew.
I cant stay here, for dey work too hard;
I'm bound to leave dis town;
I'll take my duds and tote 'em on my back
When de Glendy Burk comes down.

chorus:
Ho! for Lou'siana!
I'm bound to leave dis town;
I'll take my duds and tote 'em on my back
When de Glendy Burk comes down.
De Glendy Burk has a funny old crew
And dey sing de boatman's song,
Dey burn de pitch and de pine knot too,
For to shove de boat along.

De smoke goes up and de ingine roars
And de wheel goes round and round,
So fair you well! for I'll take a little ride
When de Glendy Burk comes down.
I'll work all night in de wind and storm,
I'll work all day in de rain,
Till I find myself on de levy dock
In New Orleans again.

Here, the singer cannot stay on the boat because the ship's crew *work too hard*. Ironically, it was while aboard an actual ship like the *Glendy Burk* that Stephen Foster began an important change in his career which led him to stop writing minstrel songs. As Shaftel notes, in 1852 (two years after he married his wife, Jane), the Fosters took a steamboat trip to New Orleans that may have altered his outlook. "It seems likely during this trip Foster was able to see slaves working on plantations. Perhaps," Shaftel suggests, "this was a rude awakening for him, or, it simply reinforced his earlier misgivings about the minstrel songs." In any event, "the trip brought him to a new realization about the nature of slavery."[188]

Whatever misgivings and changes of heart Stephen Foster later had, he left a trove of minstrel songs that most of us have sung countless times without realizing what we sang. I concede that it is *much* easier now to simply Google the lyrics of the songs we program and learn within 0.19 seconds the offensive origins of a song, whereas in 1990, the same desire to find the origins of every song we program for a concert would have involved a full day's work in a university research library. But now we can, and now, you and I know.

Once we look into the world of minstrelsy, it is stunning both how intertwined it is with our "American song collection" and how glossed over it has become. The very first song I ever learned to play on the piano was *Turkey in the Straw*. I did not know that this fiddle tune was made popular with Zip Coon lyrics, or that there was a very popular version of the text that went *N- love a watermelon, ha ha ha!*[189] If the song goes well with a banjo, describes a foolish/humorous person, and uses 'funny' pronunciations in the text (e.g. *Bile (boil) them cabbage down*), there is a good chance that you are looking at a minstrel song.

Moreover, Stephen Foster was not the only minstrel troupe composer in America. Indeed, Daniel Emmett of the Virginia Minstrels was quite prolific, and you have also sung his songs. If you gather a roomful of general music teachers and ask what song they *all* know and teach, *Dan Tucker*[190] might be high on the list. But what we might not know is that this song was written by Emmett for the Virginia Minstrels in 1843. It included such verses as:

Tucker on de wood pile--can't count 'lebben,
Put in a fedder bed--him gwine to hebben,
His nose so flat, his face so full,
De top ob his head like a bag ob wool,
Get out de way! Get out de way!
Get out de way! Old Dan Tucker,
Your too late to come to supper.

Emmitt also wrote *The Boatman's Dance*[191] for the Virginia Minstrels in 1843, which included such lyrics as:

De boatman dance, de boatman sing,
de boatman up to eb'rything.
And when de boatman get on shore,
he spends his cash and works for more.

chorus: Dance, de boatman dance!
O dance, de boatman dance.
O dance all night till broad daylight
And go home wid de gals in de morning.
Hi ho de boatman row,
Floatin' down de ribber on de Ohio!
Hi ho, de boat man row,
up an' down de ribber on de Ohio!

Yes, even *Polly Wolly Doodle* was an Emmett song composed for minstrel performance.

While Foster and Emmett may have been the Mozart and Beethoven of these minstrel songs, many later composers became like the Vaughan Williams and Bartok of this 'folk tradition,' providing well-crafted arrangements to songs that were written for minstrel troupes. I have sung Copland's *Ching-a-Ring-Chaw* many times, but had no idea that the original text (which Copland deliberately softened) was a minstrel song about enslaved people planning a trip to Haiti. This is more powerful when seen than read.[192]

Well, now you know. And the thing about knowing is that you cannot un-know. And we cannot pretend that 'everyone back then' was fine with this music, either. Frederick Douglass reviewed a minstrel troupe in Rochester in 1848, railing against the

> Virginia Minstrels, Christy's Minstrels, the Ethiopian Serenaders, or any of the filthy scum of White society, who have stolen from us a complexion denied to them by nature, in which to make money, and pander to the corrupt taste of their White fellow-citizens.[193]

This is a very real and very extensive part of America's singing history.

What do we make of this music that we have all sung for so many years, then? Is it possible to pretend that this repertoire is not problematic, now that we know that these songs were written for White people to laugh at White people dressed up as silly dumb Black people? Maybe we could redeem a controversial work like Bach's *Johannes-Passion* by pointing out how much less anti-Judaist it is in comparison to his peers' settings. But with minstrel songs, we know the point of this repertoire was *explicitly* to make entertainment and political propaganda out of people who were enslaved, traded, raped, and worked to death.

I am not making a plea for censorship. I do, however, ask us all to consider very seriously if and how we want to teach these songs, knowing now why they were written.

History pedagogue Richard Hughes asserts that we can help our students understand "the ways in which Americans in the past used both subtle and blatant cultural messages to construct race," an investigation which "allows students to deconstruct and expose racist hierarchies." In contrast to sweeping minstrelsy under the rug, "the willingness of Americans to confront, rather than ignore, the ideas embedded in minstrel music" is what lays "at the center of historical efforts at racial justice."[194] I cannot begin to imagine how uncomfortable it would be to foster a good conversation with third graders on racist hierarchies in antebellum America, but I know that it would and should feel at least as uncomfortable to harvest out the musical fruit (pitches, rhythms) of songs that are designed to mock people being so systematically harmed without doing so.

SPIRITUALS

If you asked me to name the ten most amazing choral performances I'd ever been a part of, at least five of those would include spirituals. Growing up with arrangements by William Dawson, and then living through Moses Hogan's amazing renaissance of spiritual composition and performance, I never felt as connected to my fellow singers as when we put ourselves fully into *Ezekiel Saw the Wheel* or *Soon I Will Be Done* or *Elijah Rock*. It seemed like everyone on the stage and in the audience felt the power of this amazing choral repertoire. As I grew older on the podium, I began to question whether a spiritual could rightly be framed as 'entertainment' – it seemed too easy to give short-shrift to the historical and theological importance of these works. But they remained a treasured and essential part of the choral repertoire in my mind.

In 2015, a group of students questioned the appropriateness of our singing spirituals uncritically in concert performance. I would love to say I handled this well, but the truth is that I failed to hear what they were saying, and I failed to handle these conversations with the respect that I would want if I were a concerned singer. When students came to me with concerns, I countered that they were now beginning to think about performance practice problems that we conductors have been thinking about for decades, and resolved that the spiritual is an essential choral tradition for all to sing.

And then… I did not sleep that night. To confront their concern would mean addressing a whole range of issues in America around race, politics, epistemology, and respect. I felt myself at a critical crossroads: either double down on my respected authority as a conductor and professor and show the door to students that disagree, or dive deeper into these complicated issues. When I finally did get to sleep, my life had changed, and I began working on this book.

I have loved singing and hearing spirituals my entire life. I decided to learn what I was singing about.

Clearer Context

How do we teach spirituals? A standard lesson plan around a spiritual might include basic definitions of 'work-song,' or 'ring-shout,' or 'call and response.' We might include conversation about coded language, specifically about the Underground Railroad. We might even include some scripture references and explications. And many of us leave it there, right?

Let us go back to the first term, 'work-song' and examine it further. For decades I have seen this definition glossed over, as in "a song you sing while working." We might even get lost in specifics of "to help pass the time" or "to help coordinate physical work." But if we can let the camera pan out beyond this propaganda image of happy enslaved people working and singing—an image of plantation life that we saw promoted by minstrelsy as well as by racist historians and scientists in the 19th century—we see chattel slavery in all of its horror. I will include here below two descriptions of what being an enslaved person was like that are truly horrible.

This first story comes from a woman named Sally Crane, who, at age 90, was interviewed by the Federal Writers Project in the 1930s about her life. She said:

> I been whipped from sunup till sundown. Off and on, you know. They whip me till they got tired and then they go and rest and come out and start again. They kept a bowl filled with vinegar and salt and pepper settin' nearby, and when they had whipped me till the blood come, they would take the mop and sponge the cuts with this stuff so that they would hurt more. They would whip me with the cowhide part of the time and with the birch sprouts the other part… They just whipped me because they could – because they had the privilege. It wasn't nothin' I done; they just whipped me.
>
> – Sally Crane, age 90[195]

Who can begin to imagine this level of pain and suffering? The second story comes from Frederick Douglass' autobiography in 1851 (the same year Stephen Foster produced "Swanee River"):

> I have often been awakened at the dawn of day by the most heart-rending shrieks of an own aunt of mine, whom he used to tie up to a joist, and whip upon her naked back till she was literally covered with blood. No words, no tears, no prayers, from his gory victim seemed to move his iron heart from its bloody purpose. The louder she screamed, the harder he whipped; and where the blood ran fastest, there he whipped longest. He would whip her to make her scream, and whip her to make her hush; and not until overcome by fatigue, would he cease to swing the blood-clotted cowskin. I remember the first time I ever witnessed this horrible exhibition. I was quite a child, but I well remember it. I never shall forget it whilst I remember any thing.[196]

To be an enslaved person meant to have no power or rights over your own body. You could be bought, or sold, or raped, or beaten, or killed - and you had no recourse.

In what world could we imagine that a spiritual would be sung by a group of enslaved people that was pleasant and free of this constant, life-and-death abuse?

Frederick Douglass, after he attained his freedom, never wanted to hear spirituals again. As he writes, they

> told a tale of woe which was then altogether beyond my feeble comprehension: they were tones loud, long, and deep; they breathed the prayer and complaint of souls boiling over with the bitterest anguish. Every tone was a testimony against slavery, and a prayer to God for deliverance from chains. The hearing of those wild notes always depressed my spirit, and filled me with ineffable sadness. I have frequently found myself in tears while hearing them. The mere recurrence to these songs, even now, afflicts me... To those songs I trace my first glimmering conceptions of the dehumanizing character of slavery... Those songs still follow me...[197]

In today's language we might describe those songs as a profound psychological trigger for the pain from those scars (physical and mental) from such constant abuse. When Douglass first heard those songs in the north, removed from their context, he was shocked. He writes that he has often been...

> ...utterly astonished, since I came to the north, to find persons who could speak of the singing among slaves, as evidence of their contentment and happiness. It is impossible to conceive of a greater mistake. Slaves sing most when they are most unhappy. The songs of the enslaved person(s) represent the sorrows of his heart; and he is relieved by them, only as an aching heart is relieved by its tears... Crying for joy, and singing for joy, were alike uncommon to me while in the jaws of slavery. The singing of a man cast away upon a desolate island might be as appropriately considered as evidence of contentment and happiness, as the singing of a slave; the songs of the one and of the other are prompted by the same emotion.[198]

In short, as we dwell longer on the context and framework of what it meant to be enslaved, we may arrive at the conclusion that the aesthetic entertainment value of contemporary spiritual arrangements needs to be heavily counterbalanced by the historical reality of their origins.

Again, it is not for me to say whether you can program a spiritual in your concert performance. But I do want to suggest that any performance of the music that came out of slavery be done in full awareness of that context – 250 years of whipping, raping, and killing. You could add a jazzy piano accompaniment to *Didn't My Lord Deliver Daniel*, but *should* you? You could teach *Soon I Will Be Done* without discussing why there was "weeping and wailing" in the first place, but *should* you? Consider how we (rightly) hold up the Messiaen *Quartet for the End of Time*, written in a concentration camp, as such a powerful statement of art emerging from the worst possible trauma. We would never perform that work lightly. How could we, then, sing spirituals without a similarly serious approach?

Religious Context

Once we acknowledge the essential truth that spirituals emerged from 250 years of torture, we must also acknowledge the religious depth of the words from which they get the name *spiritual*. Our first mistake would be to assume that our singers understand Biblical references. As we discussed in Chapter Six, 35% of 18-29 year-olds never go to church, and 37% go only a few times a year.[199] While past generations may have assumed a significant amount of collective biblical literacy, we should not assume that of any of our singers, regardless of their religious identity. We do these songs and our singers a disservice if we do not help our singers connect the dots on what is being referred to and what it might mean.

I would therefore strongly encourage conductors to read through texts that are being referenced in a spiritual so that singers understand the context. This is teaching *about* religion, not teaching *of* religion – our curricular goal here is to learn the context from which a text is derived, not to endorse a belief in it.

Here, briefly, are a few salient references for some of the more frequently performed spirituals:

- *Ain'a that Good News*
  - Crown – 1 Thessalonians 2:19; 2 Timothy 4:8; 1 Peter 5:4; Revelation 2:10 (all of these refer to the wealth in heaven as opposed to wealth on earth)
  - Harp – Revelation 5:8
  - Robe - Revelation 6:11
  - Shoulder up my cross – Matthew 16:24

- *Didn't My Lord Deliver Daniel?*
  - Story of the lion's den - Daniel 6
  - Jonah and the whale - Jonah 1
  - The Hebrew children (Shadrach, Meshach, and Abednego) and the fiery furnace) - Daniel 3
  - The Gospel Ship is in Matthew 8, when Jesus calms the sea

- *Every Time I Feel the Spirit*
  - Mountain/Fire/Smoke – Exodus 19
  - Jordan River – numerous, including Matthew 3 (Jesus is baptized)

- *Ezekiel Saw the Wheel*
  - Describes Ezekiel's vision in chapters 1 and 10 of the Book of Ezekiel

- *Go Down, Moses*
  - Moses warns the Pharaoh of plagues if the Israelites are not released from slavery – Exodus chapters 7 through 11

- *Hold On*
  - 'Norah' is Noah – the flood is coming and the singer wants to be saved – Genesis 6

  - Hand on the plow – leave everything/one behind for salvation – Luke 9:57-62
  - Mary's golden chain – refers to Romans 8:28-30, and the five links of theology therein: (1) foreknowledge, (2) predestination, (3) effectual calling, (4) justification, and (5) glorification.
  - Climbing the ladder (*Jacob's Ladder*) – Genesis 28

- *John the Revelator*
  - The holy number and the golden altar – Revelation 8
  - Worthy is the Lamb – Revelation 5
  - Mary and Martha weeping – John 11 (Jesus raises Lazarus)

- *Joshua Fit the Battle*
  - Joshua and the Israelites marched around Jericho for six days; then on the seventh day, blew trumpets, and the walls of the city fell down. – Joshua 6

- *Ride On, King Jesus*
  - Jesus rides a horse (donkey) into Jerusalem – John 12/Matthew 21, etc.
  - My race is run – 2 Timothy chapter 4 (in both cases, a preparation for death.)

- *Swing Low, Sweet Chariot*
  - Elijah is carried up to heaven in a chariot – 2 Kings, chapter 2

- *There Is a Balm in Gilead*
  - The prophet mourns and asks if there is a balm in Gilead – Jeremiah 8:18-22
  - Jeremiah says that the Lord proclaims "to go to Gilead and take balm" – Jeremiah 46

Without basic scriptural context, singers have no reason to make sense of why anyone would want a chariot or what a *gospel plow* might be.

Political Context

When teachers introduce spirituals, we tend to focus on the integration of these songs with the abolitionist movement and the Underground Railroad. It partners well, and it de-emphasizes the suffering that is inextricably bound to this music. I agree that it is important to teach the coded language of the texts. Marvin V. Curtis likewise notes that, "the spiritual served as both a deeply religious song and a vehicle for conveying coded messages… In the spiritual lyric, slaves found not only the source of spiritual salvation but also the means for gaining deliverance from their bondage."[200] Bob Darden provides a useful translator for some of the more common codes here[201]:

Satan = slave master

King Jesus = slave benefactor

Babylon = winter

Hell = further South

Jordan (River) = first step to freedom

Israelites = enslaved African-Americans

Egyptians = slaveholders

Canaan = land of freedom

Heaven = Canada (north)

Home = Africa

In his important book on spirituals, *Way Over in Beulah Lan'*, André Thomas suggests that excellent performance of spirituals requires careful attention to diction. Thomas speaks of his initial discomfort with the written-out dialect in spirituals and how Jester Hairston helped him to understand the connection between the dialect and West African linguistic/phonetic patterns.[202] Many singers and teachers are apprehensive to coach texts that include "hebben" for "heaven" and "chillun" for "children." Are we mocking? Caricaturing? Felicia Barber argues that the hesitation comes from a perception that African-American English dialect is somehow 'less than' or shameful. Instead, she says, "By changing our perception, we as a collective choral community take steps toward rejecting the supposition that the AAE dialect is a broken language but rather facilitate an understanding of the development of African American English as a beautiful marriage of features found in both African and English languages."[203] A common argument among many scholars of spirituals is that avoiding the diction conversation deprives the music of its sound, just as avoiding attention to French would yield a poor performance of a Poulenc *chanson*.

Another frame of reference is the communal-political act of *challenge* that is woven into these songs. As psychologist Arthur Jones notes, the "notion of the challenge attitude might well be the central thread that pulls together all of various psychological functions of the spirituals." Challenging the "pervasively pejorative views of African-American self-worth" has been, according to Jones, "seen throughout the history of the African-American experience," serving "in the face of the larger forces of cultural and institutional racism."[204] A clear example of this challenge would be in the song *I Got Shoes*, in which "everyone talking about heaven ain't going there" – i.e., those in authority are not the ones who will be redeemed. If we teach spirituals, we must be willing to look into the texts to explore how words and music challenged the status quo.

A respectful pedagogy in spirituals will include a serious consideration for the origins of this music as well as its spiritual and political significations.

Isn't Music Color-Blind?

Perhaps the most common argument made in favor of any problematic performance around race is that music is color-blind. That is, music is just notes and rhythms, and those belong to humanity, so therefore the performance cannot be racist. I concede that, at the most literal definition, music could be conceived of as simply sound waves. But that is more properly a definition for "sound"; *music* is created and performed by *people*. If we were all equals in a world where America had not been built on the backs of enslaved Black people, we could have a different conversation. But it was, and this is indeed our history.

As it stands, deciding to be color-blind is a decision that only White people can make. Negotiating the world through the perceived lens of 'other' is an outside-imposed requirement for singers of color in America every day. Though we may say that music is color-blind, the people who write and perform it are not. As J. Rodriguez writes, the "pattern of separating the art from the people leads to an appropriation of aesthetic innovation that not only 'exploits' Black cultural forms, commercially and otherwise, but also nullifies the cultural meaning those forms provide for African-Americans." Rodriguez suggests that a framework in which spirituals are simply musical art separated from African-American slave experience nullifies its cultural meaning. He further states, "color-blind ideology is consequential for popular culture because it provides those with more racial power the discursive resources to decontextualize cultural objects from the histories and experiences from whence they came."[205]

To perform a spiritual 'color-blindly' is precisely to decontextualize that cultural object (those notes and rhythms of *Soon I Will Be Done*) from the "histories and experiences from whence (it [slavery]) came." Phillip Olson and Laura Gillman point out that liberal individualism (the central paradigm of my own education) is built on an ahistorical sense of a level playing field among equals. In the musical world, this allows notes to be just notes, and performances to be color-blind. They contend that White privilege "conceals itself behind a veil of color-blindness, actively though unconsciously passing off as neutral or objective its own group-based perspectives and practices."[206] While we might want to perform this repertoire as if it were ahistorical notes and rhythms, we cannot perform it under the illusion that we are not a part of its history.

A Short History of Concertized Spirituals

It should be noted that the tradition of concertizing spirituals emerged with performances and editions by African-American choirs, notably the Fisk College Jubilee Singers led by George White, the Hampton College Choir led by Dr. R. Nathaniel Dett, and the Tuskegee Institute Choir led by William Dawson. Indeed, arrangers like Dawson and Dett made their international fame by providing concertized arrangements of spirituals, repertoire that you and I likely sang. Why would it be problematic to sing music that these African-American conductor-composers were willingly publishing for all to sing?

Let us start by asking why such repertoire ever made it onstage. When the Fisk Jubilee Singers first began touring in the 1870s, their immediately pressing need was to keep the college afloat. Not surprisingly, a new Black college in early Reconstruction-era Tennessee was not well-funded. A primary motivation for this first concertizing of spirituals came from the economic necessities imposed on the oppressed. They had to raise money to keep the school going.

Patricia Trice notes that the Jubilee Singers adapted their repertoire in response to audiences. In their initial 1871 tour, the Fisk Jubilee Singers originally programmed "anthems, Irish ballads, sentimental songs, temperance songs, patriotic songs, and a few spirituals. By the time the group reached New York City, White realized the audience appeal of the spirituals and began to devote a larger share of the program to them. By the end of the ensemble's tour in May 1872, the Jubilee Singers had raised $20,000, making possible the construction of Jubilee Hall on the Fisk campus."[207] The concert spiritual has been, from the onset, a successful commercial enterprise.

Moreover, the Jubilee Singers provided the White world with their first performance encounter from *actual* Black musicians, not Blackface minstrels. They were, in effect, reclaiming the past forty years of subject and content appropriation from minstrelsy. One contemporary American reviewer wrote: "Those who have only heard the burnt cork caricatures of negro minstrelsy have not the slightest conception of what it [Black music] really is."[208]

At Hampton College, Dr. Dett intended to perform his compositions using spiritual melodies as quite the *opposite* of light entertainment, but rather as the source material for serious artistic compositions to be performed solemnly. As he noted in a 1918 interview:

> We have this wonderful folk music-the melodies of an enslaved people, who poured out their longings, their griefs, and their aspirations in the one great, universal language. But this store will be of no value unless we utilize it, unless we treat it in such manner that it can be presented in choral form, in lyric and operatic works, in concertos and suites and salon music-unless our musical architects take the rough timber of Negro themes and fashion from it music which will prove that we, too, have national feelings and characteristics, as have the European peoples whose forms we have zealously followed for so long.[146]

Instead, what his White American administrators and funders consistently insisted on was the 'primitive' spiritual, as it would be authentically sung. Acting Director of Hampton College, George Phenix, wrote to Dr. Dett and requested that the choir sing spirituals "in the same manner that they would sing them if they had come together by chance in South Carolina or some other place, that the contrast between them and the other songs on the program would be striking."[209] Moreover, the administrators did not understand why he performed the spirituals as a separate set from concert music, holding applause and maintaining a solemn, more sacred atmosphere.

Dr. Dett was fighting a battle against what had already been centuries of a White expectation that Black people, and therefore Black music, was somehow primitive and simple. The idea that Dett would write symphonies and cantatas challenged the entire paradigm. What White sponsors and audiences wanted was 'authentic' African music. Although [major funder George Peabody] recognized the artistic value of Dett's compositions, he felt that the "strongest impact on the Europeans would come from the choir's rendition of Negro spirituals, delivered—one could always hope—in as primal a manner as possible."[210] It may help to put these conversations in the historical context of when Bingham was testing Jews to confirm their intellectual inferiority – the 1910s and 1920s.

This consistent push to other Black composition into a static, primitive category permeates the choral world that you and I have inherited. A 1930 Virginia newspaper reviewer commented on the Hampton choir's performance – no doubt trying to convey his enthusiasm – by stating, "the primitive appeal of the negro music arouses the natural impulses even of the White man, and stirs within him some deep laid understanding of simple song untutored through the ages of civilization."[211] Can we imagine what extraordinary music Dr. Dett (a graduate of Oberlin, Harvard, Columbia, and Eastman) might have written if he had been treated as an artist and colleague instead of simply 'an authentic curator of plantation songs?'

I concede that these composers, who were Black, wrote this music for public consumption, including concertized performances by White choirs. I do not agree that they therefore speak for all Black people throughout the entirety of American history. I do not agree that they wanted to write only this particular genre of music. And I do not think anyone should want this music performed thoughtlessly. Here I must note that I have been in festivals where a conductor, arriving at the end of the program, thanks the audience and singers, and then says something to the effect of "now that we've done the serious stuff, let's have some fun!" and then launches into a spiritual to conclude the program. We need to reconsider the ways we teach this music.

Finally, I note that, since. the first edition of this book, a significant range of perspectives has emerged in national discourse about performing concert spirituals. There are many highly respected Black conductors who agree that the genre of the concert spiritual deserves the same careful study as a Bach motet, and push back against the hesitancy to program this repertoire. The concern is that a performative "I don't want to get in trouble" attitude deprives singers of some of America's most important choral repertoire, erases the struggle and resilience and exceptional musical contribution from African-Americans, and opts for the path of least resistance when a thoughtful pedagogy could engage students with our complicated history. André Thomas argues that, "rather than asking, 'can we create an authentic performance (and perhaps choosing not to program an arrangement because you answer no), ask, 'what can we create instead?' What we are beholden to create is our best representation of the sound that was in the mind of the concert arranger. As long as we are honoring and respecting that and the broader tradition, we should all move ahead, secure and empowered in our right to perform this music."[212] Anton Armstrong has argued that to choose music because of "one's racial/ethnic background would be to say that I should not sing or conduct the music of Johann Sebastian Bach because I am not from eastern Germany. What is most important is that the universal messages of the music be our focus and create the connection between people."[213] And, I will also share that I know that a lot of White conductors have stayed in the initial stage of hesitance to unpack what it means that these songs are more than entertainment. My argument has never been to cancel concert spirituals. I only ask that we take the time to understand their context and our relationship to that context. It is a distinctly colonialist idea to argue that all music is just music. Lauren Michele Jackson pushes back on the 'universal themes' argument in the arts in saying that, "'no stories belong to anyone' may be true in spirit—in law and capital it is quite another matter. Ideas and practices and art and appearances accrue value the whiter they become, the whiter they are perceived as being all along. Underwriting is a money matter. And black people have been underwriting white capital for centuries."[214] She adds: "know who gets erased, but know your part in it. See yourself in the lineage that fought and killed and gerrymandered its way to being the only name in town. See and understand that, and only upon seeing, really seeing, decide if this lane needs you. Sometimes being the best you can be means stepping aside—let the doing be done."[215] Doing the deep dive into the context of the music of enslaved African-Americans may result in a highly informed and transformative performance and educational experience. It might also result in White conductors sitting with their inherited privilege and finding ways to work restoratively to repair harm.

GOSPEL MUSIC

When I was four years old, my preschool teacher asked us all to share our favorite movie. I was supposed to say something by Disney, but I was honest and said, *The Blues Brothers*. That movie was rated R, so naturally my mother received a very concerned phone call from the teacher. The reality was that I did not (nor do I yet) understand the plot – I just listened to our record of the soundtrack over and over, specifically to James Brown and the church choir's performance of *The Old Landmark*.

Of course, now I understand that the church scene in *The Blues Brothers* was a caricature on the same order as, say, Mafiosi wearing pinstripe suits and eating pasta, or a group of Irishmen wearing wool hats and drinking pints in a bar – a simplistic *mis-en-scene* of ethnic-as-entertainment. And now I also understand that James Brown was an international celebrity whose adaptation of Black church musical language into secular, sexy texts puts him at odds with many Black church-goers. But what that *record* did for me was to ignite a lifelong love of Black Gospel musical language. That relationship has always been uneasy for me, but I lacked the words to name my uneasiness. Until I started work on this book and began to look more clearly at race and music, I never knew how to approach the conversation, either for myself or for my singers. Now I understand more clearly that the *musical* language spoke to me, but that I lacked an honest understanding of and embrace for the spiritual and cultural significance of this music.

The first thing we need to establish is that Gospel is a broad category of Christian music, including music from both White and Black styles. As James Kinchen writes, Black Gospel music "emerged from the urban areas of the Northeast and Midwest during the early part of [the 20th] century. It was one of the musical expressions that Black Americans - most of whom were transplants from the rural South in search of freedom, justice, and opportunity made in symbolic and emotional response to society, religion, and the realities of life."[216] There are many songs and hymns that we call Gospel that were not written by Black musicians, for example *Blessed Assurance* (Fanny Crosby and Phoebe Knapp), *I'll Fly Away* (Albert Brumley), or *I Surrender All* (Judson Van der Vender and W. S. Weeden). These have various origins, from early American Shape-Note tradition (*Amazing Grace*) to 19th- century revival (*Softly and*

Tenderly). These songs are united by a Christian message, not by a specific racial or ethnic identity. Gospel songs preach the Gospel, a Greek word for "good news".

The second thing to remember is that Black Gospel music is not the same as Spiritual. Many White choral conductors tend to conflate the two genres. The implicit phrase we say by conflating them is "music sung by Black people about religion," though their origins differ profoundly. When we use the term (Black) Gospel music, we want to make sure we are making the following basic distinctions with (Black) spirituals:

	SPIRITUAL	GOSPEL
Origin	No specified timeline; centuries ago	Late 19th through 20th century
Geography	Predominantly south	Predominantly north
Composer	Arose in communities; commonly assigned terms like "traditional"; usually arranged by someone	A clearly defined composer, like Thomas A. Dorsey
Instrumentation	Typically a cappella	Typically with instruments, e.g. piano, bass, and drums
Text	Typically Old Testament (Daniel, Moses, Joshua)	Typically New Testament (Gospels, Epistles, Revelation)
Message	Often focused on endurance through strife (*Soon I Will Be Done*, e.g.)	Often focused on hope and redemption (*He Touched Me, Praise Is What I Do, Move On Up a Little Higher*)
Part-writing	Usually SATB	Often SAT
Political origin	Slavery, addressing liberation	Civil Rights movement

And we must understand that we are making broad generalizations here with many exceptions.

We want to make sure that we help our singers understand the distinctions, as we ourselves must also do. Gospel music clearly has Spiritual influences and contemporary settings of Spirituals are clearly influenced by Gospel. But it is as important that we understand the different roots of these genres.

Gospel music is rooted in Christian *worship*. It takes as foundational the idea that the Holy Spirit is present in a community at worship, and that we can be stirred into fuller connection with the Holy Spirit through our singing and praising. The church scene in *The Blues Brothers* caricatures a distinctly Pentecostal form of worship. The congregation invites the Spirit to move through them, using dance, call and response, improvisation, testifying, and speaking in tongues to create an experience similar to the disciples in Acts 2, in which the Spirit rushes through the faithful.

It is difficult to excise a great Gospel song from its original worshipping context. When the St. Olaf Choir records *Praise His Holy Name!*, the ensemble can unite under the school's Christian heritage and meet Dr. Hampton's composition at the point of

Christian faith, even if many of the singers do not come from this particular style of worship. But for a public school, performing Gospel music requires a very nuanced line to walk: if we undersell the theological importance of the text, we commit a profound offense to the composer and genre; if we oversell the theological importance, we teach religion, contrary to the First Amendment.

MOVING FORWARD

1. We have been raised in a musical world in which African-American music is too often equated with entertainment, while Euro-American music is equated with art, or entertainment, or whatever the composer chooses. We *must* take a closer look at the language we use when we program and teach music from African-American musical traditions. How often do we use "fun, rhythmic, and exciting" to describe music of enslavement or music of Black contemporary Christian worship? How often is our selection of music born of suffering based on sentiments like "the kids will love this" or "the audience will love going out with a bang?"
2. We must hold ourselves to the same level of critical study and analysis of Gospels and Spirituals as we do for Mozart and Bach. What does it mean when we throw a djembe into a song for rhythmic interest? Is there a performance-practice reason for adding a West African drum to a composition written in Chicago in 1990?
3. As Black Gospel music serves a worship purpose for moving the spirit, it is normal to see a choir raised in this tradition to sing this repertoire with movement, stepping, or clapping, or lifting hands in testimony. Often, in a quest for authenticity, choirs parrot these physical movements without consideration. If singers do not feel the Holy Spirit moving in their hearts, of what value is the choreography? Would we choreograph a genuflected knee whenever we arrive at *Jesu Christe* in a Mass setting, or would the conductor parrot the priest's elevation of the communion wafer during the Sanctus? If we appropriate the *accoutrements* of a performance practice without any understanding, we do a tremendous disservice to the musical tradition and the people who live it.
4. What is your *curricular goal* with your repertoire selection? There are many ways in which programming a Spiritual or Black Gospel song could be an important part of a singer's education. But the conductor must first decide what the pedagogical goal of such a decision would be, and then select repertoire that matches that goal.
5. How are we training our pre-service teachers? Julie Kailin addresses this at length in her important work, *Antiracist Education*, noting that the overwhelming majority of teachers are working- to middle-class White women who have not been raised in integrated communities, have no relationship with people of color, and do not want to teach in urban schools. She observes:

> This indeed paints a dismal picture for children of color, for they likely will be taught by people who are teaching them by default—after all, there simply won't be enough of those "suburban" teaching positions to go around. This leaves a teaching force that is highly unrepresentative and divorced from the lives of the students they teach. Since the majority of teachers are White and still live in segregated neighborhoods far distanced from their students of color, antiracist multicultural education for teachers is imperative.[217]

As a result, teachers go out into the world profoundly unprepared to negotiate the effects of such institutional racism, and thus for "many teachers, the experience of teaching in multiracial schools in which White and Black children are effectively segregated may actually lead to a sharpening or reinforcement of racial stereotypes among White teachers rather than a lessening of them."[218] Those of us who train pre-service teachers must be very intentional in teaching anti-racist pedagogy. Indeed, much of the challenge lies with how we frame music education curricula.

Darren Hamilton argues that "the Whiteness of teacher education programs and Western dominated post-secondary music programs that continue to produce music educators who are unqualified to teach Black music genres must be addressed." Hamilton adds that universities make broad commitments to anti-racism, but "there must be a willingness to create spaces for Black music in the curriculum. This includes engaging Black music educators and musicians in the education system. Teachers must also value the prior cultural knowledge and experience that Black students bring to their music classes, being prepared to facilitate dialogue about cultural music while learning themselves from their students."[219]

6. As we scroll through our repertoire choices in the past, how many compositions by African-Americans do we find? If we cross out Spirituals and Gospel selections, how many other compositions do we find? There is a dearth of choral music by African-American composers that speaks to the legacy of our institutional racism. There are no easy solutions to a problem that has been created over 400 years. Publishers must create opportunities for African-American composers that are not limited to Spirituals/Gospel. Conductors and choirs must perform these works as they become published. If we can hold space for the possibility that Eric Whitacre can write both "Water Night" and the techno-opera *Paradise Lost*, then we can hold space for the possibility that William Grant Still wrote symphonies and Nathaniel Dett wrote oratorios. Marques Garrett observes that, "trends in concert programming reveal that repertoire considerations for Black composers are often limited to spirituals, gospel, and jazz. While some arrangements are quite popular and well known, I argue that the representation of the original works of Black composers rarely receive the same attention in comparison to similar contributions of white composers..."[220] Just as we have previously discussed that "only Hannukah"

essentializes, tokenizes, and provides an incomplete picture of the tapestry of Jewish musics, only teaching songs from enslavement or Gospel essentializes, tokenizes, and provides an incomplete picture of the tapestry of Black musics. Leslie Adams, Adophus Hailstork, Betty Jackson King, B.E. Boykin, Christopher Harris, Ulysses Kay, Julius Miller, Robert Harris, Brandon Waddles, Rosephanye Powell, and so many other composers past and present are writing music that merits deep study and outstanding performance. As Julia Shaw notes, culturally responsive teaching, centered on students, "suggests that we begin the repertoire selection process by considering our students rather than by perusing a publisher's catalogue or reading through a stack of octavos."[221] Together, we need to create this new market of choral music.

7. What does anti-racism look like in choir? It has to be more than the songs you select. Jason Dungee argues that, "restorative, anti-racist pedagogy has little to do with what music is selected on our concerts, and has nothing to do with the race of the choral director.... Furthermore, it is clear that it exists as much outside of our classroom as it does inside. This is not to suggest that representation does not matter or is not impactful. It is to suggest, rather, that such decisions are low-hanging fruit, and without other anti-racist action they amount to being performative in nature."[222] Adding a motet by Nathaniel Dett does not equate with anti-racist work, and can be done harmfully as a form of representation bingo (see chapter 7). Anti-racist choral pedagogy involves humility, relationship, trust, curiosity, and personal growth.

POSTLUDE
Building Our Audience

Building Our Audience

How do we work together to create a more inclusive and respectful choral experience? We have looked at the ways we create a space for all singers, and the ways our repertoire and pedagogy honor or marginalize our singers. It is also important to remember that our choirs are singing to an audience. How will *they* process the choral experience? How do *they* engage with our music-making?

In this postlude, we consider who is impacted by our choral performances. What do we want listeners to experience? How will our work affect them? We also consider our current singers and ask how they will or will not engage in choral performances after they leave our ensembles. In the introduction, I said that I believe choral music can change the world. Now, we envision how that happens.

Who Fills the Seats?

Take time to consider who attends your choral performances. The answer will vary depending on what kinds of choir(s) you direct and what kinds of performances you share, but the exercise is always fruitful. I will discuss some of the standard choir models and share basic observations, but you know your community and its constituents best. I strongly urge you to go deeper in your own reflection than I can do here.

In a **church or synagogue choir**, Kierkegaard suggests that we sing, not to each other, but to God. "In the theater, the play is staged before an audience who are called theatergoers; but at the devotional address, God himself is present. In the most earnest sense God is the critical theatergoer, who looks on to see how the lines are spoken and how they are listened to."[223] If we accept this claim, then our task is not to give aesthetic pleasure to those in the congregation, but to offer ourselves spiritually through our singing. As for the listening audience of people, the worshippers who fill the pews likely have a vast range of educational and career backgrounds, but they are united in a religious identity and in the way the congregation worships. Since the worship experience varies significantly between an Evangelical arena-style worship center with a million- dollar sound system and a Presbyterian church with a Skinner organ, congregants generally choose a worship community where they can hear and sing the kind of music that they love and that speaks to their spirituality in a significant way. There are no doubt different musical preferences within each congregation (witness the emails directors have to field about which hymns congregants like or dislike), but the clear focus of the music is on how it connects to the worship experience.

By contrast, a **public school** audience has no obvious unifying factor of religion or politics or musical style or ethnicity or background. Most of the concert attendees are families of the students, and reflect the diversity we see in our classes. As we look around the audience at these families, we see more clearly that the unifying factor, then, is that we are all supporting these students and their music education. We come as listeners excited to see how much our children have learned, to honor their hard work, and to celebrate their progress. Of course, everyone wants the performance to go as well as possible, too!

The **private school** (K-12) shares features of both the church and the public school. It has a clear unifying goal of celebrating students' education as well as an additional identity, such as college-preparatory or parochial. In this context, the audience becomes families who want to celebrate their children's growth, and also a community that shares a common set of values, however it may be defined.

University audiences, on the other hand, may often have more college students, faculty members, and community members than family members. While a university audience may still want to honor the students' growth, there is an expectation at a university concert that a performance reflects a certain degree of research and preparation which can be interrogated critically for academic discussion.

Community choirs build a thriving audience of members throughout a region. Whereas the school choir focuses the audience's attention on the students' educational progress, the community choir must build an audience by the quality of its performances and clarity of its mission. They may also do so by emphasizing an identity, for example a Gay or Lesbian chorus, or a social movement such as a Worker's chorus.

Professional choirs earn their livelihoods producing performances of the highest quality. The audience that attends a professional choral concert tends to be lovers of choral music that expect a polished and stirring performance.

Who Is *Not* Coming?

I encourage every director to take a clear and honest look at who attends our concerts and note which members from our communities are *not* present. School directors may agree with the general observation that families come, but do all families? If some families do not come, we should investigate this. Are our concerts offered at times in conflict with work schedules? Do we charge admission that some families cannot afford? Do parents also have younger children at home who cannot stay up this late, or who need babysitting? What preconceptions about choir and the choral experience may keep some families from attending? As we consider our community population, do we see gender, age, ethnicity, educational background, and other forms of diversity represented? If not, we should explore how our work invites or marginalizes the presence of those we are not seeing. No choir can be all things to all people, but in our efforts to be as respectful and inclusive as possible, we need to take the time to acknowledge those we are not reaching.

How Do Audiences Take in Information?

Do we think our audience will know the music we are programming? How does that change their experience? One of a director's implicit motivations for programming a Christmas concert is because they know in many communities that the audience knows and loves these carols. You can enjoy something if you are familiar with it, just as it's easier for me to enjoy watching football rather than cricket. In the context of a Christmas program, even if a director programs a wild new arrangement of *Silent Night*, most of the audience will still be able to find the melody, and thus recognize what makes this new arrangement so interesting. Conversely, in order to really appreciate Liszt's piano transcription of Schubert's *Die Forelle*, the listener needs to already know the Schubert song, and ideally, something about Liszt.

How do we handle music from a style or genre that we think our audience might not know? What do we want or need for them to know about it? Will the music speak for itself or do we feel that some context or explanation is necessary? How do we approach that context-giving? These are the decisions that each director must make. How and why we make these decisions is what defines our personality and leadership as directors. Here are a few common strategies.

When my choirs sing in a foreign language at church or school, I include **translations** in the bulletin or program or supertitles on a screen. I do not expect everyone to speak Latin or French, and I want listeners to understand what we are saying. I want congregants to see how this anthem connects with the scripture readings. I want audience members to see how this builds on the theme. I want all listeners to admire how this music sets these words so aptly. I want listeners to hear how our performance communicates these words.

When my choirs sing something that is either controversial or outside our normal repertoire, I use **program notes**. I once conducted Bach's *St. John Passion*, a work which met both criteria. The libretto's use of "the Jews" has been a source of critical investigation for anti-Judaism, and I needed to address the issue directly. Anyone reading the translations thoughtfully would wonder on their own why this text kept emphasizing "the Jews" in a negative light, and if I were to say nothing, my silence would have been a problem. Further, this oratorio was a significant change from our usual mix of four-minute songs. The program notes allowed me to provide a short historical background, a case for why it was not an anti-Judaic work, a short theological exegesis, and a basic framework for how the work was constructed. Program notes allow the curious audience member enough information to listen with guided ears, and they also allow the listener to put them away or ignore them if they prefer to experience the music for themselves.

In my experience, choral directors—myself included!—have a tendency to misuse our most powerful tool for guiding the audience's experience: **brief spoken remarks**. From the audience member's perspective, from the moment they sit down in their seats until the moment they leave, they are attending a performance. Why, then, do we rehearse our choirs to the razor's edge of perfection in tuning, diction, and phrasing, but then stand at a microphone and chat extemporaneously for a few minutes? Also, we must keep in mind that most school audience members are there for the students, not us, so we are delaying what they want to experience. Finally, we have to ask ourselves what *essential* information about the upcoming song are we delivering that should be said yet does not belong in the program notes?

Despite these concerns, I believe spoken remarks can be highly impactful. Program notes communicate information – for example, "Mozart wrote this *Ave Verum Corpus* the summer before he died at age 35." Remarks, by contrast, are a form of relationship-building between you and the audience. When you speak to the audience, you break the fourth wall, acknowledging that these people are sharing in this experience with you. When you thank families for supporting their students' passion for music, you show appreciation for the time and energy they spend getting their kids to these and other events, and you advocate for its importance at the same time. When you thank colleagues and administrators, you share your gratitude and name the reality that you do not do this alone. When you share a brief story about how or why these singers connected with the upcoming song, you teach the audience the choir is about people and how they express ideas and feelings in a singing community. When you have students give these remarks, you communicate that this concert is not about you—it is about celebrating these students.

Onstage remarks, then, have the highest possibility of making or breaking our relationship with the audience. If you have information that could go in programs, such as soloists, historical context, translations, or other notes about the concert theme, let written communication do what it does best: relay information. If you have information that needs to be said as if in a conversation, let spoken communication do what it does best: convey feelings. And practice those remarks with the same level of refinement to which we rehearse our choirs.

What Kind of Experience Do We Want Our Audience to Have?

As directors, we have a significant role in shaping the concert experience for audiences. For example, if we set up a lecture-recital format for our concert, our audience will process this as an information-gathering experience. If we design the concert to be an interactive, participatory experience, the audience will get involved. If we imagine the concert to be a live recording session ("please, no clapping – we're recording this for ACDA!"), the audience will tune out visual stimuli and listen intentionally. Just as we think about the curricular goals for our singers, it is also a good practice to think about the goals we have for our audience.

Most often, I believe that directors want an audience member to have **"an enjoyable experience."** In this mode of thinking, we design our concerts the way we would design a nice multi-course meal: well-crafted short courses, each having its own distinct flavor and content, but all flowing together as one seamless meal. I think this is a template that most of us use implicitly, but I think we too often lose sight of the larger 'one seamless meal' aspect. I have found it as difficult to succeed at creating intentional pairings and groupings of songs as it is to succeed at creating an excellent multi-course meal. If we want our audience to experience the joy of a multi-course meal, we need to put a great deal of intentional planning in our initial programming phase. We need to amass a huge bank of possible repertoire, and then play with which song follows which best, considering keys, tempi, instrumentation, musical styles, languages, affects, and more. When we present such a concert, we want our audience members to feel like they had a wonderful time and enjoyed the program.

Turning our attention again to the students, our goal for the audience member might be to experience and **celebrate our students' learning**. In this context, it is okay to produce a little of the 'musical indigestion' that sometimes comes from hopping around musical styles, because our primary focus has been on teaching these students about these songs. In this mode, if our goal is to communicate our students' learning to the audience, we should have students communicate, with program notes, brief remarks, artwork and posters in the lobby, and more. We hope that the audience member has a clearer understanding of the students' progress at the end of the concert.

For some of us, the concert serves to *move* the audience, to **create a transcendent experience**. If our choirs perform at a high enough level, we may design a concert that seeks to lift audience members outside of their daily world and carry them to a thin place. In this mode, we avoid breaking the fourth wall. We use every corner of the concert hall to literally surround the listener with our singing. We play with lighting and other media. We program multiple works in a row without applause or comments. We hope that these carefully considered decisions - and the flawless singing - leave the audience member moved and even changed by the performance.

For others, the concert serves to **educate the audience and singer**. We design programs that move through historical eras of composition, often starting with medieval and renaissance music and working through baroque, classical, romantic, and contemporary periods in sequence. In both our lesson plans and our program notes or remarks, we note the stylistic changes and features of each era. We hope that, at the end of the concert, the audience member has a clearer grasp of and appreciation for choral music throughout history.

Of course, I recognize that I am speaking of these audience goals as if they were separate bins, and most of us want most of these experiences in most concerts. If attending a concert is like going out to a restaurant, we can each remember a few spectacular examples of each that seemed to fit all categories at once. But just as we avoid a lot of struggle in our teaching by having clear curricular goals, we can likewise avoid a lot of indigestion in our concert experience by having clear performance goals.

Which Is the Dog and Which Is the Tail?

I suggest that our performance goals for our audience have everything to do with *who is standing in front of us in choir*. What do *these singers* need in this next experience? If we are centered on respecting our singers, we put them first, and then build out. When I taught middle school, I pushed and pushed those students to the highest level of performance they had in them. They sang very well. They did not sing as transcendently as The Sixteen, and I was okay with that. So part of the clarity we seek is to ask if what we want from a group is within their capability.

We have responsibility for the singers we direct. In the case of those middle school students, I could have taught them every song by rote and force-fed them a good performance for every concert. But my job title was Music Teacher, and my responsibility was to help them *learn* how to read, write, hear, compose, and sing music. So we learned note names, rhythms, key signatures, intervals, *solfege*, vocalizations, and all the other skills and processes that thousands of music educators teach every day. We also learned how to perform at the highest level we could. But their performance was the tail, and their education was the dog. When our daily work in a school setting is entirely focused on concert preparation, the tail is wagging the dog.

We push our church choirs to perform at the highest level they can. We have a responsibility to our congregation to praise God "with heart and hands and voices," and if we sing transcendently, all may better feel the living presence of the Spirit. The members of our choirs are not professional singers; they are accountants, physical therapists, graphic designers, etc. They come to choir to be a part of a fellowship group, much like our Habitat for Humanity team. If we berate them into transcendent singing but lose sight of why they come to choir, we become "...a noisy gong or a clanging cymbal (1 Cor 13:1). The dog is our fellowship community of singers; the tail is how we sing our anthems. When our rehearsals in church are entirely focused on the performance, the tail is wagging the dog.

I push my college students to perform at the highest level they can. Among my singers are eighty vocal-performance majors in a pre-professional conservatory program designed to prepare them for success in vocal careers. That career will assuredly include ensemble singing. But if I teach straight-tone singing at all times because I sense we will have more aesthetic success, I ignore the important and difficult work these singers are doing to develop operatic vocal production. I have to see my role as one team member among many in their growth and education. The dog is a comprehensive training in professional singing; the tail is our concert. When I produce a great concert but the students do not learn how to navigate their voices healthily, the tail is wagging the dog.

In short, our audience will see a tail, but it is up to us to see the dog. As the owner of dogs, I know that their tails wag best when they are fed, walked, and loved. If we focus on respectful leadership for and with our singers, they will thrive. If we clarify to ourselves and to our ensembles what we want our audience to experience, they will perform more effectively. Because of our clearer goals for our singers, and then our audience, we will know more clearly what to communicate to our audience and how best to do it. And in this cycle of clear communication, we will better be able to grow our audience to be more inclusive.

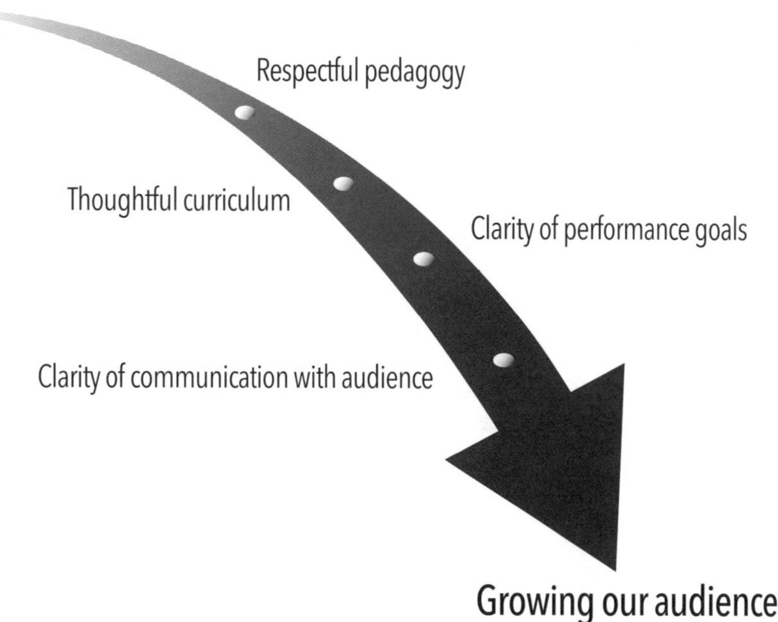

THE FUTURE AUDIENCE

Take a moment to make an estimate of the number of singers you will teach in your total career. Even if you calculate conservatively, your total will be in the *thousands*. Look back at programs from five or ten or twenty years ago if you can; if you are not that old yet, think back to programs you sang in. Study through the names of every singer. This one dropped out of choir after a semester. That one stayed in choir for two years, went to college, and became a paralegal. This one sang all the way through college, and now raises three young kids at home. Trace out the lives of all of these singers who once spent *hours* of their lives with you, watching your cut-offs, memorizing their part, singing on *solfege*, and doing their best musical work with you. How will they remember the choral experience?

Every singer who enters our room begins a new narrative about what choir is. We have no idea what their previous narrative might be. Were they told it was "gay" and enter with a fear of being judged? Were they told it was "cut-throat" and fear that they will fail? Were they told it was "easier than the other arts requirements" and look forward to doing nothing? Conductors like having a lot of power, but we do not have the power to go back in time and correct misconceptions and false narratives.

We do have the power to help our singers write a new narrative, though. When we teach with respect, we value all of our singers as people worthy of dignity. We may be creating the only space in their lives where they feel valued. When we push for excellence, but keep our attention on the people we are pushing and how they are learning, we foster their strength, resilience, and lasting success.

Our singers do not disappear when they graduate from our programs. They go on to live their lives. Will they sing in college after they leave high school? Will they sing in church or synagogue choirs? Will they join a community choir? Will they attend professional choir concerts? Will they send their kids to choir?

Our present singers are the next generation's audience. If our singers find a fulfilling experience in choir, they will seek out choral experiences and support music throughout their lives. If they do not find fulfillment in choir, they will probably never come back (think of something else you quit in 8th or 9th grade). Our singers will become advocates, either way. If choir nurtures our present singers, they will recruit for choir exponentially. If our choir shuts down and marginalizes singers, those singers will advocate against choir their whole lives. Your choir *right now* has future sports coaches, future district superintendents, future voice teachers, and future PTA boosters. How you teach those future leaders will have an immense impact on the shape of the field.

I did not grow up in choirs. I joined choir in ninth grade because my sister had had such an amazing, life-changing experience that she said I *had* to join. If Mr. Fuller hadn't been such an amazing teacher to my sister, I would not have joined choir. If he hadn't been such an amazing teacher to me, I would not have stayed in choir past ninth grade. In short, Mr. Fuller's legacy continues to send generational ripples of advocacy for the power of singing in choir long after his lifetime. The audience he built was far bigger than the number of people in the seats at his concerts.

Now I understand which kind of change we are after when we describe choir as something that can "change the world." When we teach singers how to use their voices and also acknowledge their right to a Voice in the sense of being whole people, we change their lives, infusing respect and dignity into a world torn apart by insult and division. We make a more compassionate, respectful, cooperative, thoughtful world - starting in our choir room. Our singers learn that you cannot make a great chord without other people, and that you cannot tune it without listening to those people. In this simple moment, choir sets the foundation for a better world.

RESOURCES

Resources

INCLUSIVITY

Abramo, Joseph. "Disability in the Classroom: Current Trends and Impacts on Music Education." *Music Educators Journal*, 99:1, September 2012, Sage Publications, pp.39-45.

Arao, Brian, and Clemens, Kristi. "From Safe Spaces to Brave Spaces: A New Way to Frame Dialogue Around Diversity and Social Justice." From: *The Art of Effective Facilitation*, 2013 Stylus Publishing, Sterling VA 2013, pp.135-150.

Damer, Linda K. "Inclusion and the Law." *Music Educators Journal*, 87:4, January 2001, Sage Publications, pp.19-22.

Dobbs, Teryl L. "A Critical Analysis of Disabilities Discourse in the *Journal of Research in Music Education*, 1990-2011." *Bulletin for the Council for Research in Music Education*, no. 194, Fall 2012, University of Illinois Press, pp. 7-30.

Dupont, Cheryl. "Who Should Sing? A Model of Inclusion." *Choral Journal*, 47:6, December 2006, pp. 89-91.

Eyerly, Heather E. "Redefining Performance in Choral Music Education: Part Three of a Three-part Series." *Choral Journal*, 48:5, November 2007, pp.53-55.

Fitzgerald, Margaret. "'I Send My Best Matthew to School Every Day': Music Educators Collaborating with Parents." *Music Educators Journal*, 92:4, March 2006, Sage Publications, pp.40-45.

Gabel, Susan. "Some Conceptual Problems with Critical Pedagogy." *Curriculum Inquiry* 33:2, Ontario Institute for Studies in Education, 2002, pp. 177-201.

Hourigan, Ryan and Amy. "Teaching Music to Children with Autism: Understandings and Perspectives." *Music Educators Journal*, 96:1, September 2009, Sage Publications, pp.40-45.

Jellison, Judith A. "On-task Participation of Typical Students Close to and Away from Classmates with Disabilities in an Elementary Music Classroom." *Journal of Research in Music Education*, 50:4, Winter 2002, Sage Publications, pp.343-355.

Jellison, Judith A., and Taylor, Donald M. "Attitudes Toward Inclusion and Students with Disabilities: A Review of Three Decades of Music Research." *Bulletin of the Council for Research in Music Education*, no. 172, Spring 2007, University of Illinois Press, pp.9-23.

McCord, Kimberly A. "Moving Beyond 'That's All I Can Do': Encouraging Musical Creativity in Children with Learning Disabilities." *Bulletin of the Council for*

Research in Music Education, no. 159, Winter 2004, University of Illinois Press, pp.23-32.

McCord, Kimberly and Watts, Emily H. "Collaboration and Access for Our Children: Music Educators and Special Educators Together." *Music Educators Journal*, 92:4, March 2006, Sage Publications, pp. 26-33.

Price Jr., Bryan S. "Zero Margin for Error: Effective Strategies for Teaching Music to Students with Emotional Disturbances." *Music Educators Journal*, 99:1, September 2012, Sage Publications, pp.67-72.

Smaligo, Mary A. "Resources for Helping Blind Music Students." *Music Educators Journal*, 85:2, September 1998, Sage Publications, pp.23-26+45.

Van Weelden, Kimberly. "Choral Mainstreaming Tips for Success." *Music Educators Journal*, 88:3, November 2001, Sage Publications, pp.55-60.

GENDER

Apfelstadt, Hilary. "Practices of Successful Women's Choir Conductors." The Choral Journal Dec. 1998, p.35.

Bergeron, Katherine, and Bohlman, Philip V., ed. *Disciplining Music: Musicology and Its Canons*. The University of Chicago Press: Chicago, 1992.

Coleman, Ralph O. "Acoustic Correlates of Speaker Sex Identification: Implications for the Transsexual Voice." *The Journal of Sex Research*, 19:3, August 1983, Taylor & Francis Publishing, pp.293-295.

Davis, Kathy, Mary Evans, and Judith Lorber, ed. *Handbook of Gender and Women's Studies*. Sage Publishing: Thousand Oaks, CA, 2006.

Elpus, Kenneth. "National Estimates of Male and Female Enrollment in American High School Choirs, Bands, and Orchestras." *Music Education Research* vol. 17, no. 1 (2015), p.93.

Gallagher, Kathleen. "The Everyday Classroom as Problematic: A Feminist Pedagogy." *Curriculum Inquiry* 30:1, 2000. The Ontario Institute for Studies, 2000.

Gamson, Joshua. "Messages of Exclusion: Gender, Movements, and Symbolic Boundaries." *Gender and Society*, 11:2, April 1997, pp.178-199. Sage Publications.

O'Toole, Patricia. "A Missing Chapter from Choral Methods Books: How Choirs Neglect Girls." *Choral Journal*, December 1998, p.16.

Olson, Philip, and Gillman, Laura. "Combating Racialized and Gendered Ignorance: Theorizing a Transactional Pedagogy of Friendship." *Feminist Formations*, 25:1, Spring 2013, Johns Hopkins University Press, pp. 59-83.

Ortner, Sherry B. "Gender Hegemonies." *Cultural Critique*, no. 14, The Construction of Gender and Modes of Social Division II, Winter 1989-1990, pp.35-80. University of Minnesota Press.

Palkki, Joshua. "Gender Trouble: Males, Adolescence, and Masculinity in the Choral Context." *The Choral Journal*, vol. 56, no. 4, p.30.

Spurgeon, Debra, ed. *Conducting Women's Choirs: Strategies for Success*. GIA Publications, Chicago, 2012.

Stryker, Susan, and Whittle, Stephen, ed. *The Transgender Studies Reader*. Routledge: New York, 2006.

VanWeelden, Kimberly. "Demographic Study of Choral Programs and Conductors in Four-Year Institutions in the United States." *Bulletin of the Council for Research in Music Education* No. 156 (Spring, 2003), pp. 20-30.

Wilson, Jill M. "Preferences of and Attitudes Toward Treble Choral Ensembles." *Research and Issues in Music Education*, 10:1, article 4, 2012.

Woolf, Virginia. *A Room of One's Own*. Harcourt, Orlando, Florida, 2005 (annotated edition).

SEXUALITY

Boutry, Katherine. "Between Registers: Coming In and Out Through Musical Performance in Willa Cather's 'The Song of the Lark.'" *Legacy*, 17:2, 2000, University of Nebraska Press, pp.187-198.

Bergonzi, Louis. "Sexual Orientation and Music Education: Continuing a Tradition." *Music Educators Journal*, 96:2, Sage Publications, Dec. 2009, pp. 21-25.

Peraino, Judith, and Cusick, Suzanne G., convenors. "Colloquy: Music and Sexuality." *Journal of the American Musicological Society*, 66:3, pp.825-872. American Musicological Society, 2013.

Schilt, Kristen, and Westbrook, Laurel. "Doing Gender, Doing Heteronormativity: Transgender People, and the Social Maintenance of Heterosexuality." *Gender and Society*, 23:4, Heteronormativity and Sexualities, August 2009, pp.440-464. Sage Publications.

Sedgwick, Eve. *The Epistemology of the Closet*. University of California Press, 1990.

RELIGION

Abingdon Township of Pennsylvania v Schempp (1963), found online at https://www.law.cornell.edu/supremecourt/text/374/203.

Clayton, Philip, and Railey, Mark S. "What Every Teacher of Science and Religion Needs to Know about Pedagogy." *Zygon* 33:1, March 1998, pp.121-130.

Grassie, William. "Powerful Pedagogy in the Science-and-Religion Classroom." *Zygon*, 32:3, September 1997, pp.415-421.

Lindholm, Jennifer, and Astin, Helen. "Spirituality and Pedagogy: Faculty's Spirituality and Use of Student-Centered Approaches to Undergraduate

Teaching." *The Review of Higher Education*, 31:2, Winter 2008, Johns Hopkins University Press, pp.185-207.

National Association for Music Education Position Statement on Sacred Music in Public Schools: http://www.nafme.org/about/position-statements/sacred-music-in-schools-position-statement/.

Webb, Stephen H. "The Supreme Court and the Pedagogy of Religious Studies: Constitutional Parameters for the Teaching of Religion in Public Schools." *Journal of the American Academy of Religion*, 70:1, March 2002, Oxford University Press, pp.13-157.

Zhang, Kaili C. "What Does Spirituality Have to Do with Public Schools?" *International Journal of School and Cognitive Psychology*, 2:2, 2015.

OTHERING AND ETHNICITY

Gallaher, Carolyn, Carl T. Dahlman, Mary Gilmartin, and Alison Mountz, with Peter Shirlow. *Key Concepts in Political Geography*. Sage Publishing, Los Angeles, 2009.

Baker, Geoff. "Latin American Baroque: Performance as a Post-Colonial Act?" *Early Music* 36:3, Oxford University Press, August, 2008, pp.441-448.

Bithell, Caroline, and Hill, Juniper. *The Oxford Handbook of Music Revival*. Oxford University Press: New York, 2014.

Born, Georgina, and Hesmondhalgh, David, ed. *Western Music and Its Others: Difference, Representation, and Appropriation in Music*. University of California Press: Berkeley, 2000.

Bourke, Brian. "Positionality: Reflecting on the Research Process." *The Qualitative Report*, vol. 19, 2014, pp. 1-7.

Fackler, Guido, translated from the German by Peter Logan. "Music in Concentration Camps 1933–1945." *Music & Politics*. I:1, Winter 2007.

Kim Lee, Esther. *A History of Asian American Theatre*. Cambridge University Press, 2006, pp.177-199.

Livingston, Tamara E. "Music Revivals: Towards a General Theory." *Ethnomusicology*, 43:1, Winter 1999, University of Illinois Press, pp.66-85.

Román-Velázquez, Patria. "The Embodiment of Salsa: Musicians, Instruments and the Performance of a Latin Style and Identity." *Popular Music* 18:1, January 1999, Cambridge University Press, pp.115-131.

Said, Edward. *Orientalism*. Random House, New York: 1979.

Stone, Ruth. *Theory for Ethnomusicology*. Pearson Education: Upper Saddle River, NJ, 2008.

Walker, Robert. "Multiculturalism and Music Re-attached to Music Education." *Philosophy of Music Education Review*, 8:1, Spring 2000, Indiana University Press, pp.31-39.

Villegas, Ana María and Lucas, Tamara. *Educating Culturally Responsive Teachers: A Coherent Approach*. State University of New York Press: Albany, 2002.

Williams, Patrick, and Chrisman, Laura, ed. *Colonial Discourse and Post-Colonial Theory: A Reader*. Columbia Press: New York, 1994.

Young, James O. and Brunk, Conrad G., ed. *The Ethics of Cultural Appropriation*, Wiley-Blackwell, Malden, MA, 2009.

Young, Robert J. C. *Postcolonialism: A Very Short Introduction*. Oxford University Press: New York, 2003.

RACE: AFRICAN-AMERICAN MUSIC

Coates, Ta-Nehisi. "The Case for Reparations." *The Atlantic*, June 2014, available at: http://www.theatlantic.com/magazine/archive/2014/06/the-case-for-reparations/361631/.

Coates, Ta-Nehisi. *Between the World and Me*. Spiegel & Grau, New York, 2015.

Darden, Bob. *People Get Ready! A New History of Black Gospel Music*. Continuum International Publishing, New York 2004.

Delpit, Lisa. *Other People's Children*. The New Press: New York, 1995.

Douglass, Frederick. *Narrative of the Life of Frederick Douglass, an American Slave*, HG Collins, London, 1851.

Hughes, Richard L. "Minstrel Music: The Sounds and Images of Race in Antebellum America." *The History Teacher*, Vol. 40, No. 1, November, 2006, Society for History Education, pp. 27-43.

Jones, Arthur C.. "The Foundational Influence of Spirituals in African-American Culture: A Psychological Perspective" *Black Music Research Journal*, Vol. 24, No. 2 (Autumn, 2004), pp. 251-260.

Kailin, Julie. *Antiracist Education: From Theory to Practice*. Rowman & Littlefield Publishers: Lanham, Maryland, 2002.

Kramer, Lawrence. "Powers of Blackness: Africanist Discourse in Modern Concert Music." *Black Music Research Journal*, 16:1, Spring 1996, University of Illinois Press, pp.53-70.

McIntosh, Peggy. "White Privilege: Unpacking the Invisible Knapsack" *Peace and Freedom Magazine*, July/August 1989, available at: http://nationalseedproject.org/White-privilege-unpacking-the-invisible-knapsack

Rodriquez, Jason. "Color-Blind Ideology and the Cultural Appropriation of Hip-Hop." *Journal of Contemporary Ethnography*, 35:6, December 2006, Sage Publications, pp.645-668.

Roediger, David R. *The Wages of Whiteness: Race and the Making of the American Working Class*. Verso: New York, 1999 (revised edition), pp.115-128.

Schenbeck, Lawrence. "Representing America, Instructing Europe: The Hampton Choir Tours Europe." *Black Music Research Journal*, Vol. 25, No.1/2, Spring - Fall, 2005, Center for Black Music Research, University of Illinois Press, pp. 3-42.

Shaftel, Matthew. "Singing a New Song: Stephen Foster and the New American Minstrelsy." *Music and Politics*, Volume I, Issue 2, Summer 2007, p.3.

Shaw, Julia. "The Skin that We Sing: Culturally Responsive Choral Music Education." *Music Educators Journal*, 98:4, June 2012, Sage Publications, pp. 75-81 (p.76).

Wilson, August. "The Ground on Which I Stand." From *The American Theatre Reader: Essays and Conversations From American Theatre Magazine*. Theatre Communications Group: New York, 2009, pp.152-170.

End-Notes

Prelude - Why This Book?

1 http://www.charlotteobserver.com/news/local/article66900492.html Don Sturkey, photographer. With thanks to Rev. Terry Hamilton-Poore for reminding me what it means to witness.

2 https://www.nytimes.com/2021/05/12/us/politics/domestic-terror-white-supremacists.html, accessed December 16, 2021.

3 https://www.africa.upenn.edu/Articles_Gen/Letter_Birmingham.html

4 Schelling, Thomas. *Micromotives and Macrobehavior*, p.26.

Chapter One - Growing Our Perspective

5 October 26, 2015, www.cnn.com/2015/10/26/politics/donald-trump-small-loan-town-hall/

6 http://historyproject.ucdavis.edu/ic/image_details.php?id=5005

7 www.salon.com/2012/05/22/rep_steve_king_immigrants_like_dogs/

8 https://www.law.columbia.edu/news/archive/kimberle-crenshaw-intersectionality-more-two-decades-later accessed December 17, 2021.

Chapter Two - Creating Room for All Singers

9 Safespacenetwork.tumblr.com/Safespace

10 Arao, Brian and Clemens, Kristi. "From Safe Spaces to Brave Spaces". *The Art of Effective Facilitation*. Stylus Publications, 2013, pp.139, 140.

11 www.merriam-webster.com/dictionary/trigger%20warning

12 https://www.apa.org/topics/trauma, accessed December 20, 2021.

13 Bashant, Jennifer. *Building a Trauma-Informed Compassionate Classroom*. PESI Publishing, Eau Claire, WI, 2020, p. vii.

14 https://www.npr.org/sections/health-shots/2015/03/02/387007941/take-the-ace-quiz-and-learn-what-it-does-and-doesnt-mean accessed December 20, 2021

15 https://www.cdc.gov/violenceprevention/aces/fastfact.html?CDC_AA_refVal=https%3A%2F%2Fwww.cdc.gov%2Fviolenceprevention%2Facestudy%2Ffastfact.html, accessed December 20, 2021.

16 https://burkefoundation.org/what-drives-us/adverse-childhood-experiences-aces/ accessed December 20, 2021

17 https://pubmed.ncbi.nlm.nih.gov/17485609/, accessed December 20, 2021.

18 https://www.pewresearch.org/fact-tank/2019/12/12/u-s-children-more-likely-than-children-in-other-countries-to-live-with-just-one-parent/ accessed December 20, 2021.

19 https://nicic.gov/parents-state-prisons, accessed Decemer 20, 2021.

20 https://www.childrensrights.org/newsroom/fact-sheets/foster-care/, accessed December 20, 2021.

21 https://www.air.org/centers/national-center-family-homelessness, accessed December 20, 2021.

22 https://www.simplypsychology.org/maslow.html20, accessed December 20, 2021.

23 https://www.ncbi.nlm.nih.gov/pmc/articles/PMC3181836/ accessed December 21, 2021.

24 Bashant, Jennifer. *Building a Trauma-Informed Compassionate Classroom.* PESI Publishing, Eau Claire, WI, 2020, p. 19.

25 ibid, p.21.

26 ibid, p.21.

27 ibid, p.77.

28 "The Role of Deliberate Practice in the Acquisition of Expert Performance", *Psychological Review,* 1993 100:3, pp.363-406.

29 https://medium.com/@thetopessentials/the-pygmalion-effect-the-rosenthal-experiment-abc3642de889 accessed May 30, 2022.

Chapter Three - Teaching Singers with Diverse Abilities

30 Stopableism.org/what.asp.

31 Gabel, Susan. "Some Conceptual Problems with Critical Pedagogy." *Curriculum Inquiry,* vo. 33, no. 2, 2002, pp.177-201. p.185.

32 http://www2.ed.gov/policy/speced/leg/idea/history.pdf

33 http://idea.ed.gov/explore/view/p/,root,regs,300,B,300%252E114

34 https://ldaamerica.org/advocacy/lda-position-papers/full-inclusion-of-all-students-with-learning-disabilities-in-the-regular-education-classroom/

35 www.parents.com/toddlers-preschoolers/.../inclusion-doing-our-best-for-all-children/

36 http://specialedresource.com/resource-center/self-contained-classroom-defined

37 https://ldaamerica.org/advocacy/lda-position-papers/full-inclusion-of-all-students-with-learning-disabilities-in-the-regular-education-classroom/

38 http://idea.ed.gov/explore/view/p/%2Croot%2Cdynamic%2CTopicalBrief%2C10%2C

39 Price, Jr., Bryan S. "Zero Margin for Error: Effective Strategies for Teaching Music to Students with Emotional Disturbances." *Music Educators Journal,* Vol 99 No. 1 (September 2012), pp.67-72. p.70.

40 McCord, Kimberly A. "Moving Beyond 'That's All I Can Do:' Encouraging Musical Creativity in Children with Learning Disabilities. *Bulletin of the Council for Research in Music Education,* no. 159 (Winter, 2004) (p.24).

41 Hourigan, Ryan and Amy. "Teaching Music to Children with Autism: Understandings and Perspectives." *Music Educators Journal,* vol. 96, no. 1 (September 2009), pp.40-45. p.41.

42 Hourigan, Ryan and Amy. "Teaching Music to Children with Autism: Understandings and Perspectives." *Music Educators Journal,* vol. 96, no. 1 (September 2009), pp.40-45. p.43.

43 Fitzgerald, Margaret. "'I Send My Best Matthew to School Every Day': Music Educators Collaborating with Parents." *Music Educators Journal,* vol. 92, no. 4 (March, 2006), pp.40-45, p.40.

44 ibid, p.44.

45 ibid, p.45.

46 Hourigan, Ryan and Amy. "Teaching Music to Children with Autism: Understandings and Perspectives." *Music Educators Journal,* vol. 96, no. 1 (September 2009), pp.40-45 (p.42).

47 Jellison, Judith A. "On-task Participation of Typical Students Close to and Away from Classmates with Disabilities in an Elementary Music Classroom." *Journal of Research in Music Education*, vol. 50, no. 4 (Winter, 2002), pp.343-355. p.350.

48 ibid, p.351.

49 Price, Jr., Bryan S. "Zero Margin for Error: Effective Strategies for Teaching Music to Students with Emotional Disturbances." *Music Educators Journal*, vol 99 No. 1 (September 2012), pp.67-72. p.70.

50 Hourigan, Ryan and Amy. "Teaching Music to Children with Autism: Understandings and Perspectives." *Music Educators Journal*, vol. 96, no. 1 (September 2009), pp.40-45. p.42.

51 ibid, p.72.

52 http://www.udlcenter.org/aboutudl/whatisudl , accessed August 12, 2016.

53 http://www.udlcenter.org/aboutudl/udlguidelines_theorypractice accessed August 12, 2016.

54 Howard-Jones, Paul. "Neuroscience and education: myths and messages." *Neuroscience*, Volume 15:12, 2014, pp.817-824.

Chapter Four - Choir and Gender

55 Wendy Cealy Harrison, "The Shadow and the Substance: the Sex/Gender Debate" from *Handbook of Gender and Women's Studies*, p.49.

56 Kathy Davis, Mary Evans, and Judith Lorber. *Handbook of Gender and Women's Studies*. p.2.

57 Elpus, Kenneth. "National Estimates of Male and Female Enrollment in American High School Choirs, Bands, and Orchestras." *Music Education Research* vol. 17, no. 1 (2015), p.93.

58 Patricia O'Toole, "A Missing Chapter from Choral Methods Books: How Choirs Neglect Girls", *The Choral Journal*, Dec. 1998, p.16.

59 Sherry B. Ortner, "Gender Hegemonies", *Cultural Critique*, #14, 1989-90 p.41.

60 http://qz.com/428680/there-is-less-womens-sports-coverage-on-tv-today-than-there-was-in-1989/

61 http://www.cawp.rutgers.edu/women-us-congress-2015

62 http://www.aauw.org/files/2016/02/SimpleTruth_Spring2016.pdf

63 http://www.stthomas.edu/rimeonline/vol10/wilson.htm

64 Woolf, Virginia. A Room of One's Own. Harcourt, Orlando, Florida, 2005 (annotated edition) p.43.

65 Solie, Ruth. *Disciplining Music*, p.232.

66 Snow, Sandra. *Conducting Women's Choirs*. pp.104-5.

67 ibid, p.106.

68 http://www.bls.gov/cps/aa2013/cpsaat11.pdf

69 VanWeelden, Kimberly. "Demographic Study of Choral Programs and Conductors in Four-Year Institutions in the United States" *Bulletin of the Council for Research in Music Education* No. 156 (Spring, 2003), p.21.

70 ibid, p.22.

71 ibid, p.28.

72 Apfelstadt, Hilary. "Practices of Successful Women's Choir Conductors." *The Choral Journal* Dec. 1998, p.35.

73 Gallagher, Kathleen. "Everyday Classroom as Problematic", p.73.

[74] Palkki, Joshua. "Gender Trouble: Males, Adolescence, and Masculinity in the Choral Context." *The Choral Journal*, vol. 56, no. 4, p.30.

[75] Schilt and Westbrook, *Doing Gender, Doing Heteronormativity*, p.443.

[76] Palkki, J., and Sauerland, W. "Considering gender complexity in music teacher education." Journal of Music Teacher Education, 28:3, 2019, p.78.

[76] http://www.ovc.gov/pubs/forge/sexual_numbers.html, July 11 2016.

[77] Palkki, J., and Caldwell, P. "'We are Often Invisible': a Survey on Safe Space for LGBTQU Students in Secondary School Choral Programs." *Research Studies in Music Education*, 40:1, 2018, p.35.

[78] ibid, pp.37-38.

[79] Palkki, Joshua. "'My Voice Speaks for Itself': The Experiences of Three Transgender Students in American Secondary School Choral Programs." *International Society for Music Education*, Vol 38:1, 2020, p.139)

[80] Jackson Hearns, Liz, and Kremer, Brian. *The Singing Teacher's Guide to Transgender Voices*. Plural Publishing, San Diego, CA, 2018, p.33.

[81] ibid, p.62.

Chapter Five - Choir and Sexual Identity

[82] Morris, Mitchell. "Calling Names; Taking Names." (JAMS 66:3, 2013, p.832).

[83] Sedgwick, Eve. *The Epistemology of the Closet*. University of California Press, 1990, p.8.

[84] O'Toole, Patricia. "Why I Don't Feel Included in These Musics": *Bulletin of the Council for Research in Music Education*, No. 144, (Spring, 2000), pp. 28-39 Published by: University of Illinois.

[85] Bergonzi "Sexual Orientation and Music Education: Continuing a Tradition," (*Music Educators Journal*, 96:2, Dec. 2009). p.22.

[86] ibid, p.25.

[87] http://www.cdc.gov/lgbthealth/youth.htm August 20, 2016.

[88] https://www.thetrevorproject.org/research-briefs/accepting-adults-reduce-suicide-attempts-among-lgbtq-youth/, accessed December 17, 2021

Chapter Six - Choir and Religion

[89] Templeton, Sir John. *The Humble Approach: Scientists Discover God*. Templeton Foundation Press: Philadelphia, 1995. p.3.

[90] Lindholm, Jennifer A., and Astin, Helen S. "Spirituality and Pedagogy: Faculty's Spirituality and Use of Student-Centered Approaches to Undergraduate Teaching." *The Review of Higher Education*, volume 31, no. 2, Winter 2008, pp.185-207. (185-6)

[91] Zhang, Kaili C. "What Does Spirituality Have to Do with Public Schools?" *International Journal of School and Cognitive Psychology* 2:2 (May 2015).

[92] Jacobson, Eaton, et al. "Approaches to Teaching Sacred Music in a Secular Context." *Choral Journal* March 2007, p41.

[93] Thank you to Craig Gregory for data.

[94] [https://www.law.cornell.edu/constitution/first_amendment accessed July 20, 2016].

[95] [https://www.law.cornell.edu/supremecourt/text/374/203, accessed July 20, 2016].

[96] Webb, Stephen H. "The Supreme Court and the Pedagogy of Religious Studies: Constitutional Parameters for the Teaching of Religion in Public Schools." *Journal of the American Academy of Religion*, volume 70, no. 1 (March, 2002), pp.135-157, Oxford University Press. p.136.

[97] ibid, p.138.

[98] ibid, pp. 154-5

[99] Jacobson, Joshua. "Letter to the Editor". *Choral Journal*, February 2016, pp.6-7.

[100] Clayton, Phillip, and Railey, Mark S. "What Every Teacher of Science and Religion Needs to Know about Pedagogy." *Zygon*, vol.33 no.1, March 1998, p129).

[101] http://www.nafme.org/about/position-statements/sacred-music-in-schools-position-statement/

[102] ibid.

[103] ibid.

[104] Page, Nick. "The Cultural Connection." *Choral Journal*, March 2001, p.29.

[105] ibid, p.31.

[106] [http://www.pewforum.org/religious-landscape-study/ accessed July 20, 2016.].

[107] http://www.pewforum.org/religious-landscape-study/frequency-of-reading-scripture/

[108] Clayton, Phillip, and Railey, Mark S. "What Every Teacher of Science and Religion Needs to Know about Pedagogy." *Zygon*, vol.33 no.1, March 1998, pp.122-3.

[109] Lloyd, Thomas. "Hope in the Unified Language: Teaching Sacred Music in a Secular Context". *Choral Journal*, March 2007 p.39

Chapter Seven - Choir and World Music

[110] The irony of using the Oxford English Dictionary as arbiter of what this word means, by virtue of its esteem in Euro-American culture, is not lost on me.

[111] (from "The Forms of Capital", cited in *Cultural Theory: An Anthology*, ed. by Imre Szeman and Timony Kaposy, Wiley-Blackwell, 2011, pp.83-4).

[112] *Key Concepts in Political Geography*. Carolyn Gallaher, Carl T. Dahlman, Mary Gilmartin, and Alison Mountz, with Peter Shirlow. Sage Publishing, Los Angeles, 2009. p.324.

[113] Said, Edward. *Orientalism*. Random House, New York: 1979. p.45.

[114] ibid, p.7.

[115] http://www.guidodaniele.com/images/body_painting/magnum/magnum-spice.jpg

[116] http://www.themarketingblog.co.uk/2016/05/magnum-taps-shazam%E2%80%99s-technology-for-its-new-%E2%80%9Crelease-the-beast%E2%80%9D-global-campaign/

[117] http://static3.businessinsider.com/image/4e4e934e49e2ae312c000009-506-253/nivea-pulls-racist-re-civilize-yourself-ad-after-sparking-outrage.jpg

[118] Hess, Juliet. "A 'Discomfortable' Approach to Music Education: Re-Envisioning the 'Strange Encounter.'" *Philosophy of Music Education* Review 26, no. 1 (Spring 2018), p45.

[119] ibid p.27

[120] Stone, Molly et al. "If You Don't Know, Don't Assume: Cross-Cultural Engagement in Choral Music for Social Justice." *Choral Journal*, Oct. 2018, p.41.

[121] Davis Gratto, Sharon. "More Than "Politically Correct:" Accuracy And Authenticity In World Choral Music Study And Performance." *Choral Journal*, Sept. 2010, p.66.

[122] Stone et al. "If You Don't Know..." p.42.

[123] Patricia Sheehan Campbell. *Music, Education, and Diversity: Building Cultures and Communities.* Teachers College Press, New York, 2018, p.77.

[124] ibid, p.169

[125] Young, James O. and Brunk, Conrad G., ed. *The Ethics of Cultural Appropriation*, Wiley-Blackwell, 2009, p.6.

[126] ibid, p.10.

[127] ibid, p.25.

[128] ibid, p.140.

[129] Cho, Ryan. "Cultural Appropriation and Choral Music: A Conversation That Can Make Both Our Music and Community Better," *Choral Journal* 55:10 (2015), p.59.

[130] Elizabeth Burns Coleman and Rosemary J. Coombe with Fiona MacArailt,"A Broken Record: Subjecting 'Music' to Cultural Rights," p.180. From: *The Ethics of Cultural Appropriation*, ed. by James O. Young and Conrad G. Brunk, 2009.

[131] ibid, p.175.

[132] ibid, p.180.

[133] James Young and Susan Haley. "'Nothing Comes from Nowhere': Reflections on Cultural Appropriation as the Representation of Other Cultures" – from Young and Brunk, p.270.

[134] "'The Skin Off Our Backs': Appropriation of Religion" - Brunk and Young, p.96).

[135] Jackson, Lauren Michele. *White Negroes: When Cornrows Were in Vogue... And Other Thoughts on Cultural Appropriation*. Beacon Press, Boston, 2019, p.4.

[136] Young and Haley, p.107.

[137] Ladsen-Billings, Gloria. "Culturally Relevant Pedagogy 2.0: a.k.a. the Remix". *Harvard Educational Review* Vol. 84 No. 1 Spring 2014, p.76.

[138] ibid, p.74.

[139] ibid, p.82.

[140] Gay, Geneva. "Preparing for Culturally Responsive Teaching." *Journal of Teacher Education*, Vol. 53, issue 2, March/ April 2002 106-116,p.106.

[141] Joshua Palkki, "'If it fits into their culture, then they will have a connection': Experiences of two Latina students in a select high school choir." *Research & Issues in Music Education*, Volume 12 Number 1 2014-2015, p.7

[142] Walter, Jennifer. "Global Perspectives: Making the Shift from Multiculturalism to Culturally Responsive Teaching." *General Music Today* 2018, Vol. 31(2), p.25.

[143] Shaw, Julia. "'The Music I was Meant to Sing': Adolescent Choral Students' Perceptions of Culturally Repsonsive Pedagogy." *Journal of Research in Music Education*, 2016, 64:1, p.65.

[144] Gay, Geneva. "Teaching To and Through Cultural Diversity". *Curriculum Inquiry*, Vol. 43, No. 1 (January 2013), p.63.

[145] ibid, p.65.

[146] ibid, p. 57.

[147] Sheehan Campbell, Patricia. *Music, Education, and Diversity: Building Cultures and Communities.* Teachers College Press, New York, 2018, p.143.

[148] Walker, Tiffany, "Addressing Contextual Information in Multicultural Choral Repertoire." *Choral Journal*, Nov. 2020.

[149] Stone et al. "If You Don't Know..." p.36.

[150] Sheehan Campbell, Patricia. *Music, Education, and Diversity: Building Cultures and Communities*. Teachers College Press, New York, 2018, p.178.

[151] Bond, Vanessa. "Culturally Responsive Teaching in the Choral Classroom." *Choral Journal*, Sept. 2014, p.12.

[152] ibid, p.14.

[153] Hess, Juliet. "A 'Discomfortable' Approach to Music Education: Re-Envisioning the 'Strange Encounter.'" *Philosophy of Music Education* Review 26, no. 1 (Spring 2018), p.37.

[154] Ladsen-Billings, Gloria. "Toward a Theory of Culturally Relevant Pedagogy". *American Educational Research Journal* Fall 1995, Vol. 32, No. 3, p.484.

[155] ibid, p.480.

[156] Gay, Geneva. "Teaching To and Through Cultural Diversity". *Curriculum Inquiry*, Vol. 43, No. 1 (January 2013), pp. 48-70.

[157] Gay, Geneva. "Preparing for Culturally Responsive Teaching." *Journal of Teacher Education*, Vol. 53, issue 2, March/ April 2002, p.110.

[158] Cho, Ryan. "Cultural Appropriation and Choral Music: A Conversation That Can Make Both Our Music and Community Better," Choral Journal 55:10 (2015), p.60.

Chapter Eight - Choir and African-American Music

[159] McIntosh, Peggy. "White Privilege: Unpacking the Invisible Knapsack" *Peace and Freedom Magazine*, July/August 1989, available at: http://nationalseedproject.org/White-privilege-unpacking-the-invisible-knapsack

[160] Baldwin, James, "Letter from a Region of My Mind," *The New Yorker*, 1962.

[161] Kendi, Ibram X. *How to Be an Antiracist*. One World, New York, 2019, p.9.

[162] ibid, p.10.

[163] http://www.encyclopediavirginia.org/_an_act_concerning_servants_and_slaves_1705

[164] http://www.theatlantic.com/magazine/archive/2014/06/the-case-for-reparations/361631/

[165] http://kingencyclopedia.stanford.edu/encyclopedia/encyclopedia/enc_chicago_campaign/

[166] https://www.thenation.com/article/strom-thurmonds-kid-loses-gop-bid-african-american-candidate/

[167] https://www.huduser.gov/portal/Publications/pdf/HUD-514_HDS2012_execsumm.pdf , p.11.

[168] ibid, pp.11-12.

[169] http://mediaassets.tmj4.com/document/2016/02/19/MLO%20Discrimination_HHML_32264844_ver1.0.PDF?_ga=1.3526640.1148389641.1470318751 (p.15)

[170] Mark Joseph Stern, Slate Magazine: http://www.slate.com/blogs/the_slatest/2016/07/29/fourth_circuit_strikes_down_north_carolina_voting_restrictions.html)

[171] http://www.ncbi.nlm.nih.gov/pmc/articles/PMC2151154/figure/fig3/

[172] Nott, Josiah Clark. *Types of mankind: or, Ethnological researches, based upon the ancient monuments, paintings, sculptures, and crania of races, and upon their natural, geographical, philological and Biblical history*. pp.458-459, accessed: http://quod.lib.umich.edu/cgi/t/text/text-idx?c=moa;idno=AJA7398

[173] Kajikawa, Loren. *Seeing Race Again: Countering Colorblindness Across the Disciplines*. University of California Press, 2019, p.158.

[174] (http://www.pbs.org/wgbh/pages/frontline/shows/sats/where/timeline.html)

[175] Brigham, Carl, PhD. *A Study of American Intelligence* https://archive.org/stream/studyofamericani00briguoft/studyofamericani00briguoft_djvu.txt

[176] Herrnstein, Richard, and Murray, Charles. *The Bell Curve: Intelligence and Class Structure in American Life*. Simon & Schuster, New York, 1994. p.269.

[177] http://www.museum.tv/eotv/Blackandwhim.htm

[178] http://news.bbc.co.uk/2/hi/entertainment/2223239.stm

[179] Shaftel, Matthew. "Singing a New Song: Stephen Foster and the New American Minstrelsy." *Music and Politics*, Volume I, Issue 2, Summer 2007, p.3.

[180] http://utc.iath.virginia.edu/minstrel/ounedfr.html

[181] https://www.poetryfoundation.org/poems-and-poets/poems/detail/44254 (1850).

[182] http://www.npr.org/sections/codeswitch/2014/05/11/310708342/recall-that-ice-cream-truck-song-we-have-unpleasant-news-for-you

[183] http://www.stephen-foster-songs.de/foster021.htm

[184] Shaftel, p.12.

[185] https://www.poetryfoundation.org/poems-and-poets/poems/detail/44258

[186] Shaftel, p.19.

[187] http://www.poemhunter.com/best-poems/stephen-c-foster/the-glendy-burk/

[188] Shaftel, p.12.

[189] (http://www.authentichistory.com/diversity/african/3-coon/5-chickwatermelon/19160300_Nigger_Love_A_Watermelon-Harry_C_Browne.mp3).

[190] http://utc.iath.virginia.edu/minstrel/dantuckerfr.html

[191] http://www.traditionalmusic.co.uk/old-time-music/old-time-songs/de_boatman_dance.html

[192] https://repository.library.brown.edu/studio/item/bdr:54309/

[193] http://utc.iath.virginia.edu/minstrel/miar03bt.html

[194] Hughes, Richard L. "Minstrel Music: The Sounds and Images of Race in Antebellum America" *The History Teacher*, Vol. 40, No. 1 (Nov., 2006), Society for History Education, pp. 27-43 (p.29).

[195] http://memory.loc.gov/cgi-bin/ampage?collId=mesn&fileName=022/mesn022.db&recNum=56&itemLink=D?mesnbib:3:./temp/~ammem_2BFj::

[196] *Narrative of the life of Frederick Douglass, an American slave*, HG Collins, London, 1851 p.13.

[197] ibid, pp.19-20.

[198] ibid, p.20.

[199] (http://www.pewforum.org/religious-landscape-study/age-distribution/)

[200] Curtis, Marvin V. . "The Lyric of the African-American Spiritual: The Meaning behind the Words." *Choral Journal*, August 199, p.19.

[201] Darden, Bob. *People Get Ready! A New History of Black Gospel Music*. Continuum International Publishing, New York 2004 (pp.84-5).

[202] Thomas, André. *Way Over in Beulah Lan'*. Heritage Music Press, Dayton OH, 2007. See Dr. Thomas' discussion in Chapter 4.

[203] Barber, Felicia. "Gaining Perspective: A Linguistic Approach to Dialect Found in African-American Spirituals. *Choral Journal*, February 2018 58:7, p.32.

204 Jones, Arthur C. "The Foundational Influence of Spirituals in African American Culture: A Psychological Perspective" *Black Music Research Journal*, Vol. 24, No. 2 (Autumn, 2004), pp. 251-260 (p.259).

205 J. Rodriquez, "Color-Blind Ideology and the Cultural Appropriation of Hip-Hop," *Journal of Contemporary Ethnography*, 2006. (663-664).

206 Olson, Philip, and Gillman, Laura. "Combatting Racialized and Gendered Ignorance: Theorizing a Transactional Pedagogy of Friendship" *Feminist Foundations*, V.25, Issue 1, Spring 2013, pp.59-83 (p.62).

207 Trice, Patricia J. "Choral Arrangements of Spirituals: Birth and Perpetuation of a Genre." *Choral Journal*, August 1996. p.9

208 *The Black Atlantic: Modernity and Double Consciousness*. Paul Gilroy. Verso, London, 1993, p.88.

209 Schenbeck, Lawrence. "Representing America, Instructing Europe: The Hampton Choir Tours Europe." *Black Music Research Journal*, Vol. 25, No. ½, Spring - Fall, 2005, Center for Black Music Research, University of Illinois Press, pp. 3-42 (p.15)

210 ibid, p.20.

211 ibid, p.24.

212 Thomas, André. Way Over in Beulah Lan'. Heritage Music Press, Dayton OH, 2007, p.96.

213 Penelope Cruz, Anton Armstrong, et al. "Is All Music for All People?" *Choral Journal*, November 2017 58:4, p.19.

214 Jackson, Lauren Michele. *White Negros...* p.172.

215 ibid, p.128

216 Kinchen, James. "Black Gospel Music and Its Impact on Traditional Choral Singing," *Choral Journal*, August 1986.p.11.

217 Kailin, Julie. *Anti Racist Education: From Theory to Practice*. Rowman & Littlefield Publishers, NY 2002. (p.68).

218 ibid, p.99.

219 Hamilton, Darren. "#BlackMusicMatters: Dismantling Anti-Black Racism in Music Education." *Canadian Music Educator*. 62:2, pp.25,27.

220 Garrett, Marques. "Unaccompanied Non-Idiomatic Choral Music of Black Composers." *Choral Journal* Nov. 2020, 61:4. p.17.

221 Shaw, Julia. "The Skin that We Sing: Culturally Responsive Choral Music Education." *Music Educators Journal*, 98:4, June 2012, Sage Publications, pp. 75-81 (p.76).

222 Dungee, Jason. "A Pedagogy for Living: Applying Restorative, Anti-Racist Pedagogy in the Choral Classroom." *Choral Journal*, 61:4, November 2020.P.14

Postlude - Building Our Audience

223 Kierkegaard, Søren. *Purity of Heart Is the Will to One Thing*. Start Publishing, 2012.